Lecture Notes in Artificial Intelligence 3600

Edited by J. G. Carbonell and J. Siekmann

Subseries of Lecture Notes in Computer Science

T0255573

Freek Wiedijk (Ed.)

The Seventeen Provers of the World

Foreword by Dana S. Scott

 Springer

Series Editors

Jaime G. Carbonell, Carnegie Mellon University, Pittsburgh, PA, USA
Jörg Siekmann, University of Saarland, Saarbrücken, Germany

Volume Editor

Freek Wiedijk
Radboud University
Institute for Computing and Information Sciences
Postbus 9010, 6500 GL Nijmegen, The Netherlands
E-mail: freek@cs.ru.nl

Library of Congress Control Number: 2005939043

CR Subject Classification (1998): I.2.3, I.2, F.4.1, F.4, D.2

LNCS Sublibrary: SL 7 – Artificial Intelligence

ISSN   0302-9743
ISBN-10   3-540-30704-4 Springer Berlin Heidelberg New York
ISBN-13   978-3-540-30704-4 Springer Berlin Heidelberg New York

Springer is a part of Springer Science+Business Media

springeronline.com

© Springer-Verlag Berlin Heidelberg 2006
Printed in Germany

Typesetting: Camera-ready by author, data conversion by Boller Mediendesign
Printed on acid-free paper   SPIN: 11542384   06/3142   5 4 3 2 1 0

Editorial

This volume starts a new subline of Lecture Notes in Artificial Intelligence, called

AI-SYSTEMS

focusing on the most important systems and prototypical developments in artificial intelligence.

We have chosen an initiative of the year 2004 as the starting date to commemorate the 50th anniversary of the first time a mathematical theorem was proven by a computer system: Martin Davis' implementation of the Presburger Fragment of first-order logic proved the mind-stretching result that the sum of two even numbers is again even.

While the first volumes in this category will present – for historical reasons – today's internationally most relevant systems from the field of automated reasoning, we shall soon solicit detailed presentations of individual systems as well as systems from the other major subareas of AI.

October 2005

Jörg Siekmann
Alfred Hofmann

Foreword

Our compiler, Freek Wiedijk, whom everyone interested in machine-aided deduction will thank for this thought-provoking collection, set his correspondents the problem of proving the irrationality of the square root of 2. That is a nice, straight-forward question. Let's think about it geometrically – and intuitively.

The original question involved comparing the side with the diagonal of a square. This reduces to looking at an isosceles right triangle. For such a triangle, the proof of the Pythagorean Theorem is obvious. As we can see from the figure, the squares on the legs are made up of *two copies* of the original triangle, while the square on the hypothenuse requires *four copies*. The question is whether a leg is commensurable with the hypothenuse.

Call the original triangle ABC, with the right angle at C. Let the hypothenuse $AB = p$, and let the legs $AC = BC = q$. As remarked, $p^2 = 2q^2$.

Reflect ABC around AC obtaining the congruent copy ADC. On AB position E so that $BE = q$. Thus $AE = p - q$. On CD position F so that $BF = p$. Thus $DF = 2q - p$. The triangle BFE is congruent to the original triangle ABC. EF is perpendicular to AB, the lines EF and AD are parallel.

Now, position G on AD so that $AG = EF = q$. Since $AEFG$ is a rectangle, we find $AG = q$. Thus, $DG = FG = AE = p - q$. So, the triangle DFG is an isosceles right triangle with a leg $= p - q$ and hypothenuse $= 2q - p$.

If there were commensurability of p and q, we could find an example with *integer lengths* of sides and with the perimeter $p + 2q$ a minimum. But we just constructed another example with a smaller perimeter p, where the sides are also obviously integers. Thus, assuming commensurability leads to a contradiction.

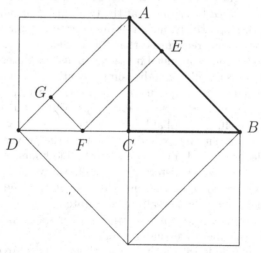

As one of the contributors remarks, this reduction of (p, q) to $(p - q, 2q - p)$ is very, very easy to accomplish with algebra – and the observation avoids the lemmas about even and odd numbers in finishing the required proof. But, what does this really mean? As I have often told students, "Algebra is smarter than you are!" By which I mean that the laws of algebra allow us to make many steps which combine information and hide tracks after simplifications, especially by cancellation. Results can be surprising, as we know from, say, the technique of generating functions.

In the case of the isosceles right triangle (from the diagonal of the square), an illumination about meaning can be obtained best from thinking about the Euclidean Algorithm. For a pair of commensurable magnitudes (a, b), the finding of "the greatest common measure" can be accomplished by setting up a sequence of pairs, starting with (a, b), and where the next pair is obtained from the preceding one by subtracting the smaller magnitude from the larger – and by replacing the larger by this difference. When, finally, equal pairs are found, this is the desired greatest common measure. (And, yes, I know this can be speeded up by use of the Division Algorithm.)

In our case we would have: (p, q), $(p - q, q)$, $(p - q, 2q - p)$, ... If we do some calculation with ratios (as the ancient Greeks knew how to do), we remark that the Pythagorean Theorem gives us first $p/q = 2q/p$. (Look at the triangles to see this: all isosceles right triangles are similar!) From this follows $(p - q)/q = (2q - p)/p$. Now switch extremes to conclude that $p/q = (2q - p)/(p - q)$. This shows that the third term of our run of the Euclidean Algorithm gives a pair with the *same* ratio (when the larger is compared with the smaller) as for the initial pair. In any run of the Euclidean Algorithm, if a ratio ever repeats, then the algorithm *never finishes*. Why? Because the pattern of larger and smaller quantities is going to repeat and, thus, no equals will be found. Hence, the magnitudes of the original pair are *incommensurable*. Indeed, Exodus knew that $a/b = c/d$ could be *defined* by saying that the two runs of the algorithm starting with (a, b) *and* (c, d), respectively, have the same patterns of larger and smaller.

In later centuries it was recognized that the Euclidean Algorithm is directly connected with the (simple) continued fraction expansion. Moreover, as Lagrange showed, the infinite, eventually periodic, simple continued fractions give *exactly* the positive irrational roots of quadratic equations (with integer coefficients). Perhaps, then, it might have been a more interesting challenge to prove the Lagrange Theorem itself, but probably fewer groups would have responded.

Alas, I have never spent any extended time with the provers/checkers represented in this collection. I did invest many profitable hours in using the equational theorem prover, Waldmeister: it is small, yet very effective on many problems involving equational deductions. Unfortunately, some theorem provers based on first-order logic do not really incorporate all the techniques of equational provers, so with certain problems time and/or space may run out before finding a proof. It is imperative that implementers of these systems now take advantage of specialized algorithms if ever mathematicians are going to become interested in using a machine-based method.

We can also see clearly from the examples in this collection that the *notations* for input and output have to be made more human readable. Several systems do generate LaTeX output for the discovered proofs, but perhaps additional thought about formatting output might be valuable. The Theorema Project (system 12 in the present list) made readability of proofs a prime requirement, and their report shows their success. However, the objective Bruno Buchberger set originally for the project was to produce a tool for pedagogic use, not research. Thus, the power of their system does not yet reach what, say, the HOL-based systems surveyed in this report have. Also, the question of the *discovery* of a proof is different from *checking* a proffered proof. Hence, any features that make a system *interactive* – and many in this collection have such – do help in finding proofs through experimentation.

Over about a decade I developed undergraduate courses using *Mathematica*. One effort was directed at Discrete Mathematics, and my colleague, Klaus Sutner, at Carnegie Mellon has expanded that effort several fold with excellent success. Most of my own thought went into a course on Projective Geometry, basically an introduction to plane algebraic curves over the complex field. What I found via the use of computer algebra was that theorems can be *proved* by asking for simplifications and interaction between equations. Technically, I used not just commutative algebra but also an implementation of the algebra of partial differential operators acting on multivariate polynomials. The details are not important, as the point was that the user of *Mathematica* had to enter the right questions and control the choices of appropriate cases (say, after a factorization of a polynomial) in order to reach the desired conclusions. In other words, though there was automatic verification and generation of algebraic facts, there is not a *deductive* facility built into *Mathematica*. And I wish there were! Some very good progress has been made in the system, however, in simplifications of logical formulae involving the equations and inequalities over the real field. But welcome as this is, it is not *general-purpose* logical deduction.

Computer algebra systems have become very powerful and are used both for applications (say, in computer-aided design of complicated surfaces) and in research (say, in group theory, for example). But we have to note that though effective, *proofs* are not generated. The user of the system has to believe that the system is doing the simplifications correctly. Usually we are able to accept results on faith, and we are happy to see what is discovered, but, strictly speaking, a proof is lacking. For a wide-ranging discussion of such issues, the reader may consult "A Skeptic's Approach to Combining HOL and Maple" by John Harrison and Laurent Théry, which appeared in the Journal of Automated Reasoning, vol. 21 (1998), pp. 279–294. (This is also to be found on John Harrison's WWW page.)

So what we have here is a dilemma to be faced by implementors of proof systems. On the one hand, interaction and experimentation can be considerably speeded up by using automatic simplification of logical and algebraic expressions – and one can hope even by rules that the user specifies himself. Alternately, new methods for large-scale Boolean satisfaction algorithms might be employed. On the other hand, for verification (either by humans or by another part of the system), *checkable proofs* have to be generated and archived. Computers are so fast now that hundreds of pages of steps of simplifications can be recorded even for simple problems. Hence, we are faced with the questions, "What really is a proof?" and "How much detail is needed?" Several different answers are offered by the systems surveyed here. But, is there a canonical answer that will satisfy the test of time – and be relevant as new systems are put forward in the future? And don't forget that probabilistic proof procedures (say, for checking whether a large number is prime) also involve the question of what constitutes a proof.

Large searches present another vexing block for understanding what a system has accomplished. The original attack by computer on the Four Color Conjecture is a case in point. As discussed in the introduction by Wiedijk, objections have now been eliminated by showing that the method for generating the necessary cases is correct, even though the total run of the program is not humanly surveyable. On the other hand, as noted, work by Hales to eliminate criticisms of his solution to Kepler's Conjecture, though making progress, still continues. Of course, there will always be people who will say that such computer calculations, no matter how well designed – and with verified design principles – do not really give us proofs. They may even say, "How do you know that there was not some quantum-mechanical glitch that threw the computer off?" Running the program again with the same results will not be convincing either. But, what I think will silence the nay-sayers is the development of *whole suites* of general-purpose programs for solving new problems. Not wishing to criticize the work on Four Color Conjecture or on Kepler's Conjecture, but it often seems that a big effort is put into solving one single problem, and that's it. When proof assistants constitute a research tool that (suitably minded) mathematicians use daily for work, then there will be recognition and acceptance. This has already happened for computer-algebra systems and for chip-design verification systems. I remain optimistic that we will sooner and not later see real progress with solid mathematics proof systems.

But human imagination can always outstrip the capabilities of machines. To bring this point home in a very clear way, I think that the two delightful books by Roger B. Nelson, *Proofs Without Words: Exercises in Visual Thinking* (1993) and *Proofs Without Words II: More Exercises in Visual Thinking* (2000), published by The Mathematical Association of America, can give a deep fund of examples and questions about how proofs can be formalized. In the books there are, of course, many of the proofs of the Pythagorean Theorem, probably the most proved theorem in mathematics. Two I especially like involve facts about similar triangles: see proof VI on p. 8 of the first volume, and XI on p. 7 of the second. Proofs like these involve augmenting the original figure by what are often called "auxiliary lines". I particularly hated this method of proof in geometry when I first saw it in school. The teacher would introduce these constructions in a way like a magician pulling a rabbit out of a hat. It did not seem fair to make a hard problem easy, because there was little made obvious about where these helpers came from. After a while, I learned to do this stuff myself, and then I liked it. But training machines to do this is another question.

A quite different method is given on p. 142 of the first book. The puzzle is taken from the article by Guy David and Carlos Tomei, "The problem of the calissons", published in the American Mathematical Monthly, vol. 96 (1989), pp. 429–431. A calisson is a French candy in the shape of two equilateral triangles joined at an edge. The problem has to do with arrangements of these (as tiles) in a hexagonal box. Thinking of a triangular grid in the plane, a calisson is the appropriate "domino" for this grid. On the usual grid of squares, there are just two orientations of a rectangular domino: vertical or horizontal. The triangular grid allows three orientations, however. What David and Tomei remarked is that when the different orientations are colored in three colors, the fact about the balance of colors used becomes "obvious" – if the observer is used to optical illusions.

It is amusing that the late Edsger W. Dijkstra in his handwritten, privately circulated note, EWD 1055, of 5 July, 1989, strongly rejected this method of argument. He writes that they "give a very unsatisfactory treatment of the problem ... [and] come up with an elaborate non proof." His note gives a rigorous proof, but I think it is one that would need some effort to automate. (Dijkstra's notes can be downloaded over the Internet, by the way.)

N.G. de Bruijn has also written on this problem in a brief paper dating initially from May 1989, which he circulated privately after 1994. In his note he remarks:

> The proof sketched [by David and Tomei] gives a very amusing intuitive argument, interpreting the box with calissons as a two-dimensional drawing of a collection of unit cubes in three dimensions. In the present note a more formal argument will be given, and a stronger result will be obtained. For any box, hexagonal or not, it will be shown that if it can be filled with calissons, then the number in each direction is uniquely determined by the box. These numbers can be found if we just know both the volume of the box and what we shall call the *weight sum* of the box. Moreover it will be shown that this weight sum can be expressed as a kind of discrete contour integral taken along the boundary of the box.

Indeed, Dijkstra proves the same result about each box determining the three numbers of orientations. But, it may be that de Bruijn adds something additional about how the shape of the box gives these numbers. Dijkstra's proof seems more "combinatorial", while de Bruijn's is more "analytical". But a closer reading might show they had equivalent ideas. Another question these authors may not have considered is the connections between the various tilings of a box. In the simple case of a hexagonal box, the counting result might be proved by "rewriting". That is, the tiles in the different orientations might be driven to different corners of the box by replacing, one after the other, a small hexagon of three tiles by one of its rotations. And it might be that the space of tilings is "path-wise connected" – in the discrete sense that one could pass from one to the other by these elementary steps. For boxes of different shapes, it might be another story.

This puzzle is only one of many amusing tiling problems which show that even simple combinatorial questions often require special techniques to automate owing to the large number of possible configurations to be considered, as many authors have remarked. In many cases, the solutions do not depend on general theorems but require searches crafted solely for the particular problem. The problem of the calissons may be an example in between; if so, it might be more interesting to study than those requiring "brute force". And all such examples make us again ask: "What is a (good) proof?"

Note Added 22 May 2005

It was just brought to my attention that the late Stanley Tennenbaum told many people about a proof of the irrationality of root 2 he discovered in the 1960's. It is of course possible that the proof has been noted often before, especially as it is not so far from what is discussed above. However, it can be explained as a 'proof without words' involving no calculations beyond what is seen in the figure.

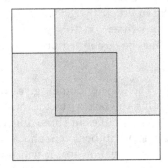

Suppose a square with integral sides is equal in area to the combination of two, smaller, congruent squares. Place the smaller squares inside the first square at two diagonally opposite corners. The two squares will have to overlap (Why?), making another square covered twice by them. But in the other corners there are two much smaller squares left uncovered. Inasmuch as the areas were supposed to add up, the two small squares must also add up to the central, overlapping square. (Why?) But the sides of these three smaller squares are obtained by subtraction, and hence must have integral values. Hence, there can be no minimal, integral configuration where the sum of two equal, integral squares adds up to another integral square.

Dana S. Scott

<dana.scott@cs.cmu.edu>

University Professor Emeritus

Carnegie Mellon University

Pittsburgh, Pennsylvania, USA

Preface

This volume is not a collection of papers but a collection of small formalizations. These formalizations all formalize a proof of the same very small theorem: the irrationality of the square root of two. After each formalization there is a description of the system used for that formalization, again not in the form of a paper but in the form of answers to a standard 'questionnaire'.

The systems shown in this volume are most of the systems that one should consider if one is interested in the formalization of mathematics, as it is very lucidly described in the QED manifesto. The purpose of this volume is not to find out which system is 'best'. The aims of the systems are too diverse to be easily comparable in a linear fashion. Instead it tries to showcase all those systems, to make clear what formalizations in all those systems look like. The main point of the volume is that these systems can be very different.

I would like to thank all the people who wrote all these very interesting formalizations. Also I would like to thank Dana Scott for his willingness to write the Foreword for this volume. I would like to thank Henk Barendregt for the concept of this collection. Finally I would like to thank Jörg Siekmann for offering to have this volume published in the LNAI series, to commemorate the 50th anniversary of the first computer-checked proof.

October 2005   Freek Wiedijk

Table of Contents

I want HOL Light to be both a cute little toy
and a macho heavyweight industrial prover.

— JOHN HARRISON

Introduction

Freek Wiedijk

By Freek Wiedijk <freek@cs.ru.nl>

Some years ago during lunch, Henk Barendregt told me about a book (*Algorithmics* by David Harel) that compared programming languages by showing the same little program in each language that was treated. Then I thought: I could do that for proof assistants! And so I mailed various people in the proof assistant community and started the collection that is now in front of you.

In the *QED manifesto* a future is sketched in which all mathematics is routinely developed and checked using proof assistants. In the comparison that you are now reading all systems have been included that one should look at when one is serious about trying to bring this *QED utopia* closer. That means that those systems are included that satisfy two criteria:

- They are designed for the formalization of mathematics, or, if not designed *specifically* for that, have been seriously used for this purpose in the past.
- They are special at something. These are the systems that in at least *one* dimension are better than all the other systems in the collection. They are the leaders in the field.

I called those systems *the provers of the world*.

Some of the people that I asked for a formalization replied to my mail by saying something like, 'Why should we do all this work for you? If you want a formalization, you go make it yourself!' But then I guessed that if the trivial proof that I was asking them for is not quite trivial in their system, then their system is not really suited for mathematics in the first place, so it then fails my first criterion, and it should not be included.

The formalizations are included in this collection in the order that I received them. In particular, I got the HOL and Mizar formalizations back on the same day that I sent my request ('Nice idea! Here it is!') However, I did not send all requests immediately: originally I only had nine systems. But then people pointed out systems that I had overlooked, and I thought of a few more myself too. So the collection grew.

I did not want to write any of the formalizations myself, as I wanted the formalizations to be 'native' to the system. I am a Coq/Mizar user, so my formalizations would have been too 'Coq-like' or 'Mizar-like' to do justice to the

F. Wiedijk (Ed.): The Seventeen Provers of the World, LNAI 3600, pp. 1–9, 2006.
© Springer-Verlag Berlin Heidelberg 2006

other systems (and even a Coq formalization by me would probably be too 'Mizar-like', while a Mizar formalization would be too 'Coq-like'.)

I had to select what proof to take for this comparison of formalizations. There are two canonical proofs that are always used to show non-mathematicians what mathematical proof is:

- The proof that there are infinitely many prime numbers.
- The proof of the irrationality of the square root of two.

From those two I selected the second, because it involves the *real numbers*. It is a lot of work to formalize the real numbers, so it is interesting which systems have done that work, and how it has turned out. In fact, not all systems in this collection have the real numbers available. In those systems the statement that was formalized was not so much the irrationality of the square root of two:

$$\sqrt{2} \notin \mathbb{Q}$$

as well just the key lemma that if a square is twice another square, then both are zero:

$$m^2 = 2n^2 \iff m = n = 0$$

I did *not* ask for a formalization of any *specific* proof. That might have given an unjustified bias to some of the systems. Instead, I just wrote about 'the standard proof by Euclid'.[1] With this I did not mean to refer to any actual historical proof of the theorem, I just used these words to refer to the theorem. I really intended everyone to take the proof that they thought to be the most appropriate. However, I *did* ask for a proof that was 'typical' for the system, that would show off how the system was meant to be used.

At first I just created a LaTeX document out of all the files that I got, but then I decided that it would be nice to have a small description of the systems to go with the formalizations. For this reason I compiled a 'questionnaire', a list of questions about the systems. I then did not try to write answers myself, but got them from the same people who gave me the formalizations. This means that the answers vary in style. Hopefully they still provide useful information about the systems.

The comparison is very much document-centric. It does not primarily focus on the interface of the systems, but instead focuses on what the *result* of proof formalization looks like. Also, it does not focus on what the result can be *made* to look like, but instead on what the proof looks like when the user of the system interacts with it while creating it. It tries to show 'the real stuff' and not only the nice presentations that some systems can make out of it.

Most formalizations needed a few lemmas that 'really should have been in the standard library of the system'. We show these lemmas together with the

---

[1] In fact the theorem does not originate with Euclid but stems from the Pythagorean tradition. Euclid did not even put it explicitly in his *Elements* (he probably would have viewed it as a trivial consequence of his X.9), although it was later added to it by others.

formalized proof: we really try to show *everything* that is needed to check the formalization on top of the standard library of the system.

One of the main aims of this comparison is comparing the appearance of proofs in the various systems. In particular, it is interesting how close that manages to get to non-formalized mathematics. For this reason there is also an 'informal' presentation of the proof included, as Section 0. On pp. 39–40 of the 4th edition of Hardy and Wright's *An Introduction to the Theory of Numbers*, one finds a proof of the irrationality of $\sqrt{2}$ (presented for humans instead of for computers):

THEOREM 43 (PYTHAGORAS' THEOREM). $\sqrt{2}$ *is irrational.*
The traditional proof ascribed to Pythagoras runs as follows. If $\sqrt{2}$ is rational, then the equation

$$a^2 = 2b^2 \tag{4.3.1}$$

is soluble in integers a, b with $(a, b) = 1$. Hence a^2 is even, and therefore a is even. If $a = 2c$, then $4c^2 = 2b^2$, $2c^2 = b^2$, and b is also even, contrary to the hypothesis that $(a, b) = 1$.   □

Ideally, a computer should be able to take this text as input and check it for its correctness. We clearly are not yet there. One of the reasons for this is that this version of the proof does not have enough detail. Therefore, Henk Barendregt wrote a very detailed informal version of the proof as Section 0. Again, ideally a proof assistant should be able to just check Henk's text, instead of the more 'computer programming language' like scripts that one needs for the current proof assistants.

There are various proofs of the irrationality of $\sqrt{2}$. The simplest proof reasons about numbers being *even* and *odd*.[2] However, some people did not just formalize the irrationality of $\sqrt{2}$, but generalized it to the irrationality of $\sqrt{p}$ for arbitrary prime numbers p. (Sometimes I even had to press them to specialize this to the irrationality of $\sqrt{2}$ at the end of their formalization.)

Conor McBride pointed out to me that if one proves the irrationality of $\sqrt{p}$ then there are two different properties of p that one can take as a assumption about p. The p can be assumed to be *irreducible* (p has just divisors 1 and itself), or it can be assumed to be *prime* (if p divides a product, it always divides one of its factors).[3] Conor observed that proving the irrationality of $\sqrt{p}$ where the assumption about p is that it is prime, is actually *easier* than proving the irrationality of $\sqrt{2}$, as the hard part will then be to prove that 2 is prime.

Rob Arthan told me that a nicer generalization than showing the irrationality of $\sqrt{p}$ for prime p, is to show that if n is an integer and $\sqrt{n}$ is not, then this $\sqrt{n}$ is in fact irrational. According to him at a very detailed level this is even slightly easier to prove than the irrationality of prime numbers.

---

[2] This becomes especially easy when a binary representation for the integers is used.
[3] In ring theory one talks about 'irreducible elements' and 'prime ideals', and this is the terminology that we follow here. In number theory a 'prime number' is generally defined with the property of being 'an irreducible element', but of course both properties characterize prime numbers there.

I had some discussion with Michael Beeson about whether the proof of the irrationality of $\sqrt{2}$ necessarily involves an inductive argument. Michael convinced me in the end that it is reasonable to take the lemma that every fraction can be put in lowest terms (which itself generally also is proved with induction) as *background knowledge*, and that therefore the irrationality proof can be given without an inductive argument. The Hardy & Wright proof seems to show that this also is how mathematicians think about it.

Each section in this document follows the same structure. They are all divided into four subsections. The third subsection is the main thing: it is the formalization, typeset as closely as possible as it appears in the files that people sent me. However, that subsection sometimes is quite long and incomprehensible. For clarity I wanted to highlight the syntax of statements, and the syntax of definitions. For this reason, I took the final statement that was proved, and some sample definitions from the formalization or system library, and put them in the first and second subsections. Therefore, those first two subsections are not part of the formalization, but *excerpts* from the third subsection. The fourth subsection, finally, is the description of the system in the form of answers to the questionnaire.

One of the main reasons for doing the comparison between provers is that I find it striking how different they can be. Seeing HOL, Mizar, Otter, ACL2 and Metamath next to each other, I feel that they hardly seem to have something in common. When one only knows a few systems, it is tempting to think that all proof assistants necessarily have to be like that. The point of this comparison is that this turns out not to be the case.

Some of the differences between the systems are apparent from the following 'consumer test' table:

proof assistant	HOL	Mizar	PVS	Coq	Otter/Ivy	Isabelle/Isar	Alfa/Agda	ACL2	PhoX	IMPS	Metamath	Theorema	Lego	Nuprl	Ωmega	B method	Minlog
small proof kernel ('proof objects')[4]	+	−	−	+	+	+	+	−	+	−	+	−	+	−	+	−	+
calculations can be proved automatically[5]	+	−	+	+	+	+	−	+	+	+	−	+	+	+	+	+	+
extensible/programmable by the user	+	−	+	+	−	+	−	−	−	−	−	−	−	+	+	−	+
powerful automation	+	−	+	−	+	+	−	+	−	+	−	+	−	−	+	+	−
readable proof input files	−	+	−	−	−	+	−	+	−	−	−	+	−	−	−	−	−
constructive logic supported	−	−	−	+	−	+	+	−	−	−	+	−	+	+	−	−	+
logical framework	−	−	−	−	−	+	−	−	−	−	−	+	−	−	−	−	−
typed	+	+	+	+	−	+	+	−	+	+	−	−	+	+	+	−	+
decidable types	+	+	−	+	−	+	+	−	+	+	−	−	+	−	+	−	+
dependent types	−	+	+	+	−	−	+	−	−	−	−	−	+	+	−	−	−
based on higher order logic	+	−	+	+	−	+	+	−	+	+	−	+	+	+	+	−	−
based on ZFC set theory	−	+	−	−	+	+	−	−	−	−	+	−	−	−	−	+	−
large mathematical standard library	+	+	+	+	−	+	−	−	−	+	−	−	−	+	−	−	−
statement about $\mathbb{R}$	+	+	+	+	−	+	−	+	−	+	+	+	−	−	+	−	+
statement about $\sqrt{}$	+	+	+	+	−	+	−	−	−	+	+	+	−	−	+	−	−

Some of the properties shown in this table (like 'powerful automation' and 'large library') are rather subjective, but we still hope that the table gives some indication about the variation between the systems. For instance, some people believe that 'ZF style' set theory is only a theoretical vehicle, and cannot be used to do realistic proofs. But this table shows that four of the systems are in fact able to formalize a *lot* of real mathematics on such a set theoretical foundation!

The systems in this comparison are all potential candidates for realization of a *QED manifesto*-like future. However, in this comparison only very small proofs in these systems are shown. Recently some very *large* proofs have been formalized, and in this introduction we would like to show a little bit of that as well. These formalizations were all finished at the end of 2004 and the beginning of 2005.

Prime Number Theorem. This formalization was written by Jeremy Avigad of Carnegie Mellon University, with the help of Kevin Donnelly, David Gray and Paul Raff when they were students there. The system that they used was Isabelle (see Section 6 on page 41). The size of the formalization was:

$$1,021,313 \text{ bytes} = 0.97 \text{ megabytes}$$
$$29,753 \text{ lines}$$
$$43 \text{ files}$$

Bob Solovay has challenged the proof assistant community to do a formalization of the analytic proof of the Prime Number Theorem. (He claims that proof assistant technology will not be up to this challenge for decades.[6]) This challenge is still open, as the proof of the Prime Number Theorem that Jeremy Avigad formalized was the 'elementary' proof by Atle Selberg. The files of this formalization also contain a proof of the Law of Quadratic Reciprocity.

The statement that was proved in the formalization was:

```
lemma PrimeNumberTheorem:
  "(%x. pi x * ln (real x) / (real x)) ----> 1";
```

which would in normal mathematical notation be written as:

$$\lim_{x\to\infty} \frac{\pi(x)\ln(x)}{x} = 1$$

In this statement the function $\pi(x)$ appears, which in the formalization was defined by:

---

[4] This is also called the *de Bruijn criterion*.
[5] This is also called the *Poincaré principle*.
[6] Others who are more optimistic about this asked me to add this footnote in which I encourage the formalization community to prove Bob Solovay wrong.

```
consts
  pi          ::   "nat => real"
defs
  pi_def: "pi(x) == real(card(y. y<=x & y:prime))"
```

meaning that the $\pi(x)$ function counts the number of primes below x.

Four Color Theorem. This formalization was written by Georges Gonthier of Microsoft Research in Cambridge, UK, in collaboration with Benjamin Werner of the École Polytechnique in Paris. The system that he used was Coq (see Section 4 on page 28). The size of the formalization was:

$$2,621,072 \text{ bytes} = 2.50 \text{ megabytes}$$
$$60,103 \text{ lines}$$
$$132 \text{ files}$$

About one third of this was generated automatically from files that were already part of the original Four Color Theorem proof:

$$918,650 \text{ bytes} = 0.88 \text{ megabytes}$$
$$21,049 \text{ lines}$$
$$65 \text{ files}$$

The proof of the Four Color Theorem caused quite a stir when it was found back in the seventies of the previous century. It did not just involve clever mathematics: an essential part of the proof was the execution of a computer program that for a long time searched through endlessly many possibilities. At that time it was one of very few proofs that had that property, but nowadays this kind of proof is more common. Still, many mathematicians do not consider such a proof to have the same status as a 'normal' mathematical proof. It is felt that one cannot be as sure about the correctness of a (large) computer program, as one can be about a mathematical proof that one can follow in one's own mind.

What Georges Gonthier has done is to take away this objection for the Four Color Theorem proof, by formally proving the computer programs of this proof to be correct. However he did not stop there, but also formalized all the graph theory that was part of the proof. In fact, that latter part turned out to be the majority of the work. So the mathematicians are wrong: it is actually *easier* to verify the correctness of the program than to verify the correctness of the pen-and-paper mathematics.

The statement that was proved in the formalization was:

```
Variable R : real_model.

Theorem four_color : (m : (map R))
  (simple_map m) -> (map_colorable (4) m).
```

This statement contains notions `simple_map` and `map_colorable` which need explanation. Here are some of the relevant Coq definitions leading up to these notions, to give some impression of what the statement actually means:

```
Inductive point : Type := Point : (x, y : R) point.

Definition region : Type := point -> Prop.

Definition map : Type := point -> region.

Record proper_map [m : map] : Prop := ProperMap {
  map_sym : (z1, z2 : point) (m z1 z2) -> (m z2 z1);
  map_trans : (z1, z2 : point) (m z1 z2) -> (subregion (m z2) (m z1))
  }.

Record simple_map [m : map] : Prop := SimpleMap {
  simple_map_proper :> (proper_map m);
  map_open : (z : point) (open (m z));
  map_connected : (z : point) (connected (m z))
  }.

Record coloring [m, k : map] : Prop := Coloring {
  coloring_proper :> (proper_map k);
  coloring_inmap : (subregion (inmap k) (inmap m));
  coloring_covers : (covers m k);
  coloring_adj : (z1, z2 : point) (k z1 z2) -> (adjacent m z1 z2) -> (m z1 z2)
  }.

Definition map_colorable [nc : nat; m : map] : Prop :=
  (EXT k | (coloring m k) & (size_at_most nc k)).
```

This says that a `proper_map` is a partial equivalence relation on the type of points, where a `point` is a pair of real numbers. And then such a `proper_map` is called a `simple_map` when all the regions in the map (i.e., the equivalence classes of the relation) are open and connected.

Jordan Curve Theorem. This formalization was written by Tom Hales of the University of Pittsburgh. The system that he used was HOL Light (see Section 1 on page 11). The size of the formalization was:

$$2,257,363 \text{ bytes} = 2.15 \text{ megabytes}$$
$$75,242 \text{ lines}$$
$$15 \text{ files}$$

In 1998, Tom Hales proved the Kepler Conjecture (which states that the optimal way of packing spheres in space is in the way that one stacks cannon-balls or oranges) with a proof that is in the same category as the Four Color Theorem proof in that it relies on a large amount of computer computation. For this reason the referees of the Annals of Mathematics, where he submitted this proof, did not feel that they could check his work. And then he decided to *formalize* his proof to force them to admit that it was correct. He calculated that this formalization effort would take around twenty man-years, and he decided that that was feasible. He called this project '*Flyspeck*', after '*F*ormal *p*roof of *k*epler'.

Then, as a first start for the Flyspeck project he formalized the Jordan Curve Theorem. This theorem states that a closed continuous curve in the plane (called a Jordan curve) divides the plane in exactly two connected components. This theorem is well-known for being very natural to state, but surprisingly difficult to prove.

The final statement of the formalization was proved like:

```
let JORDAN_CURVE_THEOREM = prove_by_refinement(
  '!C. simple_closed_curve top2 C ==>
     (?A B.   top2 A /\ top2 B /\
        connected top2 A /\ connected top2 B /\
     ~(A = EMPTY) /\ ~(B = EMPTY) /\
      (A INTER B = EMPTY) /\ (A INTER C = EMPTY) /\
         (B INTER C = EMPTY) /\
          (A UNION B UNION C = euclid 2))',
  (* {{{ proof *)
  [
  ...
  (* Tue Jan 18 20:44:12 EST 2005 *)
  ]);;
  (* }}} *)
```

(In the place of the dots there are the HOL Light tactics of the last fragment
of the formalization.) All the definitions that are needed to understand this
statement have in the formalization been conveniently collected together in
one lemma:

```
let JORDAN_CURVE_DEFS = prove_by_refinement(
  '(!x. euclid 2 x = (!n. 2 <=| n ==> (x n = &0))) /\
   (top2 = top_of_metric (euclid 2,d_euclid)) /\
   (!(X:A->bool) d. top_of_metric (X,d) =
        {A | ?F. F SUBSET open_balls (X,d) /\ (A = UNIONS F) }) /\
   (!(X:A->bool) d. open_balls(X,d) =
        {B | ?x r. (B = open_ball (X,d) x r) }) /\
   (!X d (x:A) r. open_ball (X,d) x r =
        {y | X x /\ X y /\ d x y < r}) /\
   (!U (Z:A->bool). connected U Z =
        Z SUBSET UNIONS U /\
        (!A B.
            U A /\ U B /\ (A INTER B = {}) /\ Z SUBSET A UNION B
            ==> Z SUBSET A \/ Z SUBSET B)) /\
   (!(C:A->bool) U. simple_closed_curve U C =
        (?f. (C = IMAGE f {x | &0 <= x /\ x <= &1}) /\
            continuous f (top_of_metric (UNIV,d_real)) U /\
            INJ f {x | &0 <= x /\ x < &1} (UNIONS U) /\
            (f (&0) = f (&1)))) /\
   (!(f:A->B) U V. continuous f U V =
        (!v. V v ==> U { x | (UNIONS U) x /\ v (f x) })) /\
   (!x y. d_real x y = abs  (x - y)) /\
   (!x y. euclid 2 x /\ euclid 2 y
        ==> (d_euclid x y =
            sqrt (sum (0,2) (\i. (x i - y i) * (x i - y i)))))',
  ...);;
```

(All the other notions that occur in these statements are defined in the
standard HOL Light library.)

These three formalizations show that the field of proof assistants is in rapid
development. Theorems that for a long time have seemed to be out of reach of
proof checking technology are now getting their proofs formalized! It is therefore very exciting to dream about what it will be like when the *QED utopia* is

finally realized in all its glory. Personally I am convinced that this will happen, eventually. And hopefully this collection of samples from all the provers of the world will play a small part in bringing this future nearer.

0 Informal

Henk Barendregt

Text by Henk Barendregt <henk@cs.ru.nl>.

0.1 Statement

$$\sqrt{2} \notin \mathbb{Q}$$

0.2 Definitions

Definition of P

Define on $\mathbb{N}$ the predicate

$$P(m) \Leftrightarrow \exists n.\, m^2 = 2n^2 \,\&\, m > 0.$$

0.3 Proof

Lemma 1. *For $m, n \in \mathbb{N}$ one has*

$$m^2 = 2n^2 \Rightarrow m = n = 0.$$

Proof. Define on $\mathbb{N}$ the predicate

$$P(m) \Leftrightarrow \exists n.\, m^2 = 2n^2 \,\&\, m > 0.$$

Claim: $P(m) \Rightarrow \exists m' < m.\, P(m')$. Indeed suppose $m^2 = 2n^2$ and $m > 0$. It follows that m^2 is even, but then m must be even, as odds square to odds. So $m = 2k$ and we have

$$2n^2 = m^2 = 4k^2$$
$$\Rightarrow n^2 = 2k^2$$

Since $m > 0$, if follows that $m^2 > 0$, $n^2 > 0$ and $n > 0$. Therefore $P(n)$. Moreover, $m^2 = n^2 + n^2 > n^2$, so $m^2 > n^2$ and hence $m > n$. So we can take $m' = n$.

By the claim $\forall m \in \mathbb{N}.\, \neg P(m)$, since there are no infinite descending sequences of natural numbers.

Now suppose $m^2 = 2n^2$. If $m \neq 0$, then $m > 0$ and hence $P(m)$. Contradiction. Therefore $m = 0$. But then also $n = 0$.

Corollary 1.

$$\sqrt{2} \notin \mathbb{Q}.$$

Proof. Suppose $\sqrt{2} \in \mathbb{Q}$, i.e. $\sqrt{2} = p/q$ with $p \in \mathbb{Z}$, $q \in \mathbb{Z} - \{0\}$. Then $\sqrt{2} = m/n$ with $m = |p|$, $n = |q| \neq 0$. It follows that $m^2 = 2n^2$. But then $n = 0$ by the lemma. Contradiction shows that $\sqrt{2} \notin \mathbb{Q}$.

F. Wiedijk (Ed.): The Seventeen Provers of the World, LNAI 3600, p. 10, 2006.
© Springer-Verlag Berlin Heidelberg 2006

1 HOL

John Harrison, Konrad Slind, and Rob Arthan

Formalizations by John Harrison <johnh@ichips.intel.com> (version in HOL Light), Konrad Slind <slind@cs.utah.edu> (version in HOL4) and Rob Arthan <rda@lemma-one.com> (version in ProofPower). Answers by John Harrison.

1.1 Statement

~rational(sqrt(&2))

1.2 Definitions

Definition of sqrt

```
let root = new_definition
  'root(n) x = @u. (&0 < x ==> &0 < u) /\ u pow n = x';;

let sqrt = new_definition
  'sqrt(x) = root(2) x';;
```

1.3 Proof

```
loads "Examples/analysis.ml";;
loads "Examples/transc.ml";;
loads "Examples/sos.ml";;
```

Definition of rationality (& = natural injection $\mathbb{N} \to \mathbb{R}$).

```
let rational = new_definition
  'rational(r) = ?p q. ~(q = 0) /\ abs(r) = &p / &q';;
```

Prove the key property as a lemma about natural numbers.

```
let NSQRT_2 = prove
 ('!p q. p * p = 2 * q * q ==> q = 0',
  MATCH_MP_TAC num_WF THEN REWRITE_TAC[RIGHT_IMP_FORALL_THM] THEN
  REPEAT STRIP_TAC THEN FIRST_ASSUM(MP_TAC o AP_TERM 'EVEN') THEN
  REWRITE_TAC[EVEN_MULT; ARITH] THEN REWRITE_TAC[EVEN_EXISTS] THEN
  DISCH_THEN(X_CHOOSE_THEN 'm:num' SUBST_ALL_TAC) THEN
  FIRST_X_ASSUM(MP_TAC o SPECL ['q:num'; 'm:num']) THEN
  POP_ASSUM MP_TAC THEN CONV_TAC SOS_RULE);;
```

Hence the irrationality of $\sqrt{2}$.

```
let SQRT_2_IRRATIONAL = prove
 ('~rational(sqrt(&2))',
  SIMP_TAC[rational; real_abs; SQRT_POS_LE; REAL_POS; NOT_EXISTS_THM] THEN
  REPEAT GEN_TAC THEN DISCH_THEN(CONJUNCTS_THEN2 ASSUME_TAC MP_TAC) THEN
  DISCH_THEN(MP_TAC o AP_TERM '\x. x pow 2') THEN
  ASM_SIMP_TAC[SQRT_POW_2; REAL_POS; REAL_POW_DIV; REAL_POW_2; REAL_LT_SQUARE;
               REAL_OF_NUM_EQ; REAL_EQ_RDIV_EQ] THEN
  ASM_MESON_TAC[NSQRT_2; REAL_OF_NUM_EQ; REAL_OF_NUM_MUL]);;
```

F. Wiedijk (Ed.): The Seventeen Provers of the World, LNAI 3600, pp. 11–19, 2006.
© Springer-Verlag Berlin Heidelberg 2006

1.4 Another Formalization: Version in HOL4

Challenge from Freek Wiedijk: the square root of two is not rational. I've adapted a proof in HOL Light by John Harrison.

```
load ["transcTheory"];   open arithmeticTheory BasicProvers;
```

A predicate on reals that picks out the rational ones

```
val Rational_def = Define 'Rational r = ?p q. ~(q=0) /\ (abs(r) = &p / &q)';
```

Trivial lemmas

```
val EXP_2 = Q.prove
('!n:num. n**2 = n*n',
 RW_TAC arith_ss [EXP,MULT_CLAUSES,TWO,ONE]);

val EXP2_LEM = Q.prove
('!x y:num. ((2*x)**2 = 2*(y**2)) = (2*(x**2) = y**2)',
 RW_TAC arith_ss [EXP_2,TWO,GSYM MULT_ASSOC]
 THEN PROVE_TAC [MULT_ASSOC,MULT_SYM]);
```

Main lemma

```
val lemma = Q.prove
('!m n. (m**2 = 2 * n**2) ==> (m=0) /\ (n=0)',
 completeInduct_on 'm' THEN NTAC 2 STRIP_TAC THEN
   '?k. m = 2*k' by PROVE_TAC[EVEN_DOUBLE,EXP_2,EVEN_MULT,EVEN_EXISTS]
               THEN VAR_EQ_TAC THEN
   '?p. n = 2*p' by PROVE_TAC[EVEN_DOUBLE,EXP_2,EVEN_MULT,EVEN_EXISTS,EXP2_LEM]
               THEN VAR_EQ_TAC THEN
  'k**2 = 2*(p**2)' by PROVE_TAC [EXP2_LEM] THEN
  '(k=0) \/ k < 2*k' by numLib.ARITH_TAC
 THENL [FULL_SIMP_TAC arith_ss [EXP_2],
        PROVE_TAC [MULT_EQ_0, DECIDE (Term '~(2 = 0n)')]]);


local open realTheory transcTheory
in
val SQRT_2_IRRATIONAL = Q.prove
('~Rational (sqrt 2r)',
 RW_TAC std_ss [Rational_def,abs,SQRT_POS_LE,REAL_POS]
   THEN Cases_on 'q = 0' THEN ASM_REWRITE_TAC []
   THEN SPOSE_NOT_THEN (MP_TAC o Q.AP_TERM '\x. x pow 2')
   THEN RW_TAC arith_ss [SQRT_POW_2, REAL_POS, REAL_POW_DIV,
                         REAL_EQ_RDIV_EQ,REAL_LT, REAL_POW_LT]
   THEN REWRITE_TAC [REAL_OF_NUM_POW, REAL_MUL, REAL_INJ]
   THEN PROVE_TAC [lemma])
end;
```

1.5   Another Formalization: Version in ProofPower

This section presents a "geometrical" proof of the irrationality of $\sqrt{2}$. It is an extract from a much longer document which gives three different proofs, and that can be found on the web at <http://www.lemma-one.com/papers/papers.html>.

We begin with the ML commands to create a theory to hold the results. It builds on the theory of analysis in the mathematical case studies.

SML
```
set_pc "basic_hol1"; open_theory "analysis"; new_theory "sqrt2";
```

The ProofPower user interface uses a special font for mathematical symbols. The font also includes symbols for drawing the lines that make up the Z-like syntax for defining HOL constants. The definitions of the rationals and the square root function below appear to me on the screen in a reasonably close character-based approximation to what you see in the document.[1]

HOL Constant

$\mathbb{Q} : \mathbb{R} \; SET$

$\mathbb{Q} = \{x \mid \exists a \; b : \mathbb{N} \bullet \neg b = 0 \land (x = a/b \lor x = \sim(a/b))\}$

HOL Constant

$\boldsymbol{Sqrt} : \mathbb{R} \to \mathbb{R}$

$\forall x \bullet \mathbb{NR} \; 0 \le x \Rightarrow \mathbb{NR} \; 0 \le Sqrt \; x \land (Sqrt \; x)\hat{\;}2 = x$

The implicit definition of the square root function requires a consistency proof. Before we embark on this and the rest of the proofs, we set up the proof context to deal with the vocabulary of real numbers and sets as well as the HOL basics.

SML
```
set_merge_pcs["'ℝ", "'sets_alg", "basic_hol1" ];
```

The existence of square roots has already been proved in the the theory of analysis. We just have to use the existence theorem to provide a witness.

SML
```
push_consistency_goal ⌜Sqrt⌝;
a(prove_∃_tac THEN REPEAT strip_tac);
a(cases_tac⌜NR 0 ≤ x'⌝ THEN asm_rewrite_tac[]);
a(bc_thm_tac square_root_thm1 THEN REPEAT strip_tac);
save_consistency_thm ⌜Sqrt⌝ (pop_thm());
```

Now we sneak up on the result in a series of lemmas.
Step 1: if $x^2 = 2y^2$, then $y < x \le (3/2)y$, and $(2y - x)^2 = 2(x - y)^2$:

---

[1] See in particular figure 3 of the Xpp User Guide <http://www.lemma-one.com/ProofPower/doc/doc.html#PPXpp>, which shows a proof in progress.

SML
```
set_goal([], ⌜∀x y•
          NR 0 ≤ x ∧ NR 0 < y ∧ x ^ 2 = NR 2 * y ^ 2
       ⇒  y < x ∧ NR 2 * x ≤ NR 3 * y
       ∧  (NR 2 * y − x) ^ 2 = NR 2 * (x − y) ^ 2 ⌝);
a(rewrite_tac[R_N_exp_square_thm] THEN contr_tac);
(* *** Goal "1" *** *)
a(cases_tac⌜y = x⌝ THEN1 all_var_elim_asm_tac1);
(* *** Goal "1.1" *** *)
a(LEMMA_T⌜x*x = NR 0⌝ ante_tac THEN1 PC_T1 "R_lin_arith" asm_prove_tac[]);
a(rewrite_tac[R_times_eq_0_thm] THEN  PC_T1 "R_lin_arith" asm_prove_tac[]);
(* *** Goal "1.2" *** *)
a(lemma_tac⌜x*y < y*y⌝ THEN1
          once_rewrite_tac[R_times_comm_thm] THEN1
          bc_thm_tac R_times_mono_thm THEN1
                PC_T1 "R_lin_arith" asm_prove_tac[]);
a(lemma_tac⌜x*x ≤ x*y⌝ THEN1
          bc_thm_tac R_≤_times_mono_thm THEN1
                PC_T1"R_lin_arith" asm_prove_tac[]);
a(LEMMA_T⌜y * NR 0 < y*y⌝ (strip_asm_tac o rewrite_rule[]) THEN1
          bc_thm_tac R_times_mono_thm THEN1
                PC_T1"R_lin_arith" asm_prove_tac[]);
a(all_fc_tac[R_≤_less_trans_thm]
          THEN PC_T1"R_lin_arith" asm_prove_tac[]);
(* *** Goal "2" *** *)
a(lemma_tac⌜(NR 3*y)*(NR 2*x) < (NR 2*x)*(NR 2*x)⌝ THEN1
          conv_tac(RANDS_C (eq_match_conv R_times_comm_thm)) THEN1
          bc_thm_tac R_times_mono_thm THEN1
                PC_T1 "R_lin_arith" asm_prove_tac[]);
a(lemma_tac⌜(NR 3*y)*(NR 3*y) ≤ (NR 3*y)*(NR 2*x)⌝ THEN1
          bc_thm_tac R_≤_times_mono_thm THEN1
                PC_T1"R_lin_arith" asm_prove_tac[]);
a(LEMMA_T⌜x * NR 0 < x*x⌝ (strip_asm_tac o rewrite_rule[]) THEN1
          bc_thm_tac R_times_mono_thm THEN1
                PC_T1"R_lin_arith" asm_prove_tac[]);
a(all_fc_tac[R_≤_less_trans_thm]
          THEN PC_T1"R_lin_arith" asm_prove_tac[]);
(* *** Goal "3" *** *)
a(PC_T1"R_lin_arith" asm_prove_tac[]);
val proof1_lemma1 = save_pop_thm "proof1_lemma1";
```

Step 2: step 1 recast for the natural numbers:

SML
```
set_goal([], ⌜∀m n•
          NR m ^ 2 = NR 2 * NR n ^ 2 ∧ 0 < n
       ⇒  n < m ∧ 2 * m ≤ 3 * n
       ∧  NR (2 * n − m) ^ 2 = NR 2 * NR (m − n) ^ 2 ⌝);
a(REPEAT ∀_tac THEN ⇒_tac);
```

```
a(lemma_tac ⌜∀i j•j ≤ i ⇒ NR(i − j) = NR i − NR j⌝);
(* *** Goal "1" *** *)
a(rewrite_tac[≤_def] THEN REPEAT strip_tac THEN
        all_var_elim_asm_tac1);
a(rewrite_tac[∀_elim⌜i'⌝ plus_order_thm,
        NR_plus_homomorphism_thm]
                THEN PC_T1 "R_lin_arith" prove_tac[]);
(* *** Goal "2" *** *)
a(lemma_tac ⌜NR 0 ≤ NR m ∧ NR 0 < NR n⌝ THEN1
        asm_rewrite_tac[NR_≤_thm, NR_less_thm]);
a(ALL_FC_T (MAP_EVERY ante_tac) [proof1_lemma1]);
a(rewrite_tac[NR_≤_thm, NR_less_thm,
        NR_times_homomorphism_thm1] THEN REPEAT strip_tac);
a(lemma_tac⌜m ≤ 2∗n ∧ n ≤ m⌝ THEN1 PC_T1 "lin_arith" asm_prove_tac[]);
a(ALL_ASM_FC_T asm_rewrite_tac[]);
val proof1_lemma2 = save_pop_thm "proof1_lemma2";
```

Step 3: if m and n are positive integer solutions to $m^2 = 2n^2$, then there is a solution with smaller n:

SML

```
set_goal([], ⌜ ∀m n•
        NR m ^ 2 = NR 2 ∗ NR n ^ 2 ∧ 0 < n
⇒        ∃m1 n1•0 < n1 ∧ n1 < n ∧ NR m1 ^ 2 = NR 2 ∗ NR n1 ^ 2 ⌝);
a(REPEAT strip_tac THEN all_fc_tac[proof1_lemma2]);
a(∃_tac⌜2∗n − m⌝ THEN ∃_tac⌜m − n⌝ THEN asm_rewrite_tac[]);
a(LEMMA_T ⌜n ≤ m⌝ (strip_asm_tac o rewrite_rule[≤_def])
        THEN1 PC_T1 "lin_arith" asm_prove_tac[]);
a(all_var_elim_asm_tac1);
a(rewrite_tac[∀_elim⌜i⌝ plus_order_thm]);
a(PC_T1 "lin_arith" asm_prove_tac[]);
val proof1_lemma3 = save_pop_thm "proof1_lemma3";
```

Step 4: the induction that shows the only natural number solution to $m^2 = 2n^2$ has $m = 0$:

SML

```
set_goal([], ⌜ ∀n m• NR m ^ 2 = NR 2 ∗ NR n ^ 2 ⇒ n = 0 ⌝);
a(∀_tac THEN cov_induction_tac⌜n:N⌝ THEN REPEAT strip_tac);
a(contr_tac THEN lemma_tac ⌜0 < n⌝ THEN1
        PC_T1 "lin_arith" asm_prove_tac[]);
a(all_fc_tac[proof1_lemma3]);
a(all_asm_fc_tac[] THEN all_var_elim_asm_tac1);
val proof1_lemma4 = save_pop_thm "proof1_lemma4";
```

... which gives what we wanted, expressed explicitly:

SML

```
set_goal([], ⌜ ∀a b• ¬b = 0 ⇒ ¬(a/b)^2 = NR 2 ∧ ¬(∼(a/b)^2) = NR 2 ⌝);
a(REPEAT ∀_tac THEN ⇒_tac);
a(lemma_tac⌜¬NR b = NR 0 ∧ ∼(a/b)^2 = (a/b)^2⌝ THEN1
          asm_rewrite_tac[NR_one_one_thm, R_N_exp_square_thm]
                    THEN1 PC_T1 "R_lin_arith" prove_tac[]);
a(asm_rewrite_tac[R_frac_def] THEN REPEAT strip_tac
          THEN ALL_FC_T rewrite_tac[R_over_times_recip_thm]);
a(contr_tac THEN LEMMA_T⌜
          (NR a * NR b ⁻¹) ^ 2 * NR b ^ 2 = NR 2 * NR b ^ 2⌝ ante_tac
          THEN1 asm_rewrite_tac[]);
a(rewrite_tac[]);
a(LEMMA_T⌜∀x y z:R•(x*y)^2*z^2 = (x*z*y)^2⌝ rewrite_thm_tac THEN1
          (rewrite_tac[R_N_exp_square_thm]
                    THEN PC_T1"R_lin_arith" prove_tac[]));
a(ALL_FC_T rewrite_tac[R_times_recip_thm]);
a(contr_tac THEN all_fc_tac[proof1_lemma4]);
val proof1_thm1 = save_pop_thm "proof1_thm1";
```

...or in terms of the square root function and the set ℚ.

SML

```
set_goal([], ⌜ ¬Sqrt (NR 2) ∈ ℚ ⌝);
a(rewrite_tac[get_spec⌜ℚ⌝] THEN REPEAT_UNTIL is_∨ strip_tac);
a(cases_tac ⌜b = 0⌝ THEN asm_rewrite_tac[]);
a(contr_tac THEN
          (LEMMA_T ⌜Sqrt(NR 2)^2 = NR 2⌝ ante_tac THEN1
                    bc_tac(map (rewrite_rule[]) (fc_canon (get_spec⌜Sqrt⌝))))
                    THEN ALL_FC_T asm_rewrite_tac[proof1_thm1]);
val proof1_thm2 = save_pop_thm "proof1_thm2";
```

1.6   System

What is the home page of the system?

    <http://www.cl.cam.ac.uk/users/jrh/hol-light/index.html>

What are the books about the system? There are no books specifically about the HOL Light system, but it has much in common with 'HOL88', described in the following book:

> Michael J. C. Gordon and Thomas F. Melham, *Introduction to HOL: a theorem proving environment for higher order logic* , Cambridge University Press, 1993.

and there is a preliminary user manual on the above Web page.

What is the logic of the system? Classical higher-order logic with axioms of infinity, extensionality and choice, based on simply typed lambda-calculus with polymorphic type variables. HOL Light's core axiomatization is close to the usual definition of the internal logic of a topos, and so is intuitionistic in style, but once the Axiom of Choice in the form of Hilbert's ε is added, the logic becomes classical.

What is the implementation architecture of the system? HOL Light follows the LCF approach. The system is built around a 'logical core' of primitive inference rules. Using an abstract type of theorems ensures that theorems can only be constructed by applying these inference rules. However, these can be composed in arbitrarily sophisticated ways by additional layers of programming.

What does working with the system look like? One normally works inside the read-eval-print loop of the implementation language, Objective CAML. However, since the system is fully programmable, other means of interaction can be, and have been, written on top.

What is special about the system compared to other systems? HOL Light is probably the system that represents the LCF ideal in its purest form. The primitive rules of the logic are very simple, with the entire logical core including support functions consisting of only 433 lines of OCaml (excluding comments and blank lines). Yet from this foundation some quite powerful decision procedures and non-trivial mathematical theories are developed, and the system has been used for some substantial formal verification projects in industry.

What are other versions of the system?

- HOL88, hol90 and hol98:
    `<http://www.cl.cam.ac.uk/Research/HVG/HOL/HOL.html#getting>`
- HOL4:
    `<http://hol.sourceforge.net/>`
- ProofPower:
    `<http://www.lemma-one.com/ProofPower/index/index.html>`

Who are the people behind the system? HOL Light was almost entirely written by John Harrison. However, it builds on earlier versions of HOL, notably the original work by Gordon and Melham and the improved implementation by Konrad Slind, not to mention the earlier work on Edinburgh and Cambridge LCF.

What are the main user communities of the system? HOL Light was originally an experimental 'reference' version of HOL and little active effort was made to develop a large user community, though it has been used quite extensively inside Intel to formally verify floating-point algorithms. Recently it has attracted more users based on its role in the Flyspeck project to formalize the proof by Hales of Kepler's conjecture:

`<http://www.math.pitt.edu/~thales/flyspeck/>`

What large mathematical formalizations have been done in the system?

- Analysis: Construction of the real numbers, real analysis up to fundamental theorem of calculus, complex numbers up to the fundamental theorem of algebra, multivariate calculus up to inverse function theorem.
- Topology: Elementary topological notions, classic theorems about Euclidean space including Brouwer's fixpoint theorem and the Jordan curve theorem.
- Logic: classic metatheorems of first order logic (compactness, Lowenheim-Skolem etc.), Tarski's theorem on the undefinability of truth, Gödel's first incompleteness theorem.
- Number theory: Basic results on primality and divisibility, weak prime number theorem, Bertrand's theorem, proof that exponentiation is diophantine.

In addition, many large formal verification proofs, and some of these have used non-trivial mathematics including series expansions for transcendentals, results from diophantine approximation and certification of primality, as well as many general results about floating-point rounding.

What representation of the formalization has been put in this paper? A tactic script in the form of interpreted OCaml source code.

What needs to be explained about this specific proof? Most of the mathematical interest is in the lemma `NSQRT_2`. This is proved by wellfounded induction followed by the usual even/odd case analysis. (Note that all the variables in this lemma are natural numbers, inferred by HOL from context rather than given explicitly.) `SOS_RULE`, which appears in the last line, uses an external semidefinite programming package to find a certificate that HOL can use to verify some nonlinear reasoning. To avoid any reliance on external tools, one can replace the last line with a slightly more laborious alternative such as the following:

```
ONCE_REWRITE_TAC[ARITH_RULE
  'q * q = 2 * m * m <=> (2 * m) * (2 * m) = 2 * q * q'] THEN
ASM_REWRITE_TAC[ARITH_RULE '(q < 2 * m ==> m = 0) <=> 2 * m <= q'] THEN
DISCH_THEN(MP_TAC o MATCH_MP LE_MULT2 o W CONJ) THEN
ASM_REWRITE_TAC[ARITH_RULE '2 * x <= x <=> x = 0'; MULT_EQ_0]);;
```

The final result is a reduction of the main theorem to that lemma on natural numbers using straightforward but rather tedious simplification with a suite of basic properties such as $0 \leq x \Rightarrow (\sqrt{x})^2 = x$ and $0 < z \Rightarrow (x = y/z \Leftrightarrow x \cdot z = y)$.

A simpler proof of `NSQRT_2` was later pointed out to me by Rob Arthan. Instead of an even/odd case analysis, we can drive the wellfounded induction by the observation that if $p^2 = 2q^2$ then $(2q - p)^2 = 2(p - q)^2$. All the necessary algebraic manipulations and inequality reasoning can be dealt with automatically by `SOS_RULE` (note that `EXP` denotes exponentiation):

```
let LEMMA_1 = SOS_RULE
  'p EXP 2 = 2 * q EXP 2
   ==> (q = 0 \/ 2 * q - p < p /\ ~(p - q = 0)) /\
       (2 * q - p) EXP 2 = 2 * (p - q) EXP 2';;
```

Now we can get NSQRT_2 simply by wellfounded induction followed by trivial
first-order reasoning.

```
let NSQRT_2 = prove
 ('!p q. p * p = 2 * q * q ==> q = 0',
  REWRITE_TAC[GSYM EXP_2] THEN MATCH_MP_TAC num_WF THEN MESON_TAC[LEMMA_1]);;
```

2 Mizar

Andrzej Trybulec

Formalization and answers by Andrzej Trybulec
<trybulec@math.uwb.edu.pl>.

2.1 Statement

```
sqrt 2 is irrational
```

2.2 Definitions

Definition of sqrt

```
reserve a for real number;

definition let a;
 assume  0 <= a;
  func sqrt a -> real number means
:: SQUARE_1:def 4
 0 <= it & it^2 = a;
end;
```

Definition of irrational

```
reserve x for set,
        m,n for Integer;

definition
 func RAT means
:: RAT_1:def 1
   x in it iff ex m,n st x = m/n;
 end;

definition let r be number;
 attr r is rational means
:: RAT_1:def 2
   r in RAT;
end;

reserve x for real number;

notation let x;
 antonym x is irrational for x is rational;
 end;
```

2.3 Proof

```
environ
 vocabulary SQUARE_1,IRRAT_1,ARYTM_3,RAT_1,INT_1;
 constructors NAT_1,PREPOWER,PEPIN,MEMBERED;
 notations XCMPLX_0,XREAL_0,INT_1,NAT_1,RAT_1,SQUARE_1,IRRAT_1;
 registrations XREAL_0,INT_1,MEMBERED;
 theorems INT_1,SQUARE_1,REAL_2,INT_2,XCMPLX_1,NAT_1,RAT_1,NEWTON;
 requirements ARITHM,REAL,NUMERALS,SUBSET;
begin
```

F. Wiedijk (Ed.): The Seventeen Provers of the World, LNAI 3600, pp. 20–23, 2006.
© Springer-Verlag Berlin Heidelberg 2006

```
theorem
  sqrt 2 is irrational
proof
 assume sqrt 2 is rational;
 then consider i being Integer, n being Nat such that
W1: n<>0 and
W2: sqrt 2=i/n and
W3: for i1 being Integer, n1 being Nat st n1<>0 & sqrt 2=i1/n1 holds n<=n1
        by RAT_1:25;
A5: i=sqrt 2*n by W1,XCMPLX_1:88,W2;
C: sqrt 2>=0 & n>0 by W1,NAT_1:19,SQUARE_1:93;
   then i>=0 by A5,REAL_2:121;
   then reconsider m = i as Nat by INT_1:16;
A6: m*m = n*n*(sqrt 2*sqrt 2) by A5
   .= n*n*(sqrt 2)^2 by SQUARE_1:def 3
   .= 2*(n*n) by SQUARE_1:def 4;
   then 2 divides m*m by NAT_1:def 3;
   then 2 divides m by INT_2:44,NEWTON:98;
   then consider m1 being Nat such that
W4: m=2*m1 by NAT_1:def 3;
   m1*m1*2*2 = m1*(m1*2)*2
      .= 2*(n*n) by W4,A6,XCMPLX_1:4;
   then 2*(m1*m1) = n*n by XCMPLX_1:5;
   then 2 divides n*n by NAT_1:def 3;
   then 2 divides n by INT_2:44,NEWTON:98;
   then consider n1 being Nat such that
W5: n=2*n1 by NAT_1:def 3;
A10: m1/n1 = sqrt 2 by W4,W5,XCMPLX_1:92,W2;
A11: n1>0 by W5,C,REAL_2:123;
   then 2*n1>1*n1 by REAL_2:199;
 hence contradiction by A10,W5,A11,W3;
end;
```

2.4 System

What is the home page of the system?

<http://mizar.org/>

What are the books about the system?

- Bonarska, E., *An Introduction to PC Mizar*, Fondation Philippe le Hodey, Brussels, 1990.
- Muzalewski, M., *An Outline of PC Mizar*, Fondation Philippe le Hodey, Brussels, 1993.
- Nakamura, Y. et al., *Mizar Lecture Notes* (4-th Edition, Mizar Version 6.1.12), Shinshu University, Nagano, 2002.

What is the logic of the system? Mizar is based on classical logic and the Jaskowski system of natural deduction (composite logic). It is a formal system of general applicability, which as such has little in common with any set theory. However, its huge library of formalized mathematical data, Mizar Mathematical Library, is based on the Tarski-Grothendieck set theory.

What is the implementation architecture of the system? It is the standard way of writing compilers – a multipass system consisting of: tokenizer, parser and a separated grammatical analyzer, as well as logical modules: checker, schematizer and reasoner. The system is coded in Pascal and is currently available for several platforms: Microsoft Windows, Intel-based Linux, Solaris and FreeBSD, and also Darwin/Mac OS X on PowerPC.

What does working with the system look like? One may call it a 'lazy interaction': the article is written in plain ASCII and is processed as whole by the verifier. The best writing technique is the stepwise refinement, where one starts with a proof plan and then fills the gaps reported by the verifier.

What is special about the system compared to other systems? It is easy to use and very close to the mathematical vernacular. Around 1989 we started the systematic collection of Mizar articles. Today the Mizar Mathematical Library contains the impressive number of 900 articles with almost 40000 theorems (about 65 MB of formalized texts).

What are other versions of the system? A very small part of the Mizar language, called Mizar MSE (or sometimes Baby Mizar), has been implemented separately. It can hardly be used for formalizing mathematics, but it has proved to be quite useful for teaching and learning logic.

Who are the people behind the system? Andrzej Trybulec is the author of the Mizar language, he is also the head of the team implementing the Mizar verifier:

- Grzegorz Bancerek
- Czeslaw Bylinski
- Adam Grabowski
- Artur Kornilowicz
- Robert Milewski
- Adam Naumowicz
- Andrzej Trybulec
- Josef Urban

Adam Grabowski is the head of the Library Committee of the Association of Mizar Users (SUM) and is in charge of the Mizar Mathematical Library (MML).

What are the main user communities of the system? The most active user communities are concentrated at University of Bialystok, Poland and Shinshu University, Japan. However, more than 160 authors from 10 countries have contributed their articles to the Mizar library since its establishing in 1989. Recently, we also observe the revival of the (once numerous) community who use Mizar for teaching purposes.

What large mathematical formalizations have been done in the system? The greatest challenge was the formalizing of the book 'A Compendium of Continuous Lattices' by G. Gierz, K. H. Hofmann, K. Keimel, J. D. Lawson, M. Mislove, and D. S. Scott. So far, about 60 per cent of the book's theory has been covered in the Mizar library by 16 Mizar authors. There are also several successful developments aimed at formalizing well-known theorems, e.g. Alexander's Lemma, the Banach Fixed Point Theorem for compact spaces, the Brouwer Fixed Point Theorem, the Birkhoff Variety Theorem for manysorted algebras, Fermat's Little Theorem, the Fundamental Theorem of Algebra, the Fundamental Theorem of Arithmetic, the Goedel Completeness Theorem, the Hahn-Banach Theorem for complex and real spaces, the Jordan Curve Theorem for special polygons, the Reflection Theorem, and many others.

What representation of the formalization has been put in this paper? It is the Mizar script, as prepared by the author and checked by the system.

What needs to be explained about this specific proof? The actual proof in Mizar would now be as follows:

```
sqtr 2 is irrational by IRRAT_1:1, INT_2:44;
```

The presented proof is an adjusted version of the proof that the square root of any prime number is irrational (IRRAT_1:1). So, this is what the proof would have looked like if Freek Wiedijk had not submitted the IRRAT_1 article to the MML in 1999.

3 PVS

Bart Jacobs and John Rushby

Formalization by Bart Jacobs <bart@cs.ru.nl> and John Rushby
<rushby@csl.sri.com>. It builds on the NASA PVS library at:

<http://shemesh.larc.nasa.gov/fm/ftp/larc/PVS-library/pvslib.html>

In particular the definition of sqrt below comes from this library. Answers by John Rushby.

3.1 Statement

```
NOT Rational?(sqrt(2))
```

3.2 Definitions

Definition of sqrt

```
nnx, nnz: VAR nonneg_real

sqrt(nnx): {nnz | nnz*nnz = nnx}

sqrt_pos: JUDGEMENT sqrt(px: posreal) HAS_TYPE posreal
```

TCCs for this definition

```
% Existence TCC generated (at line 19, column 2) for
    % sqrt(nnx): {nnz | nnz * nnz = nnx}
  % proved - complete
sqrt_TCC1: OBLIGATION
  EXISTS (x1: [nnx: nonneg_real -> {nnz: nonneg_real | nnz * nnz = nnx}]):
    TRUE;

% Judgement subtype TCC generated (at line 21, column 34) for  sqrt(px)
    % expected type  posreal
  % proved - complete
sqrt_pos: OBLIGATION FORALL (px: posreal): sqrt(px) > 0;
```

Proof of sqrt_TCC1

```
("" (LEMMA "sqrt_exists") (PROPAX))
```

Proof of sqrt_pos

```
("" (SKOSIMP*) (ASSERT))
```

Definition of Rational?

```
Rational? : PRED[real] =
  { t : real | EXISTS(n:int, m:posnat) : t = n/m }
```

F. Wiedijk (Ed.): The Seventeen Provers of the World, LNAI 3600, pp. 24–27, 2006.
© Springer-Verlag Berlin Heidelberg 2006

3.3 Proof

```
SQRT2 : THEORY
BEGIN

  reals : LIBRARY = "/usr/local/share/pvslib/reals"

  IMPORTING reals@sqrt

  even_or_odd : LEMMA
    FORALL(n:nat) : even?(n) XOR odd?(n)

  square_even_odd : LEMMA
    FORALL(n:nat) : (even?(n) IMPLIES even?(n*n))
                      AND
                    (odd?(n) IMPLIES odd?(n*n))

  sqrt2 : LEMMA
    FORALL(n,m:nat) : n>0 IMPLIES NOT n*n = 2*m*m
```

Non-rationality result. Note that **rational?** is introduced *axiomatically* in the prelude, and therefore not useable here.

```
  Rational? : PRED[real] =
    { t : real | EXISTS(n:int, m:posnat) : t = n/m }

  sqrt2_non_rational : LEMMA
    NOT Rational?(sqrt(2))

END SQRT2
```

Proof of even_or_odd

```
("" (INDUCT-AND-SIMPLIFY "n" :IF-MATCH NIL) (INST 2 "j!2+1") (ASSERT))
```

Proof of square_even_odd

```
(""
 (INDUCT-AND-SIMPLIFY "n" :IF-MATCH NIL)
 (("1" (INST 2 "j!3+j!1") (ASSERT)) ("2" (INST 2 "1+j!2+j!1") (ASSERT))
  ("3" (INST 2 "j!2-1") (ASSERT))))
```

Proof of sqrt2

```
(""
 (INDUCT "n" :NAME "NAT_induction")
 (SKOSIMP*)
 (USE "even_or_odd")
 (EXPAND* "XOR" "/=")
 (BDDSIMP)
 (("1"
   (EXPAND "even?")
   (SKOSIMP*)
   (INST -2 "m!1")
   (GROUND)
   (("1"
     (INST -1 "j!2")
     (LEMMA "nonzero_times3")
     (GRIND :IF-MATCH ALL))
```

```
("2"
 (LEMMA "gt_times_gt_pos1")
 (INST -1 "j!1" "j!1" "m!1" "m!1")
 (ASSERT)
 (LEMMA "pos_times_gt")
 (GRIND :IF-MATCH ALL))))
("2" (USE "square_even_odd") (GRIND))))
```

Proof of sqrt2_non_rational

```
(""
 (EXPAND "Rational?")
 (SKOSIMP)
 (LEMMA "sqrt2")
 (INST - "abs(n!1)" "abs(m!1)")
 (CASE-REPLACE "n!1*n!1=2*m!1*m!1")
 (("1" (GRIND))
  ("2" (USE "sqrt_def") (GRIND) (USE "div_cancel3") (ASSERT))))
```

3.4   System

What is the home page of the system?

<http://pvs.csl.sri.com/>

What are the books about the system? There are currently no books on PVS, but the system guide, language reference, and prover guide are available at:

<http://pvs.csl.sri.com/manuals.html>

What is the logic of the system? PVS is based on classical higher-order logic.

What is the implementation architecture of the system? PVS is written primarily in Common Lisp.

What does working with the system look like? The user interface is built on Emacs. The user normally creates specification files, typechecks them, and proves formulas interactively. There are a large number of commands for proofchain analysis, browsing, and specification and proof development and maintenance.

What is special about the system compared to other systems? It has predicate subtypes, dependent types, aggressive use of decision procedures, tight integration of typechecking and theorem proving, and theory interpretations. PVS is integrated with a number of outside systems, including a BDD-based model checker, MONA (a decision procedure for WS1S), abstraction, and a fast ground evaluator. LaTeX output may be generated for both specifications and proofs.

What are other versions of the system? The first version of PVS was introduced in 1993. Version 3.0 will be released shortly.

Who are the people behind the system? The formal methods group at SRI:

<http://www.csl.sri.com/programs/formalmethods/>

What are the main user communities of the system? It's used worldwide in both academia and industry – see:

<http://pvs.csl.sri.com/users.html>

What large mathematical formalizations have been done in the system? There is an analysis library, finite sets, domain theory, program semantics, graph theory, set theory, etc.

What representation of the formalization has been put in this paper? This is one of many possible representations in PVS, as functions may be defined ax-iomatically, constructively, or, as in this case, by putting it into the types. This particular representation builds on the definition of sqrt in the reals library at NASA.

What needs to be explained about this specific proof? The TCCs (type-correctness conditions) are proof obligations generated by the PVS typechecker. Judgements provide additional information to the typechecker, so that further TCCs are minimized; in this case after the judgement the typechecker knows that the sqrt of a positive number is positive.

The cited formulas ge_times_ge_pos and nonzero_times3 are from the PVS 'prelude' (a built-in library of several hundred proven properties outside the scope of PVS decision procedures).

These proofs are the result of an interaction with the PVS prover, which builds a sequent-based proof tree based on commands provided by the user.

4 Coq

Laurent Théry, Pierre Letouzey, and Georges Gonthier

Formalizations by Laurent Théry <laurent.thery@sophia.inria.fr>,
Pierre Letouzey <Pierre.Letouzey@lri.fr> and Georges Gonthier
<gonthier@microsoft.com>. Answers by Laurent Théry.

4.1 Statement

irrational (sqrt 2%nat).

4.2 Definitions

Definition of irrational

```
Definition irrational (x : R) : Prop :=
   forall (p : Z) (q : nat), q <> 0 ->  x <> (p / q)%R.
```

4.3 Proof

```
Require Import ArithRing.
Require Import Wf_nat.
Require Import Peano_dec.
Require Import Div2.
Require Import Even.
```

Properties of div2 and double (these theorems should be in Div2.v)

```
Theorem double_div2: forall (n : nat),  div2 (double n) = n.
simple induction n; auto with arith.
intros n0 H.
rewrite double_S; pattern n0 at 2; rewrite <- H; simpl; auto.
Qed.

Theorem double_inv: forall (n m : nat), double n = double m ->  n = m.
intros n m H; rewrite <- (double_div2 n); rewrite <- (double_div2 m); rewrite H;
 auto.
Qed.

Theorem double_mult_l: forall (n m : nat),  double (n * m) = double n * m.
unfold double; auto with arith.
Qed.

Theorem double_mult_r: forall (n m : nat),  double (n * m) = n * double m.
unfold double; intros; ring.
Qed.
```

If the power to the 2 of a number is even, then this number is even

```
Theorem even_is_even_times_even: forall (n : nat), even (n * n) ->  even n.
intros n H; (try case (even_or_odd n)); auto.
intros; apply even_mult_inv_r with (1 := H); auto.
Qed.
```

F. Wiedijk (Ed.): The Seventeen Provers of the World, LNAI 3600, pp. 28–35, 2006.
© Springer-Verlag Berlin Heidelberg 2006

Useful fact $4 \cdot (n/2) \cdot (n/2) = n \cdot n$ if n is even

```
Theorem main_thm_aux:
 forall (n : nat), even n ->  double (double (div2 n * div2 n)) = n * n.
intros; rewrite double_mult_l; rewrite double_mult_r;
 (repeat rewrite <- even_double); auto.
Qed.
```

Main theorem

We do the proof of the theorem by well founded induction: Suppose that we have $n \cdot n = 2 \cdot p \cdot p$

if $n = 0$ then $p = 0$
if $n \neq 0$ then
- n is even $(n = 2n')$ and p is even $(p = 2p')$
- we have $n' \cdot n' = 2 \cdot p' \cdot p'$ and $n' < n$
- by the induction hypothesis we have $p' = 0$
- so $p = 0$

```
Theorem main_thm: forall (n p : nat), n * n = double (p * p) ->  p = 0.
intros n; pattern n; apply lt_wf_ind; clear n.
intros n H p H0.
case (eq_nat_dec n 0); intros H1.
generalize H0; rewrite H1; case p; auto; intros; discriminate.
assert (H2: even n).
apply even_is_even_times_even.
apply double_even; rewrite H0; rewrite double_div2; auto.
assert (H3: even p).
apply even_is_even_times_even.
rewrite <- (double_inv (double (div2 n * div2 n)) (p * p)).
apply double_even; rewrite double_div2; auto.
rewrite main_thm_aux; auto.
assert (H4: div2 p = 0).
apply (H (div2 n)).
apply lt_div2; apply neq_0_lt; auto.
apply double_inv; apply double_inv; (repeat rewrite main_thm_aux); auto.
rewrite (even_double p); auto; rewrite H4; auto.
Qed.
```

Coercions from nat and Z to R

```
Require Import Reals.
Require Import Field.
Coercion INR : nat >-> R.
Coercion IZR : Z >-> R.
```

Definition of irrational

```
Definition irrational (x : R) : Prop :=
   forall (p : Z) (q : nat), q <> 0 ->  x <> (p / q)%R.
```

Final theorem

```
Theorem irrational_sqrt_2: irrational (sqrt 2%nat).
intros p q H HO; case H.
apply (main_thm (Zabs_nat p)).
replace (Div2.double (q * q)) with (2 * (q * q));
 [idtac | unfold Div2.double; ring].
case (eq_nat_dec (Zabs_nat p * Zabs_nat p) (2 * (q * q))); auto; intros H1.
case (not_nm_INR _ _ H1); (repeat rewrite mult_INR).
rewrite <- (sqrt_def (INR 2)); auto with real.
rewrite HO; auto with real.
assert (q <> 0%R :> R); auto with real.
field; auto with real; case p; simpl; intros; ring.
Qed.
```

Proof term of `main_thm`

```
main_thm =
fun n : nat =>
lt_wf_ind n
  (fun n0 : nat => forall p : nat, n0 * n0 = Div2.double (p * p) -> p = 0)
  (fun (n0 : nat)
     (H : forall m : nat,
          m < n0 -> forall p : nat, m * m = Div2.double (p * p) -> p = 0)
     (p : nat) (HO : n0 * n0 = Div2.double (p * p)) =>
   match Peano_dec.eq_nat_dec n0 0 with
   | left H1 =>
       let H2 :=
         eq_ind_r (fun n : nat => n * n = Div2.double (p * p) -> p = 0)
           match p as n return (0 * 0 = Div2.double (n * n) -> n = 0) with
           | 0 => fun H2 : 0 * 0 = Div2.double (0 * 0) => H2
           | S n0 =>
               fun H2 : 0 * 0 = Div2.double (S n0 * S n0) =>
               let H3 :=
                 eq_ind (0 * 0)
                   (fun ee : nat =>
                    match ee with
                    | 0 => True
                    | S _ => False
                    end) I (Div2.double (S n0 * S n0)) H2 in
               False_ind (S n0 = 0) H3
           end H1 in
       H2 HO
   | right H1 =>
       let H2 :=
         even_is_even_times_even n0
           (double_even (n0 * n0)
              (eq_ind_r (fun n : nat => n = Div2.double (div2 n))
                 (eq_ind_r
                    (fun n : nat => Div2.double (p * p) = Div2.double n)
                    (refl_equal (Div2.double (p * p)))
                    (double_div2 (p * p))) HO)) in
       let H3 :=
         even_is_even_times_even p
           (eq_ind (Div2.double (div2 n0 * div2 n0))
              (fun n : nat => even n)
```

```
              (double_even (Div2.double (div2 n0 * div2 n0))
                 (eq_ind_r
                    (fun n : nat =>
                     Div2.double (div2 n0 * div2 n0) = Div2.double n)
                    (refl_equal (Div2.double (div2 n0 * div2 n0)))
                    (double_div2 (div2 n0 * div2 n0))))
              (p * p)
              (double_inv (Div2.double (div2 n0 * div2 n0))
                 (p * p)
                 (eq_ind_r (fun n : nat => n = Div2.double (p * p)) H0
                    (main_thm_aux n0 H2)))) in
        let H4 :=
          H (div2 n0) (lt_div2 n0 (neq_0_lt n0 (sym_not_eq H1)))
            (div2 p)
            (double_inv (div2 n0 * div2 n0) (Div2.double (div2 p * div2 p))
               (double_inv (Div2.double (div2 n0 * div2 n0))
                  (Div2.double (Div2.double (div2 p * div2 p)))
                  (eq_ind_r
                     (fun n : nat =>
                      n =
                      Div2.double
                        (Div2.double (Div2.double (div2 p * div2 p))))
                     (eq_ind_r (fun n : nat => n0 * n0 = Div2.double n) H0
                        (main_thm_aux p H3)) (main_thm_aux n0 H2)))) in
        eq_ind_r (fun p0 : nat => p0 = 0)
          (eq_ind_r (fun n1 : nat => Div2.double n1 = 0) (refl_equal 0) H4)
          (even_double p H3)
    end)
     : forall n p : nat, n * n = Div2.double (p * p) -> p = 0
```

4.4 Another Formalization: Using the Binary Representation of the Integers

```
Require Import BinPos.
Open Scope positive_scope.

Ltac mysimpl := simplify_eq; repeat rewrite Pmult_xO_permute_r.

Theorem main_thm: forall p q: positive, 2*(q*q)<>p*p.
Proof.
induction p; simpl; intro; mysimpl.
destruct q; mysimpl; firstorder.
Qed.

Require Import Reals Field.
Open Scope R_scope.

(* IPR: Injection from Positive to Reals *)
(* Should be in the standard library, close to INR and IZR *)

Definition IPR (p:positive):= (INR (nat_of_P p)).
Coercion IPR : positive >-> R.

Lemma mult_IPR : forall p q, IPR (p * q) = (IPR p * IPR q)%R.
unfold IPR; intros; rewrite nat_of_P_mult_morphism; auto with real.
Qed.
Lemma IPR_eq : forall p q, IPR p = IPR q -> p = q.
unfold IPR; intros; apply nat_of_P_inj; auto with real.
Qed.
```

```
Lemma IPR_nonzero : forall p, IPR p <> 0.
unfold IPR; auto with real.
Qed.
Hint Resolve IPR_eq IPR_nonzero.
(* End of IPR *)

Ltac myfield := field; rewrite <- mult_IPR; auto.

Lemma main_thm_pos_rat : forall (p q:positive), 2 <> (p/q)*(p/q).
Proof.
red; intros.
assert (2*(q*q)=p*p).
  rewrite H; myfield.
clear H; change 2 with (IPR 2) in H0.
apply main_thm with p q; auto.
repeat rewrite <- mult_IPR in H0; auto.
Qed.

Coercion IZR : Z >-> R.

Lemma main_thm_rat : forall (p:Z)(q:positive), 2 <> (p/q)*(p/q).
Proof.
destruct p; simpl; intros.
replace (0 / q * (0 / q)) with 0.
discrR.
field; rewrite <- mult_IPR; auto.
exact (main_thm_pos_rat p q).
replace (INR (nat_of_P p)) with (IPR p); auto.
replace (- p / q * (- p / q)) with ((p/q)*(p/q)); try myfield.
exact (main_thm_pos_rat p q).
Qed.

Definition irrational (x:R) : Prop := forall (p:Z)(q:positive), x <> (p/q).

Lemma Sqrt2_irr : irrational (sqrt 2).
Proof.
 red; intros p q H.
 assert (H1: 2 = sqrt 2 * sqrt 2).
   symmetry; apply sqrt_sqrt; auto with real.
 rewrite H in H1; apply main_thm_rat with p q; auto.
Qed.
```

4.5   Another Formalization: Coq in the Style of Georges Gonthier

```
Section Sqrt2.

Variable R : real_model.
Coercion Local fracR := (fracr R).

Theorem sqrt2_irrational : ~(EX f : frac | 'f = sqrt 2').
Proof.
Move=> [f Df]; Step [Hf22 H2f2]: '(mulf f f) = F2'.
  Apply: (eqr_trans (fracr_mul ? ? ?)); Apply: eqr_trans (fracrz R (Znat 2)).
  By Apply: eqr_trans (square_sqrt (ltrW (ltr02 R))); Apply mulr_morphism.
Step Df2: (eqf F2 (mulf f f)) By Apply/andP; Split; Apply/(fracr_leqPx R ? ?).
Move: f Df2 {Hf22 H2f2 Df} => [d m]; Rewrite: /eqf /= -eqz_leq; Move/eqP.
Rewrite: scalez_mul -scalez_scale scalez_mul mulzC {-1 Zpos}lock /= -lock.
Step []: (Zpos (S d)) = (scalez d (Znat 1)).
  By Apply esym; Apply: eqP; Rewrite scalez_pos; Elim d.
Step [n []]: (EX n | (mulz (Zpos n) (Zpos n)) = (mulz m m)).
```

```
Case: m => [n | n]; LeftBy Exists n.
  By Exists (S n); Rewrite: -{1 (Zneg n)}oppz_opp mulz_oppl -mulz_oppr.
Pose i := (addn (S d) n); Move: (leqnn i) {m}; Rewrite: {1}/i.
Elim: i n d => // [i Hrec] n d Hi Dn2; Move/esym: Dn2 Hi.
Rewrite: -{n}odd_double_half double_addnn !zpos_addn; Move/half: n (odd n) => n.
Case; [Move/((congr oddz) ? ?) | Move/((congr halfz) ? ?)].
  By Rewrite: !mulz_addr oddz_add mulzC !mulz_addr oddz_add !oddz_double.
Rewrite: addOn addnC -addnA addOz mulz_addr !halfz_double mulzC mulz_addr.
Case: n => [|n] Dn2 Hi; LeftBy Rewrite: !mulz_nat in Dn2.
Apply: Hrec Dn2; Apply: (leq_trans 3!i) Hi; Apply: leq_addl.
Qed.

End Sqrt2.
```

4.6 System

What is the home page of the system?

<http://pauillac.inria.fr/coq/>

What are the books about the system? The Coq'Art book

> Yves Bertot and Pierre Castéran, *Interactive Theorem Proving and Program Development, Coq'Art: The Calculus of Inductive Constructions*, Texts in Theoretical Computer Science. An EATCS Series, 2004, 469 pp., ISBN 3-540-20854-2.

provides a pragmatic introduction to the development of proofs and certified programs using Coq. Its web page is:

<http://www.labri.fr/Perso/~casteran/CoqArt/>

Otherwise a reference manual and a tutorial are available at:

<http://pauillac.inria.fr/coq/doc/main.html>
<http://pauillac.inria.fr/coq/doc/tutorial.html>

What is the logic of the system? Coq is based on the *Calculus of Inductive Construction*, a lambda calculus with a rich type system with dependent types.

What is the implementation architecture of the system? The system is written in ocaml (a dialect of ML). Following Curry-Howard's isomorphism, the kernel of the system is a type-checking algorithm that checks the correctness of proofs.

What does working with the system look like? The system has a specification language called Gallina. It allows the user to write its own specification by developing theories. Theories are built from axioms, hypotheses, parameters, lemmas, theorems and definitions of constants, functions, predicates and sets. Proofs are constructed interactively using the usual LCF tactics approach.

User may interact with the system using the standard shell window but there are also three available graphical user-interfaces:

- CoqIde an integrated gtk-based user interface
- Proof General `<http://zermelo.dcs.ed.ac.uk/~proofgen/>` an Emacs-based interface
- Pcoq `<http://www-sop.inria.fr/lemme/pcoq/>` a java-based interface

What is special about the system compared to other systems? First of all, the logic of Coq is very expressive allowing to define rich mathematical objects. Second, Coq manipulates explicit proof objects. A consequence is that the integrity of the system only relies on the correct implementation of a typechecking algorithm. Finally, a program extractor synthesizes computer programs obeying their formal specifications written as logical assertions in the language.

What are other versions of the system? There is only one supported implementation of the system. The current version is 8.0.

Who are the people behind the system? The main developers of the system are from the Logical group at INRIA France (`<http://logical.inria.fr/>`).

What are the main user communities of the system? The main user communities are in France (INRIA, LIX, ENS, LRI) and in Holland (Nijmegen).

What large mathematical formalizations have been done in the system? The user contributions are listed at the following address:

http://pauillac.inria.fr/coq/contribs-eng.html.

Here are some relevant ones:

- A proof of the four colour theorem by Georges Gonthier, in collaboration with Benjamin Werner
- Constructive Category Theory by Amokrane Saïbi
- Rational Numbers represented as Stern-Brocot Trees by Milad Niqui
- Elements of Constructive Geometry, Group Theory, and Domain Theory by Gilles Kahn
- High School Geometry and Oriented Angles of Vectors in the Plane by Frédérique Guilhot
- Basics notions of algebra by Loïc Pottier
- Fundamental Theorem of Algebra by Herman Geuvers, Freek Wiedijk, Jan Zwanenburg, Randy Pollack, Henk Barendregt
- Proof of Buchberger's algorithm by Laurent Théry, Henrik Persson
- Rem Theorem in Baire space by Henk Barendregt
- Real analysis by Micaela Mayero (standard library)
- A Proof of the Three Gap Theorem (Steinhaus Conjecture) by Micaela Mayero

What representation of the formalization has been put in this paper? What is presented is the exact script one has to feed Coq with so it accepts the final theorem.

After the script a proof term of one of the lemmas is shown.

What needs to be explained about this specific proof? In this proof we have decided to use as much as possible the notions that were already present in the system. The predicates *even* and *odd* are mutually defined in the theory Even. The function *div2* and *double* are defined in Div2. The key point of the main proof (main_thm) is the application of the well founded induction *lt_wf_ind* (second line of the script) whose statement is:

$$\forall p, P. \, (\forall n. \, (\forall m. \, m < n \to (P \, m)) \to (Pn)) \to (P \, p)$$

The reals are defined in the standard library Reals.

What needs to be explained about the second proof? The second formalization has been inspired by the Minlog entry (page 151). It takes advantage of the *positive* datatype of Coq, that encodes strictly positive numbers in a binary way. This allows to easily check whether a number is even or not, and also to stick to normal induction instead of well-founded induction.

What needs to be explained about the third proof? This formalization uses a few basic libraries of the Colour Theorem proof, including a construction of the classic reals, which has been extended with a definition of the square root (not shown). The type frac is the representation of the rational numbers used in the construction of the real numbers.

The proof script uses the extended Coq v7 tactics developed for the Four Colour Theorem proof. It is self-contained: the first four lines reduce the problem from $\mathbb{R}$ to $\mathbb{Q}$, the next two from $\mathbb{Q}$ $\mathbb{Z}$, the next five from $\mathbb{Z}$ to $\mathbb{N}$, the next two lines set up an induction on the size of the fraction, which is completed in the last six lines.

5 Otter/Ivy

Michael Beeson and William McCune

Formalization from Larry Wos <wos@mcs.anl.gov> by Michael Beeson
<beeson@mathcs.sjsu.edu> and William McCune <mccune@mcs.anl.
gov>. Answers by William McCune.

5.1 Statement

m(a,a) = m(2,m(b,b))

5.2 Definitions

Definition of m

```
m(1,x) = x.                          % identity
m(x,1) = x.
m(x,m(y,z)) = m(m(x,y),z).           % associativity
m(x,y) = m(y,x).                     % commutativity
m(x,y) != m(x,z) | y = z.            % cancellation
```

5.3 Proof

Here's an input file that gets a proof quickly. Note that he has a cancellation
rule for multiplication.

```
set(auto).
set(ur_res).
assign(max_distinct_vars, 1).
list(usable).
x = x.
m(1,x) = x.                          % identity
m(x,1) = x.
m(x,m(y,z)) = m(m(x,y),z).           % associativity
m(x,y) = m(y,x).                     % commutativity
m(x,y) != m(x,z) | y = z.            % cancellation
-d(x,y) | m(x,f(x,y)) = y.           % this and next line define divides
m(x,z) != y | d(x,y).
-d(2,m(x,y)) | d(2,x) | d(2,y).      % 2 is prime
m(a,a) = m(2,m(b,b)).                % a/b = √2
-d(x,a) | -d(x,b) | x = 1.           % a/b is in lowest terms
2 != 1.                              % I almost forgot this!
end_of_list.
```

F. Wiedijk (Ed.): The Seventeen Provers of the World, LNAI 3600, pp. 36–40, 2006.
© Springer-Verlag Berlin Heidelberg 2006

Proof part of the output

----> UNIT CONFLICT at   0.25 sec ----> 1273 [binary,1272.1,1261.1] $F.

Length of proof is 16. Level of proof is 10.

---------------- PROOF ----------------

```
1 [] m(x,y)!=m(x,z)|y=z.
2 [] -d(x,y)|m(x,f(x,y))=y.
3 [] m(x,y)!=z|d(x,z).
4 [] -d(2,m(x,y))|d(2,x)|d(2,y).
5 [] -d(x,a)| -d(x,b)|x=1.
6 [] 2!=1.
7 [factor,4.2.3] -d(2,m(x,x))|d(2,x).
13 [] m(x,m(y,z))=m(m(x,y),z).
14 [copy,13,flip.1] m(m(x,y),z)=m(x,m(y,z)).
16 [] m(x,y)=m(y,x).
17 [] m(a,a)=m(2,m(b,b)).
18 [copy,17,flip.1] m(2,m(b,b))=m(a,a).
30 [hyper,18,3] d(2,m(a,a)).
39 [para_from,18.1.1,1.1.1] m(a,a)!=m(2,x)|m(b,b)=x.
42 [hyper,30,7] d(2,a).
46 [hyper,42,2] m(2,f(2,a))=a.
48 [ur,42,5,6] -d(2,b).
50 [ur,48,7] -d(2,m(b,b)).
59 [ur,50,3] m(2,x)!=m(b,b).
60 [copy,59,flip.1] m(b,b)!=m(2,x).
145 [para_from,46.1.1,14.1.1.1,flip.1] m(2,m(f(2,a),x))=m(a,x).
189 [ur,60,39] m(a,a)!=m(2,m(2,x)).
190 [copy,189,flip.1] m(2,m(2,x))!=m(a,a).
1261 [para_into,145.1.1.2,16.1.1] m(2,m(x,f(2,a)))=m(a,x).
1272 [para_from,145.1.1,190.1.1.2] m(2,m(a,x))!=m(a,a).
1273 [binary,1272.1,1261.1] $F.
```

Final part of the output

-------------- statistics --------------

clauses given	231
clauses generated	5020
clauses kept	1192
clauses forward subsumed	2515
clauses back subsumed	299
Kbytes malloced	830

---------- times (seconds) -----------

user CPU time	0.25	(0 hr, 0 min, 0 sec)
system CPU time	0.06	(0 hr, 0 min, 0 sec)
wall-clock time	0	(0 hr, 0 min, 0 sec)
hyper_res time	0.00	
UR_res time	0.01	
para_into time	0.02	
para_from time	0.00	
for_sub time	0.05	
back_sub time	0.01	
conflict time	0.01	
demod time	0.01	

That finishes the proof of the theorem.

Process 14745 finished Wed Mar 2 15:38:41 2005

Ivy proof object

```
;; BEGINNING OF PROOF OBJECT
(
(1 (input) (or (not (= (m v0 v1) (m v0 v2))) (= v1 v2)) (1))
(2 (input) (or (not (d v0 v1)) (= (m v0 (f v0 v1)) v1)) (2))
(3 (input) (or (not (= (m v0 v1) v2)) (d v0 v2)) (3))
(4 (input) (or (not (d (2) (m v0 v1))) (or (d (2) v0) (d (2) v1))) (4))
(5 (input) (or (not (d v0 (a))) (or (not (d v0 (b))) (= v0 (1)))) (5))
(6 (input) (not (= (2) (1))) (6))
(7 (instantiate 4 ((v0 . v1))) (or (not (d (2) (m v1 v1))) (or (d (2) v1) (d (2)
   v1))) NIL)
(8 (propositional 7) (or (not (d (2) (m v1 v1))) (d (2) v1)) NIL)
(9 (instantiate 8 ((v1 . v0))) (or (not (d (2) (m v0 v0))) (d (2) v0)) (7))
(10 (input) (= (m v0 (m v1 v2)) (m (m v0 v1) v2)) (13))
(11 (flip 10 ()) (= (m (m v0 v1) v2) (m v0 (m v1 v2))) (14))
(12 (input) (= (m v0 v1) (m v1 v0)) (16))
(13 (input) (= (m (a) (a)) (m (2) (m (b) (b)))) (17))
(14 (flip 13 ()) (= (m (2) (m (b) (b))) (m (a) (a))) (18))
(15 (instantiate 3 ((v0 . (2))(v1 . (m (b) (b)))(v2 . (m (a) (a))))) (or (not (=
   (m (2) (m (b) (b))) (m (a) (a)))) (d (2) (m (a) (a)))) NIL)
(16 (resolve 15 (1) 14 ()) (d (2) (m (a) (a))) (30))
(17 (instantiate 1 ((v0 . (2))(v1 . (m (b) (b)))(v2 . v66))) (or (not (= (m (2)
   (m (b) (b))) (m (2) v66))) (= (m (b) (b)) v66)) NIL)
(18 (paramod 14 (1) 17 (1 1 1)) (or (not (= (m (a) (a)) (m (2) v66))) (= (m (b)
   (b)) v66)) NIL)
(19 (instantiate 18 ((v66 . v0))) (or (not (= (m (a) (a)) (m (2) v0))) (= (m (b)
   (b)) v0)) (39))
(20 (instantiate 9 ((v0 . (a)))) (or (not (d (2) (m (a) (a)))) (d (2) (a))) NIL)
(21 (resolve 20 (1) 16 ()) (d (2) (a)) (42))
(22 (instantiate 2 ((v0 . (2))(v1 . (a)))) (or (not (d (2) (a))) (= (m (2) (f (2)
   (a))) (a))) NIL)
(23 (resolve 22 (1) 21 ()) (= (m (2) (f (2) (a))) (a)) (46))
(24 (instantiate 5 ((v0 . (2)))) (or (not (d (2) (a))) (or (not (d (2) (b))) (=
   (2) (1)))) NIL)
(25 (resolve 24 (1) 21 ()) (or (not (d (2) (b))) (= (2) (1))) NIL)
(26 (resolve 25 (2) 6 ()) (not (d (2) (b))) (48))
(27 (instantiate 9 ((v0 . (b)))) (or (not (d (2) (m (b) (b)))) (d (2) (b))) NIL)
(28 (resolve 27 (2) 26 ()) (not (d (2) (m (b) (b)))) (50))
(29 (instantiate 3 ((v0 . (2))(v2 . (m (b) (b))))) (or (not (= (m (2) v1) (m (b)
   (b)))) (d (2) (m (b) (b)))) NIL)
(30 (resolve 29 (2) 28 ()) (not (= (m (2) v1) (m (b) (b)))) NIL)
(31 (instantiate 30 ((v1 . v0))) (not (= (m (2) v0) (m (b) (b)))) (59))
(32 (flip 31 ()) (not (= (m (b) (b)) (m (2) v0))) (60))
(33 (instantiate 11 ((v0 . (2))(v1 . (f (2) (a)))(v2 . v66))) (= (m (m (2) (f (2)
   (a))) v66) (m (2) (m (f (2) (a)) v66))) NIL)
(34 (paramod 23 (1) 33 (1 1)) (= (m (a) v66) (m (2) (m (f (2) (a)) v66))) NIL)
(35 (flip 34 ()) (= (m (2) (m (f (2) (a)) v66)) (m (a) v66)) NIL)
(36 (instantiate 35 ((v66 . v0))) (= (m (2) (m (f (2) (a)) v0)) (m (a) v0))
   (145))
(37 (instantiate 19 ((v0 . (m (2) v64)))) (or (not (= (m (a) (a)) (m (2) (m (2)
   v64)))) (= (m (b) (b)) (m (2) v64))) NIL)
(38 (instantiate 32 ((v0 . v64))) (not (= (m (b) (b)) (m (2) v64))) NIL)
(39 (resolve 37 (2) 38 ()) (not (= (m (a) (a)) (m (2) (m (2) v64)))) NIL)
(40 (instantiate 39 ((v64 . v0))) (not (= (m (a) (a)) (m (2) (m (2) v0)))) (189))
(41 (flip 40 ()) (not (= (m (2) (m (2) v0)) (m (a) (a)))) (190))
(42 (instantiate 12 ((v0 . (f (2) (a)))(v1 . v64))) (= (m (f (2) (a)) v64 (m v64
   (f (2) (a)))) NIL)
```

```
(43 (instantiate 36 ((v0 . v64))) (= (m (2) (m (f (2) (a)) v64)) (m (a) v64))
   NIL)
(44 (paramod 42 (1) 43 (1 2)) (= (m (2) (m v64 (f (2) (a)))) (m (a) v64)) NIL)
(45 (instantiate 44 ((v64 . v0))) (= (m (2) (m v0 (f (2) (a)))) (m (a) v0))
   (1261))
(46 (instantiate 41 ((v0 . (m (f (2) (a)) v0)))) (not (= (m (2) (m (2) (m (f (2)
   (a)) v0))) (m (a) (a)))) NIL)
(47 (paramod 36 (1) 46 (1 1 2)) (not (= (m (2) (m (a) v0)) (m (a) (a)))) (1272))
(48 (instantiate 47 ((v0 . (f (2) (a))))) (not (= (m (2) (m (a) (f (2) (a)))) (m
   (a) (a)))) NIL)
(49 (instantiate 45 ((v0 . (a)))) (= (m (2) (m (a) (f (2) (a)))) (m (a) (a)))
   NIL)
(50 (resolve 48 () 49 ()) false (1273))
)
;; END OF PROOF OBJECT
```

5.4   System

What is the home page of the system?

<http://www.mcs.anl.gov/AR/otter/>

What are the books about the system?

- W. McCune and R. Padmanabhan. *Automated Deduction in Equational Logic and Cubic Curves*, volume 1095 of *Lecture Notes in Computer Science (AI subseries)*. Springer-Verlag, Berlin, 1996.
- J. Kalman. *Automated Reasoning with Otter*. Rinton Press, Princeton, New Jersey, 2001.
- L. Wos and G. Pieper. *A Fascinating Country in the World of Computing: Your Guide to Automated Reasoning*. World Scientific, Singapore, 1999.
- L. Wos. *The Automation of Reasoning: An Experimenter's Notebook with Otter Tutorial*. Academic Press, New York, 1996.
- A. Quaife. *Automated Development of Fundamental Mathematical Theories*. Kluwer Academic, 1992.

What is the logic of the system? Untyped first-order logic with equality.

What is the implementation architecture of the system? Resolution, paramodulation, rewriting, with indexing.

What does working with the system look like? Command-line interface.

What is special about the system compared to other systems? Stable, robust.

What are other versions of the system? Various experimental versions.

Who are the people behind the system? William McCune, Larry Wos, Robert Veroff, Ross Overbeek, Rusty Lusk.

What are the main user communities of the system? Mathematicians, logicians.

What large mathematical formalizations have been done in the system? Otter users don't ordinarily work in 'large' theories. However, large set theory projects have been done with Otter by Art Quaife and Johan Belinfante.

6 Isabelle/Isar

Markus Wenzel and Larry Paulson

Formalizations by Markus Wenzel <makarius@gmx.de> (Isar style version
in Isabelle/HOL) and by Larry Paulson <lcp@cl.cam.ac.uk> (script versions in Isabelle/HOL and Isabelle/ZF). Answers by Markus Wenzel.

6.1 Statement

$sqrt\ (real\ (2::nat)) \notin \mathbb{Q}$

6.2 Definitions

Definition of $\mathbb{Q}$

constdefs
  rationals :: *real set*   ($\mathbb{Q}$)
  $\mathbb{Q} \equiv \{x.\ \exists\, m\ n.\ n \neq 0 \wedge |x| = real\ (m::nat)\ /\ real\ (n::nat)\}$

Definition of sqrt

constdefs
  root :: *nat* $\Rightarrow$ *real* $\Rightarrow$ *real*
  $root\ n\ x \equiv (SOME\ u::real.\ (0 < x \longrightarrow 0 < u) \wedge u\,\hat{}\,n = x)$

  sqrt :: *real* $\Rightarrow$ *real*
  $sqrt\ x \equiv root\ 2\ x$

6.3 Proof

theory $Sqrt = Primes + Complex\text{-}Main$:

Preliminaries

The set of rational numbers, including the key representation theorem.

constdefs
  rationals :: *real set*   ($\mathbb{Q}$)
  $\mathbb{Q} \equiv \{x.\ \exists\, m\ n.\ n \neq 0 \wedge |x| = real\ (m::nat)\ /\ real\ (n::nat)\}$

theorem *rationals-rep*: $x \in \mathbb{Q} \Longrightarrow$
  $\exists\, m\ n.\ n \neq 0 \wedge |x| = real\ m\ /\ real\ n \wedge gcd\ (m,\ n) = 1$
proof −
  assume $x \in \mathbb{Q}$
  then obtain $m\ n :: nat$ **where**

F. Wiedijk (Ed.): The Seventeen Provers of the World, LNAI 3600, pp. 41–49, 2006.
© Springer-Verlag Berlin Heidelberg 2006

$n: n \neq 0$ **and** x-*rat:* $|x| = real\ m\ /\ real\ n$
  by (*unfold rationals-def*) *blast*
let $?gcd = gcd\ (m, n)$
from n **have** *gcd:* $?gcd \neq 0$ **by** (*simp add: gcd-zero*)
let $?k = m\ div\ ?gcd$
let $?l = n\ div\ ?gcd$
let $?gcd' = gcd\ (?k, ?l)$
have $?gcd\ dvd\ m$ .. **then have** *gcd-k:* $?gcd * ?k = m$
  by (*rule dvd-mult-div-cancel*)
have $?gcd\ dvd\ n$ .. **then have** *gcd-l:* $?gcd * ?l = n$
  by (*rule dvd-mult-div-cancel*)

from n **and** *gcd-l* **have** $?l \neq 0$
  by (*auto iff del: neq0-conv*)
moreover
have $|x| = real\ ?k\ /\ real\ ?l$
proof −
  from *gcd* **have** $real\ ?k\ /\ real\ ?l =$
    $real\ (?gcd * ?k)\ /\ real\ (?gcd * ?l)$
    by (*simp add: mult-divide-cancel-left*)
  also from *gcd-k* **and** *gcd-l* **have** ... $= real\ m\ /\ real\ n$ **by** *simp*
  also from x-*rat* **have** ... $= |x|$ ..
  finally show *?thesis* ..
qed
moreover
have $?gcd' = 1$
proof −
  have $?gcd * ?gcd' = gcd\ (?gcd * ?k, ?gcd * ?l)$
    by (*rule gcd-mult-distrib2*)
  with *gcd-k gcd-l* **have** $?gcd * ?gcd' = ?gcd$ **by** *simp*
  with *gcd* **show** *?thesis* **by** *simp*
qed
ultimately show *?thesis* **by** *blast*
qed

lemma [*elim?*]: $r \in \mathbb{Q} \Longrightarrow$
$(\bigwedge m\ n.\ n \neq 0 \Longrightarrow |r| = real\ m\ /\ real\ n \Longrightarrow gcd\ (m, n) = 1 \Longrightarrow C)$
  $\Longrightarrow C$
  using *rationals-rep* **by** *blast*

Main theorem

The square root of any prime number (including 2) is irrational.

theorem *sqrt-prime-irrational:* $p \in prime \Longrightarrow sqrt\ (real\ p) \notin \mathbb{Q}$
proof
  assume p-*prime:* $p \in prime$
  then have $p: 1 < p$ **by** (*simp add: prime-def*)
  assume $sqrt\ (real\ p) \in \mathbb{Q}$
  then obtain $m\ n$ **where**
    $n: n \neq 0$ **and** *sqrt-rat:* $|sqrt\ (real\ p)| = real\ m\ /\ real\ n$

    and *gcd:* *gcd* $(m, n) = 1$ ..
have *eq:* $m^2 = p * n^2$
proof −
  from *n* **and** *sqrt-rat* **have** *real* $m = |sqrt\ (real\ p)| * real\ n$ **by** *simp*
  then have *real* $(m^2) = (sqrt\ (real\ p))^2 * real\ (n^2)$
    by (*auto simp add: power2-eq-square*)
  also have $(sqrt\ (real\ p))^2 = real\ p$ **by** *simp*
  also have $\ldots * real\ (n^2) = real\ (p * n^2)$ **by** *simp*
  finally show *?thesis* ..
qed
have $p\ dvd\ m \land p\ dvd\ n$
proof
  from *eq* **have** $p\ dvd\ m^2$ ..
  with *p-prime* **show** $p\ dvd\ m$ **by** (*rule prime-dvd-power-two*)
  then obtain *k* **where** $m = p * k$ ..
  with *eq* **have** $p * n^2 = p^2 * k^2$ **by** (*auto simp add: power2-eq-square mult-ac*)
  with *p* **have** $n^2 = p * k^2$ **by** (*simp add: power2-eq-square*)
  then have $p\ dvd\ n^2$ ..
  with *p-prime* **show** $p\ dvd\ n$ **by** (*rule prime-dvd-power-two*)
qed
then have $p\ dvd\ gcd\ (m, n)$ ..
with *gcd* **have** $p\ dvd\ 1$ **by** *simp*
then have $p \leq 1$ **by** (*simp add: dvd-imp-le*)
with *p* **show** *False* **by** *simp*
qed

corollary *sqrt* $(real\ (2::nat)) \notin \mathbb{Q}$
  by (*rule sqrt-prime-irrational*) (*rule two-is-prime*)

Variations

Here is an alternative version of the main proof, using mostly linear forward-reasoning. While this results in less top-down structure, it is probably closer to proofs seen in mathematics.

theorem $p \in prime \implies sqrt\ (real\ p) \notin \mathbb{Q}$
proof
  assume *p-prime:* $p \in prime$
  then have *p:* $1 < p$ **by** (*simp add: prime-def*)
  assume *sqrt* $(real\ p) \in \mathbb{Q}$
  then obtain *m n* **where**
    n: $n \neq 0$ **and** *sqrt-rat:* $|sqrt\ (real\ p)| = real\ m\ /\ real\ n$
    and *gcd:* *gcd* $(m, n) = 1$ ..
  from *n* **and** *sqrt-rat* **have** *real* $m = |sqrt\ (real\ p)| * real\ n$ **by** *simp*
  then have *real* $(m^2) = (sqrt\ (real\ p))^2 * real\ (n^2)$
    by (*auto simp add: power2-eq-square*)
  also have $(sqrt\ (real\ p))^2 = real\ p$ **by** *simp*
  also have $\ldots * real\ (n^2) = real\ (p * n^2)$ **by** *simp*
  finally have *eq:* $m^2 = p * n^2$ ..
  then have $p\ dvd\ m^2$ ..

   with *p-prime* **have** *dvd-m*: *p dvd m* **by** (*rule prime-dvd-power-two*)
   then obtain *k* **where** *m = p ∗ k* ..
   with *eq* **have** $p * n^2 = p^2 * k^2$ **by** (*auto simp add: power2-eq-square mult-ac*)
   with *p* **have** $n^2 = p * k^2$ **by** (*simp add: power2-eq-square*)
   then have $p \ dvd \ n^2$ ..
   with *p-prime* **have** *p dvd n* **by** (*rule prime-dvd-power-two*)
   with *dvd-m* **have** *p dvd gcd* (*m, n*) **by** (*rule gcd-greatest*)
   with *gcd* **have** *p dvd 1* **by** *simp*
   then have *p ≤ 1* **by** (*simp add: dvd-imp-le*)
   with *p* **show** *False* **by** *simp*
qed

end

6.4 Another Formalization: Script Version in Isabelle/HOL

theory *Sqrt-Script = Primes + Complex-Main*:

Preliminaries

lemma *prime-nonzero*: *p ∈ prime ⟹ p ≠ 0*
  by (*force simp add: prime-def*)

lemma *prime-dvd-other-side*:
   n ∗ n = p ∗ (k ∗ k) ⟹ p ∈ prime ⟹ p dvd n
  apply (*subgoal-tac p dvd n ∗ n, blast dest: prime-dvd-mult*)
  apply (*rule-tac j = k ∗ k in dvd-mult-left, simp*)
  done

lemma *reduction*: *p ∈ prime ⟹*
   0 < k ⟹ k ∗ k = p ∗ (j ∗ j) ⟹ k < p ∗ j ∧ 0 < j
  apply (*rule ccontr*)
  apply (*simp add: linorder-not-less*)
  apply (*erule disjE*)
   apply (*frule mult-le-mono, assumption*)
   apply *auto*
  apply (*force simp add: prime-def*)
  done

lemma *rearrange*: (*j::nat*) ∗ (*p ∗ j*) = *k ∗ k ⟹ k ∗ k = p ∗ (j ∗ j)*
  by (*simp add: mult-ac*)

lemma *prime-not-square*:
   p ∈ prime ⟹ (⋀k. 0 < k ⟹ m ∗ m ≠ p ∗ (k ∗ k))
  apply (*induct m rule: nat-less-induct*)
  apply *clarify*
  apply (*frule prime-dvd-other-side, assumption*)
  apply (*erule dvdE*)
  apply (*simp add: nat-mult-eq-cancel-disj prime-nonzero*)
  apply (*blast dest: rearrange reduction*)
  done

The set of rational numbers

constdefs
  rationals :: real set   (ℚ)
  ℚ ≡ {x. ∃ m n. n ≠ 0 ∧ |x| = real (m::nat) / real (n::nat)}

Main theorem

The square root of any prime number (including *2*) is irrational.

theorem *prime-sqrt-irrational*:
    $p \in prime \Longrightarrow x * x = real\ p \Longrightarrow 0 \le x \Longrightarrow x \notin \mathbb{Q}$
  apply (*simp add: rationals-def real-abs-def*)
  apply *clarify*
  apply (*erule-tac P = real m / real n * ?x = ?y in rev-mp*)
  apply (*simp del: real-of-nat-mult*
              add: divide-eq-eq prime-not-square real-of-nat-mult [symmetric])
  done

lemmas *two-sqrt-irrational =*
  prime-sqrt-irrational [OF two-is-prime]

end

6.5   Another Formalization: Script Version in Isabelle/ZF

lemma *prime-dvd-other-side*:
    ⟦n#∗n = p#∗(k#∗k); p ∈ prime; n ∈ nat⟧ ⟹ p dvd n
  apply (*subgoal-tac p dvd n#∗n*)
   apply (*blast dest: prime-dvd-mult*)
  apply (*rule-tac j = k#∗k in dvd-mult-left*)
   apply (*auto simp add: prime-def*)
  done

lemma *reduction*:
    ⟦k#∗k = p#∗(j#∗j); p ∈ prime; 0 < k; j ∈ nat; k ∈ nat⟧
      ⟹ k < p#∗j & 0 < j
  apply (*rule ccontr*)
  apply (*simp add: not-lt-iff-le prime-into-nat*)
  apply (*erule disjE*)
   apply (*frule mult-le-mono, assumption+*)
  apply (*simp add: mult-ac*)
  apply (*auto dest!: natify-eqE*
          simp add: not-lt-iff-le prime-into-nat mult-le-cancel-le1)
  apply (*simp add: prime-def*)
  apply (*blast dest: lt-trans1*)
  done

lemma *rearrange: j #∗ (p#∗j) = k#∗k ⟹ k#∗k = p#∗(j#∗j)*
  by (*simp add: mult-ac*)

lemma *prime-not-square*:
  $\llbracket m \in nat; \; p \in prime \rrbracket \implies \forall k \in nat. \; 0 < k \longrightarrow m\#*m \neq p\#*(k\#*k)$
apply (*erule complete-induct, clarify*)
apply (*frule prime-dvd-other-side, assumption*)
apply *assumption*
apply (*erule dvdE*)
apply (*simp add: mult-assoc mult-cancel1 prime-nonzero prime-into-nat*)
apply (*blast dest: rearrange reduction ltD*)
done

6.6 System

What is the home page of the system? The official Isabelle home page is available at `<http://www.cl.cam.ac.uk/Research/HVG/Isabelle/>` (Cambridge) or `<http://isabelle.in.tum.de>` (Munich). There is also an Isabelle/Isar specific page at `<http://isabelle.in.tum.de/Isar/>`.

What are the books about the system? Quite a number of texts covering certain aspects of Isabelle have emerged over the last decade; several manuals are part of the official Isabelle distribution. At present, the most important documents are as follows.

- Tobias Nipkow, Lawrence C. Paulson, and Markus Wenzel. *Isabelle/HOL — A Proof Assistant for Higher-Order Logic*. LNCS 2283, Springer Verlag, 2002.
  This tutorial covers the practically important Isabelle object-logic of HOL from an end-user perspective. It focuses on common specification techniques and development of unstructured proof scripts.
- Tobias Nipkow. Structured Proofs in Isar/HOL. In *Types for Proofs and Programs (TYPES 2002)*, LNCS 2646, Springer Verlag, 2002.
  This paper is an introduction to the basic constructs of the Isar proof language.
- Markus Wenzel. *The Isabelle/Isar Reference Manual*, TU Munich, 2002. `<http://isabelle.in.tum.de/doc/isar-ref.pdf>`
  This manual is the definitive reference on all 'new-style' theory language elements of Isabelle/Isar, subsuming both structured and unstructured proofs.
- Markus Wenzel. *Isabelle/Isar — a versatile environment for human-readable formal proof documents*. PhD thesis, Institut für Informatik, TU Munich, 2002.   `<http://tumb1.biblio.tu-muenchen.de/publ/diss/in/2002/wenzel.html>`
  This thesis covers all aspects of the structured Isar proof language, with logical foundations, general proof techniques, and applications from several domains. It is not exactly a tutorial on authoring Isar proofs, but shows many practical proof patterns.

What is the logic of the system? Isabelle is a logical framework, where object-logics (e.g. HOL or ZF) are embedded into a general natural deduction environment of minimal higher-order logic ('Pure').

Speaking in type-theoretic terms, Isabelle/Pure corresponds to λ-HOL as discussed in H. Barendregt and H. Geuvers, 'Proof Assistants using Dependent Type Systems' (in A. Robinson and A. Voronkov (eds.), *Handbook of Automated Reasoning*, Elsevier, 2001), for example. Conceptually, there are three levels of λ-calculus, with a non-dependent arrow $\Rightarrow$ for syntactic functions, a dependent arrow $\bigwedge$ for universal quantification (local parameters), and another non-dependent arrow $\Longrightarrow$ for implication (logical entailment). Isabelle provides an optional view of primitive Isabelle/Pure proofs as actual λ-terms, due to Stefan Berghofer.

Isabelle/HOL is a classical formulation of simply-typed set-theory within the Pure framework. It uses several generic proof tools of Isabelle (higher-order rewriting, classical proof search, arithmetic etc.), and implements a number of derived specification mechanisms on top of the existing kernel (inductive sets and datatypes, recursive functions, extensible records etc.).

Isabelle/ZF is full untyped set-theory according to the classic Zermelo-Fraenkel axiomatization (optionally with Axiom of Choice). There are similar proof tools and specification mechanisms as in Isabelle/HOL, but fewer advanced tools such as arithmetic decision procedures and records. Type-checking in ZF needs to be performed as explicit set-membership reasoning. Isabelle/ZF is mainly useful for formalizing pure mathematics.

What is the implementation architecture of the system? Isabelle is fully expansive, like the HOL system and Milner's original LCF: all proofs expand to primitive inferences in the kernel. The Curry-Howard propositions-as-types principle may be employed as well; then all primitive inferences are recorded as λ-terms for independent checking, program extraction etc. The Isabelle/Isar language layer resides on top of the Pure inference environment; object-logics (HOL, ZF, etc.) all benefit from the Isar infrastructure. Derived principles (specification schemes, proof methods etc.) may be added at any time without breaching the integrity of the system.

What does working with the system look like? Theory and proof development is highly interactive, both for unstructured tactic scripts and structured Isar proof texts. The basic idea is to compose the source of a formal theory text in an incremental manner, stepping back and forth according to the purposes of experimentation and debugging.

The Proof General interface   `<http://proofgeneral.inf.ed.ac.uk>` by David Aspinall provides a specific Isabelle/Isar instance. It holds up the perception of 'life editing' of formal proof documents fairly well, although truly hierarchic checking of Isar sub-proofs is not supported.

Final document output is produced in batch-mode with (PDF-LaTeX). Thus recipients may access formal proof documents without any special tools required, apart from a standard PDF viewer.

What is special about the system compared to other systems? Isabelle/Pure offers a generic environment for building formal logic applications in general. The Isabelle/Isar layer provides a rich infrastructure for high-level proof schemes, with a special focus on human-readable formal proof documents. Structured and unstructured proofs may be freely intermixed within Isabelle/Isar theory developments. The Isabelle distribution includes Isabelle/HOL as an end-user environment with many proven applications in mathematical modeling and verification. There is also a document preparation system for turning the Isabelle theory sources into high-quality typeset output (as a side-effect of formal processing).

What are other versions of the system? There is essentially just one main trunk of Isabelle development, which evolves over time in a linear fashion (Isabelle2002, Isabelle2003, Isabelle2004 etc.).

Who are the people behind the system? The key players are Lawrence C. Paulson (Cambridge), Tobias Nipkow (Munich), and Markus Wenzel (Munich). Stefan Berghofer (Munich) and Gerwin Klein (Munich and Sydney) have made substantial contributions. Many other people have participated in Isabelle development.

What are the main user communities of the system? Researchers and students of computer-science and mathematics worldwide. A significant number of Isabelle users are from outside of the original sites of Cambridge or Munich.

What large mathematical formalizations have been done in the system? A massive body of Isabelle applications have emerged over the years. The largest one is the Java formalization of the projects Bali <http://isabelle.in.tum.de/bali/> and VerifiCard <http://isabelle.in.tum.de/verificard/>, which were later combined into a unified whole <http://www.in.tum.de/~nipkow/Jinja/> (as described by Gerwin Klein and Tobias Nipkow in 'A Machine-Checked Model for a Java-Like Language, Virtual Machine and Compiler', to be published in *TOPLAS*). Some properly 'mathematical' ones are part of the standard library, such as <http://isabelle.in.tum.de/library/HOL/HOL-Algebra/document.pdf> or <HOL-Complex/HahnBanach/document.pdf>. The largest of these is the formalization of Gödel's proof of the relative consistency of the axiom of choice, <http://isabelle.in.tum.de/library/ZF/Constructible/document.pdf>.

The Archive of Formal Proofs <http://afp.sourceforge.net/> is a collection of proof libraries, examples, and larger scientific developments, mechanically checked in Isabelle. It is organized in the way of a scientific journal. Submissions are refereed.

What representation of the formalization has been put in this paper? The formalization follows common mathematical practice; both HOL and ZF provide an adequate background theory for standard mathematics.

What needs to be explained about this specific proof? Isabelle/Isar proof texts are meant to be self-explanatory, at least well-written ones. The present example has been conducted realistically in the sense that any 'omissions' of the existing background library are included in full. The main proofs have been laid out to represent the logical structure of the argument adequately, without having excessive formal detail clutter the text. The general style of writing is up to the author; the Isar proof language is very flexible in that respect.

The Isabelle/HOL and Isabelle/ZF variants given in tactical style represent the typical manner of unstructured proof composition in Isabelle. The unstructured Isabelle/HOL proof uses the same background library as the structured Isar text.

The formalizations of the irrationality of $\sqrt{2}$ from this section can be found in the Isabelle2004 distribution as:

```
src/HOL/Complex/ex/Sqrt.thy
src/HOL/Complex/ex/Sqrt_Script.thy
src/ZF/ex/Primes.thy
```

7 Alfa/Agda

Formalization and answers by Thierry Coquand
<coquand@cs.chalmers.se>.

7.1 Statement

$prime\, p\ \rightarrow\ noether\, A\ (multiple\, p)\ \rightarrow\ isNotSquare\, p$

7.2 Definitions

Definition of noether

$noether\ (A\ \in\ Set, R\ \in\ rel\, A)\ \in\ Type$
$noether\, A\, R\ \equiv$
$(P\ \in\ pred\, A)\ \rightarrow\ (x\ \in\ A)\ \rightarrow\ ((y\ \in\ A)\ \rightarrow\ (R\, y\, x\ \rightarrow\ P\, y)\ \rightarrow\ P\, x)\ \rightarrow\ (x\ \in\ A)\ \rightarrow\ P\, x$

Definition of multiple

$multiple\ (p\ \in\ A)\ \in\ rel\, A$
$multiple\, p\ \equiv\ \lambda\, x\, y\ \rightarrow\ (p\cdot\, x)\ ==\, y$

Definition of prime

$prime\ \in\ pred\, A$
$prime\ \equiv\ \lambda\, p\ \rightarrow\ (x, y\ \in\ A)\ \rightarrow\ (p\,|\,(x\cdot\, y))\ \rightarrow\ (p\,|\,x)\ \vee\ (p\,|\,y)$

Definition of isNotSquare

$isNotSquare\ \in\ pred\, A$
$isNotSquare\ \equiv\ \lambda\, p\ \rightarrow\ (x, y\ \in\ A)\ \rightarrow\ \neg\ ((p\cdot\, square\, x)\ ==\, square\, y)$

7.3 Proof

File `noether.alfa`

some general logical concepts and principles

$rel\ (A\ \in\ Set)\ \in\ Type$
$rel\, A\ \equiv\ A\ \rightarrow\ A\ \rightarrow\ Set$

$pred\ (A\ \in\ Set)\ \in\ Type$
$pred\, A\ \equiv\ A\ \rightarrow\ Set$

$exists\ \in\ (A\ \in\ Set, B\ \in\ A\ \rightarrow\ Set)\ \rightarrow\ Set$
$exists\ \equiv\ \lambda\, A\, B\ \rightarrow\ \textbf{data}\ \{\, \textbf{Witness}\,(u\ \in\ A, v\ \in\ B\, u)\,\}$

$existsElim\ \in\ (h1\ \in\ exists\, A\, B, h2\ \in\ (x\ \in\ A)\ \rightarrow\ B\, x\ \rightarrow\ C)\ \rightarrow\ C$
$(A\ \in\ Set, B\ \in\ A\ \rightarrow\ Set, C\ \in\ Set)$

F. Wiedijk (Ed.): The Seventeen Provers of the World, LNAI 3600, pp. 50–54, 2006.
© Springer-Verlag Berlin Heidelberg 2006

$existsElim \equiv \lambda h1\, h2 \to$ case $h1$ of $\{$ Witness $u\,v \to h2\,u\,v\}$

$\wedge\, (A, B \in Set) \in Set$
$A \wedge B \equiv$ data $\{$ Pair $(a \in A, b \in B)\}$

$andElimLeft \in (A \wedge B) \to A \qquad (A, B \in Set)$
$andElimLeft \equiv \lambda h \to$ case h of $\{$ Pair $a\,b \to a\}$

$andElimRight \in (A \wedge B) \to B \qquad (A, B \in Set)$
$andElimRight \equiv \lambda h \to$ case h of $\{$ Pair $a\,b \to b\}$

$\vee\, (A, B \in Set) \in Set$
$A \vee B \equiv$ data $\left\{\begin{array}{l} \text{Inl}\,(a \in A) \\ \text{Inr}\,(b \in B) \end{array}\right\}$

$orElim \in (A \to C) \to (B \to C) \to (A \vee B) \to C \qquad (A, B, C \in Set)$
$orElim \equiv \lambda h1\, h2\, h3 \to$ case $h3$ of $\left\{\begin{array}{l} \text{Inl}\,a \to h1\,a \\ \text{Inr}\,b \to h2\,b \end{array}\right\}$

$noether\,(A \in Set, R \in rel\,A) \in Type$
$noether\,A\,R \equiv$
$(P \in pred\,A) \to (x \in A) \to ((y \in A) \to (R\,y\,x \to P\,y) \to P\,x) \to (x \in A) \to P\,x$

$\bot \in Set$
$\bot \equiv$ data $\{\}$

$\neg\,(A \in Set) \in Set$
$\neg A \equiv A \to \bot$

The principle of infinite descent, following Fermat

$infiniteDescent\,(A \in Set, R \in rel\,A, P \in pred\,A) \in$
$noether\,A\,R \to (x \in A) \to (P\,x \to exists\,A\,\lambda x1 \to R\,x1\,x \wedge P\,x1) \to (x \in A) \to \neg\,(P\,x)$
$infiniteDescent\,A\,R\,P \equiv \lambda h1\, h2\, x \to h1\,\lambda y \to \neg\,(P\,y)\,\lambda z\, h3\, h4 \to$
$existsElim\,(h2\,z\,h4)\,\lambda y\, h5 \to h3\,y\,(andElimLeft\,h5)\,(andElimRight\,h5)\,x$

File `lem.alfa`

`import` *noether.alfa*

Definition of commutative monoid; for the main proof, it will be the monoid $\mathbb{N}^*$ for multiplication

$AbMonoid\,(A \in Set, == \in rel\,A) \in Set$
$AbMonoid\,A\,(==) \equiv$

sig $\left\{\begin{array}{l} ref \in (x \in A) \to x == x \\ sym \in (x, y \in A) \to (x == y) \to y == x \\ trans \in (x, y, z \in A) \to (x == y) \to (y == z) \to x == z \\ ss \in A \to A \to A \\ cong \in (x1, x2, y1, y2 \in A) \to (x1 == x2) \to (y1 == y2) \to (x1\cdot y1) == (x2\cdot y2) \\ assoc \in (x, y, z \in A) \to (x\cdot (y\cdot z)) == ((x\cdot y)\cdot z) \\ comm \in (x, y \in A) \to (x\cdot y) == (y\cdot x) \end{array}\right\}$

A beginning of the theory of commutative monoid

`package` *ThAbMonoid* $(A \in Set, == \in rel\,A, m \in AbMonoid\,A\,(==))$
`with`
  `open` *m* `use` *ref, sym, trans, cong, ·, assoc, comm*

  $square\,(x \in A) \in A$
  $square\,x \equiv x\cdot x$

$multiple\ (p \in A) \in rel\,A$
$multiple\ p \equiv \lambda\,x\,y\ \rightarrow\ (p \cdot x)\ == y$

$congLeft \in (y == z)\ \rightarrow\ (y \cdot x)\ == (z \cdot x)$ $(x, y, z \in A)$
$congLeft \equiv \lambda\,h\ \rightarrow\ cong\,h\ (ref\,x)$

$congRight \in (y == z)\ \rightarrow\ (x \cdot y)\ == (x \cdot z)$ $(x, y, z \in A)$
$congRight \equiv \lambda\,h\ \rightarrow\ cong\ (ref\,x)\ h$

$lemma0 \in (x == z)\ \rightarrow\ (y == z)\ \rightarrow\ x == y$ $(x, y, z \in A)$
$lemma0 \equiv \lambda\,h\,h'\ \rightarrow\ trans\,h\ (sym\,y\,z\,h')$

$lemma2 \in (x == y)\ \rightarrow\ square\,x == square\,y$ $(x, y \in A)$
$lemma2 \equiv \lambda\,h\ \rightarrow\ cong\,h\,h$

$lemma3 \in (x \cdot (y \cdot z))\ == (y \cdot (x \cdot z))$ $(x, y, z \in A)$
$lemma3 \equiv lemma0\ assoc\ (trans\ assoc\ (congLeft\ comm))$

$lemma4 \in (x \cdot (x \cdot square\,y))\ == square\ (x \cdot y)$ $(x, y \in A)$
$lemma4 \equiv trans\ (congRight\ lemma3)\ assoc$

$lemma5 \in ((p \cdot y1)\ == y)\ \rightarrow\ (p \cdot (p \cdot square\,y1))\ == square\,y$ $(p, y, y1 \in A)$
$lemma5 \equiv \lambda\,h\ \rightarrow\ trans\ lemma4\ (lemma2\,h)$

File `lem1.alfa`

import *lem.alfa*

Cancelative abelian monoid; $\mathbb{N}^*$ is cancelative for the multiplication

$isCancel\ (A \in Set, == \in rel\,A, m \in AbMonoid\,A\ (==)) \in Set$
$isCancel\,A\ (==)\ m \equiv (x, y, z \in A)\ \rightarrow\ (m.ss\,z\,x == m.ss\,z\,y)\ \rightarrow\ x == y$

package *square* $(A \in Set, == \in rel\,A, m \in AbMonoid\,A\ (==), cancel \in isCancel\,A\ (==)\ m)$
with
  open *m* **use** *ref, sym, trans, cong, ·, assoc, comm*
  open *ThAbMonoid A* $(==)$ *m* **use** *square, multiple*

$lemma1 \in ((p \cdot u)\ == w)\ \rightarrow\ ((p \cdot v)\ == w)\ \rightarrow\ u == v$ $(p, u, v, w \in A)$
$lemma1 \equiv \lambda\,h2\,h3\ \rightarrow\ cancel\,u\,v\,p\ ((ThAbMonoid\,A\ (==)\ m).lemma0\ (p \cdot u)\ (p \cdot v)\ w\,h2\,h3)$

$lemma2 \in ((p \cdot square\,x)\ == square\,y)\ \rightarrow\ ((p \cdot y1)\ == y)\ \rightarrow\ (p \cdot square\,y1)\ == square\,x$
$(p, x, y, y1 \in A)$
$lemma2 \equiv \lambda\,h1\,h2\ \rightarrow\ lemma1\ ((ThAbMonoid\,A\ (==)\ m).lemma5\,p\,y\,y1\,h2)\ h1$

$\exists \in pred\,A\ \rightarrow\ Set$
$\exists \equiv exists\,A$

$| \in rel\,A$
$| \equiv \lambda\,x\,y\ \rightarrow\ \exists z\ ((x \cdot z)\ == y)$

$prime \in pred\,A$
$prime \equiv \lambda\,p\ \rightarrow\ (x, y \in A)\ \rightarrow\ (p\,|\ (x \cdot y))\ \rightarrow\ (p\,|\,x) \vee (p\,|\,y)$

$lemma3 \in prime\,p\ \rightarrow\ (p\,|\ square\,x)\ \rightarrow\ p\,|\,x$ $(p, x \in A)$
$lemma3 \equiv \lambda\,h1\,h2\ \rightarrow\ orElim\,\lambda\,h\ \rightarrow\ h\,\lambda\,h\ \rightarrow\ h\ (h1\,x\,x\,h2)$

$lemma4 \in prime\,p\ \rightarrow\ ((p \cdot square\,x)\ == square\,y)\ \rightarrow$
$\exists y1\ (((p \cdot y1)\ == y) \wedge ((p \cdot square\,y1)\ == square\,x))$ $(p, x, y \in A)$

$$lemma4 \equiv \lambda\,h1\,h2\ \rightarrow\ \mathbf{let}\ \begin{bmatrix} rem \in p\,|\,y \\ rem \equiv lemma3\,h1\ (\mathrm{Witness}\ (square\,x)\ h2) \end{bmatrix}$$
$\quad\quad \mathbf{in}\ existsElim\,rem\,\lambda\,y1\,h3\ \rightarrow\ \mathrm{Witness}\,y1\ (\mathrm{Pair}\,h3\ (lemma2\,h2\,h3))$

$Square \in rel\,A$
$Square \equiv \lambda\,p\,x \rightarrow \exists\,y\,((p \cdot square\,x) == square\,y)$

$lemma5\,(h2 \in prime\,p, x \in A, h3 \in Square\,p\,x) \in \exists\,x1\,(((p \cdot x1) == x) \wedge Square\,p\,x1)$
$(p \in A)$
$lemma5\,h2\,x\,h3 \equiv existsElim\,h3\,\lambda\,y\,h4 \rightarrow existsElim\,(lemma4\,h2\,h4)\,\lambda\,y1\,h5 \rightarrow$

$$\text{let} \begin{bmatrix} rem1 \in (p \cdot y1) == y \\ rem1 \equiv andElimLeft\,h5 \\ rem2 \in (p \cdot square\,y1) == square\,x \\ rem2 \equiv andElimRight\,h5 \end{bmatrix}$$

$$\text{in } existsElim\,(lemma4\,h2\,rem2)\,\lambda\,x1\,h6 \rightarrow \text{ let} \begin{bmatrix} rem3 \in (p \cdot x1) == x \\ rem3 \equiv andElimLeft\,h6 \\ rem4 \in (p \cdot square\,x1) == square\,y1 \\ rem4 \equiv andElimRight\,h6 \end{bmatrix}$$
$$\text{in Witness } x1\,(\text{Pair } rem3\,(\text{Witness } y1\,rem4))$$

$isNotSquare \in pred\,A$
$isNotSquare \equiv \lambda\,p \rightarrow (x, y \in A) \rightarrow \neg\,((p \cdot square\,x) == square\,y)$

$theorem\,(p \in A) \in prime\,p \rightarrow noether\,A\,(multiple\,p) \rightarrow isNotSquare\,p$
$theorem\,p \equiv$

$$\lambda\,h1\,h2 \rightarrow \text{ let} \begin{bmatrix} rem \in (x \in A) \rightarrow \neg\,(Square\,p\,x) \\ rem \equiv infiniteDescent\,A\,(multiple\,p)\,(Square\,p)\,h2\,(lemma5\,h1) \end{bmatrix}$$
$$\text{in } \lambda\,x\,y\,h3 \rightarrow rem\,x\,(\text{Witness } y\,h3)$$

This is the main result; it applies to the case where A is $\mathbb{N}^*$ and p is 2, but it shows as well that any prime cannot be a square of a rational

7.4   System

What is the home page of the system?

<http://www.cs.chalmers.se/~catarina/agda/>

What are the books about the system? No book directly on the system, but it is inspired by:

Nordstrom, Petersson, Smith, *Programming in Type Theory*, Oxford University Press.

What is the logic of the system? Described in Per Martin-Löf, 'An intuitionistic theory of types', 1972. It can be found in:

G. Sambin and J. Smith (eds.), *25 years of constructive type theory*, Oxford University Press.

This is extended by general data type declaration and case notation.

What is the implementation architecture of the system? Described in <http://www.cs.chalmers.se/~catarina/agda/>.

What does working with the system look like? It feels like programming in a functional language with dependent types. The construction of the proof/program can be done interactively with place-holders/meta-variables. Actually the syntax is very close to the functional language Cayenne, designed by Lennart Augustsson, `<http://www.cs.chalmers.se/~augustss/cayenne/>`.

What is special about the system compared to other systems? Identification of proofs and functional programs with dependent types + meta-variables.

What are other versions of the system? A first version (1990) was written by Thierry Coquand (caml) and Lennart Augustsson (C). Then (1992) version Lena Magnusson (SML) and Johan Nordlander (C).

Alfa is the interface of the system. It has been written by Thomas Hallgren. There is also an Emacs interface, following ideas of Dan Synek, written by Catarina Coquand,

Who are the people behind the system? The meta-variable idea comes from Bengt Nordstrom, refined later by Thierry Coquand and Lena Magnusson. The previous version Half was designed by Thierry Coquand (gofer) and Dan Synek (C). The actual version is designed by Catarina Coquand (haskell).

What are the main user communities of the system? Peter Hancock and Anton Setzer.

What large mathematical formalizations have been done in the system? Localic version of Hahn-Banach was done by Jan Cederquist in Half.

8 ACL2

Ruben Gamboa

Formalization from J Strother Moore <moore@cs.utexas.edu> by Ruben
Gamboa <ruben@gamboas.org>. Answers by Ruben Gamboa.

8.1 Statement

```
(implies (equal (* x x) 2)
         (and (realp x)
              (not (rationalp x))))
```

8.2 Definitions

Definition of even-induction

```
(defun even-induction (x)
  "Induct by going two steps at a time"
  (if (or (zp x) (equal x 1))
      x
      (1+ (even-induction (1- (1- x))))))
```

8.3 Proof

```
(in-package "ACL2")
```

This book presents the proof that $\sqrt{2}$ is an irrational number. The proof proceeds
by observing that p^2 is even precisely when p is even. Thus, if $p^2 = 2q^2$, p must
be even. But then, p^2 isn't just even, it's a multiple of 4, so $q^2 = p^2/2$ must also
be even. But since q^2 is even, so is q. Now, letting p be the numerator of $\sqrt{2}$ and
q the denominator of $\sqrt{2}$, we find that both the numerator and denominator are
even – but this is an impossibility. Hence, we can conclude that 2 is not rational.

The proof is completed by observing that $\sqrt{2}$ is not complex. The reason is
that if x is complex, x^2 is real only when x is a pure imaginary number. But in
those cases, x^2 is negative

```
(include-book "../arithmetic/top"
              :load-compiled-file nil)
```

Step 1: We begin by proving that p^2 is even precisely when p is even.

```
(encapsulate
 ()
```

Since ACL2 is so strong in induction, it is common to use induction to prove
simple number theoretic results. But to induce over the even numbers requires
that each time through the induction we 'step' by 2, not the usual 1. So we start
by introducing the induction scheme for the even numbers.

F. Wiedijk (Ed.): The Seventeen Provers of the World, LNAI 3600, pp. 55–66, 2006.
© Springer-Verlag Berlin Heidelberg 2006

```
(local
 (defun even-induction (x)
   "Induct by going two steps at a time"
   (if (or (zp x) (equal x 1))
       x
     (1+ (even-induction (1- (1- x)))))))
```

Now we can prove that if p^2 is even, so is p. Because we're doing this inductively, we only consider the even naturals to begin with.

```
(local
 (defthm lemma-1
   (implies (and (integerp p)
                 (<= 0 p)
                 (evenp (* p p)))
            (evenp p))
   :hints (("Goal"
            :induct (even-induction p)))
   :rule-classes nil))
```

Technically, we do not need to worry about the negative integers in this proof, since both the numerator and denominator of $\sqrt{2}$ (if they existed) are positive. But it's easy enough to prove this, and it gets rid of the 'non-negative' hypothesis. In general, it is good to get rid of hypothesis in ACL2 rewrite rules.

```
(local
 (defthm lemma-2
   (implies (and (integerp p)
                 (<= p 0)
                 (evenp (* p p)))
            (evenp p))
   :hints (("Goal"
            :use (:instance lemma-1 (p (- p)))))
   :rule-classes nil))
```

Now, we can prove that if p^2 is even, so is p. But the converse is trivial, so we could show that p^2 is even iff p is even. Because equalities are more powerful rewrite rules than implications, we prefer to do so, even though we don't really need the stronger equality for this proof. So we prove the converse here: if p is even, so is p^2.

```
(local
 (defthm lemma-3
   (implies (and (integerp p)
                 (evenp p))
            (evenp (* p p)))
   :rule-classes nil))
```

Now, we simply collect the results above to find that p^2 is even if and only if p is even. This is the only theorem that is exported from this event.

```
(defthm even-square-implies-even
  (implies (integerp p)
           (equal (evenp (* p p)) (evenp p))))
```

```
  :hints (("Goal"
            :use ((:instance lemma-1)
                  (:instance lemma-2)
                  (:instance lemma-3)))))
)
```

Step 2. Suppose p^2 is even. Then, p is even, so p^2 is more than even – it is a multiple of 4. We prove this here, since it is the key fact allowing us to conclude that q^2 is even when we know that $p^2 = 2 \cdot q^2$.

```
(defthm even-square-implies-even-square-multiple-of-4
  (implies (and (integerp p)
                (evenp (* p p)))
           (evenp (* 1/2 p p)))
  :hints (("Goal"
            :use ((:instance even-square-implies-even)
                  (:instance (:theorem (implies (integerp x) (integerp (* x x))))
                             (x (* 1/2 p))))
            :in-theory (disable even-square-implies-even))))
```

In the proofs below, we disable ACL2's definition of even, but we need to remember that $2 \cdot n$ is always even. So we prove that rewrite rule here.

```
(defthm evenp-2x
  (implies (integerp x)
           (evenp (* 2 x))))
```

Step 3. Suppose $p^2 = 2 \cdot q^2$. Then we can conclude that p is even, since p^2 is even.

```
(defthm numerator-sqrt-2-is-even
  (implies (and (integerp p)
                (integerp q)
                (equal (* p p)
                       (* 2 (* q q))))
           (evenp p))
  :hints (("Goal"
            :use ((:instance even-square-implies-even)
                  (:instance evenp-2x (x (* q q))))
            :in-theory (disable even-square-implies-even
                                evenp-2x
                                evenp)))))
```

Step 4. Suppose $p^2 = 2 \cdot q^2$. Then we can conclude that q is even, since p^2 is a multiple of 4, so q^2 is even.

```
(defthm denominator-sqrt-2-is-even
  (implies (and (integerp p)
                (integerp q)
                (equal (* p p)
                       (* 2 (* q q))))
           (evenp q))
  :hints (("Goal"
            :use ((:instance even-square-implies-even-square-multiple-of-4)
                  (:instance even-square-implies-even (p q))
```

```
            (:instance evenp-2x
                       (x (* q q)))
            (:instance equal-*-/-1
                       (x 2)
                       (y (* p p))
                       (z (* q q))))
      :in-theory (disable even-square-implies-even-square-multiple-of-4
                          even-square-implies-even
                          evenp-2x
                          evenp
                          equal-*-/-1))))
```

Step 5. Those are all the pieces we need to prove that $\sqrt{2}$ is not rational. For we observe that if $p = \texttt{numerator}(\sqrt{2})$ and $q = \texttt{denominator}(\sqrt{2})$, the theorems above show that both p and q are even, and that's an absurdity.

```
(encapsulate
 ()
```

ACL2's algebraic prowess is modest. In the proof of the main theorem below, it builds the expression p^2/q^2 where $x = p/q$, but it does not reduce the expression further to x^2. We add a rewrite rule to take care of that.

```
(local
 (defthm lemma-1
   (implies (rationalp x)
            (equal (* (/ (denominator x))
                      (/ (denominator x))
                      (numerator x)
                      (numerator x))
                   (* x x)))
   :hints (("Goal"
            :use ((:instance Rational-implies2)
                  (:instance *-r-denominator-r (r x)))
            :in-theory (disable Rational-implies2
                                *-r-denominator-r)))))
```

Now we can prove that the square root of 2 is not rational. This involves using the theorems defined above, as well as some algebraic lemmas to help reduce the terms. The most important hint, however, is the inclusion of the axiom Lowest-Terms, because it is not enabled in the ACL2 world.

```
(defthm sqrt-2-not-rational
  (implies (equal (* x x) 2)
           (not (rationalp x)))
  :hints (("Goal"
           :use ((:instance numerator-sqrt-2-is-even
                            (p (numerator x))
                            (q (denominator x)))
                 (:instance denominator-sqrt-2-is-even
                            (p (numerator x))
                            (q (denominator x)))
                 (:instance Lowest-Terms
                            (n 2)
                            (r (/ (numerator x) 2))
```

```
                              (q (/ (denominator x) 2)))
                    (:instance equal-*-/-1
                              (x (/ (* (denominator x) (denominator x))))
                              (y 2)
                              (z (* (numerator x) (numerator x)))))
              :in-theory (disable equal-*-/-1
                                 numerator-sqrt-2-is-even
                                 denominator-sqrt-2-is-even))))
)
```

Step 6. Now that the rationals are ruled out, we need to weed out the remaining $\sqrt{2}$ suspects. One possibility is that $\sqrt{2}$ is a complex number. We explore that here. Because ACL2 has very little knowledge of the complex numbers, we have to start with some basic facts. First, we show that $(a+bi)^2 = (a^2-b^2)+(ab+ab)i$.

```
(encapsulate
 ()
```

We start out with the desired theorem when the complex number is written as $a+bi$ instead of (complex a b). Here, the result follows from simple algebra and the fact that $i^2 = -1$.

```
(local
 (defthm lemma-1
   (equal (* (+ x (* #c(0 1) y))
            (+ x (* #c(0 1) y)))
         (+ (- (* x x) (* y y))
            (* #c(0 1) (+ (* x y) (* x y)))))
   :rule-classes nil))
```

Now we rewrite the right-hand side of the rewrite rule into the final form of (complex $(a^2 - b^2)$ $(ab + ab)$).

```
(local
 (defthm lemma-2
   (implies (and (realp x)
                 (realp y))
           (equal (* (+ x (* #c(0 1) y))
                    (+ x (* #c(0 1) y)))
                 (complex (- (* x x) (* y y))
                         (+ (* x y) (* x y)))))
   :hints (("Goal"
            :use ((:instance lemma-1)
                  (:instance complex-definition
                            (x (- (* x x) (* y y)))
                            (y (+ (* x y) (* x y)))))))
   :rule-classes nil))
```

And finally we rewrite the left-hand side of the rewrite rule into the final form of (complex a b)^2.

```
(defthm complex-square-definition
  (implies (and (realp x)
                (realp y))
          (equal (* (complex x y) (complex x y))
```

```
                    (complex (- (* x x) (* y y))
                             (+ (* x y) (* x y)))))
      :hints (("Goal"
               :use ((:instance complex-definition)
                     (:instance lemma-2))))
      :rule-classes nil)
   )
```

Step 7. Since $(a + bi)^2 = (a^2 - b^2) + (ab + ab)i$, it follows that it is real if and only if a or b is zero, i.e., if and only if the number is real or pure imaginary. Since we're interested only in the non-real complex numbers (the ones for which complexp is true), we can conlude that only pure imaginaries have real squares.

```
(encapsulate
 ()
```

First we show that $(a + bi)^2 = (a^2 - b^2) + (ab + ab)i$ is real if and only $ab + ab$ is zero.

```
(local
  (defthm lemma-1
    (implies (and (complexp x)
                  (realp (* x x)))
             (equal (+ (* (realpart x) (imagpart x))
                       (* (realpart x) (imagpart x)))
                    0))
    :hints (("Goal"
             :use (:instance complex-square-definition
                             (x (realpart x))
                             (y (imagpart x)))))
    :rule-classes nil))
```

The following rewrite rule allows us to conclude that a real number x is zero whenever $x + x$ is zero.

```
(local
  (defthm lemma-2
    (implies (and (realp x)
                  (equal (+ x x) 0))
             (= x 0))))
```

The two lemmas above conclude that ab is zero whenever $(a + bi)^2$ is zero, and since b is assumed non-zero (because $a + bi$ is complex), we have that a must be zero, and $a + bi = bi$ is a pure imaginary number.

```
(defthm complex-squares-real-iff-imaginary
  (implies (and (complexp x)
                (realp (* x x)))
           (equal (realpart x) 0))
  :hints (("Goal"
           :use ((:instance lemma-1)
                 (:instance lemma-2
                           (x (* (realpart x) (imagpart x)))))))
  )
```

Step 7. Trivially, the square of a pure imaginary number bi is a negative real, since $(bi)^2 = -b^2$.

```
(defthm imaginary-squares-are-negative
  (implies (and (complexp x)
                (equal (realpart x) 0))
           (< (* x x) 0))
  :hints (("Goal"
           :use (:instance complex-square-definition
                           (x 0)
                           (y (imagpart x)))))))
```

Step 8. From the theorems above, we can conclude that $\sqrt{2}$ is not a complex number, because the only candidates are the pure imaginary numbers, and their squares are all negative.

```
(defthm sqrt-2-not-complexp
  (implies (complexp x)
           (not (equal (* x x) 2)))
  :hints (("Goal"
           :use ((:instance complex-squares-real-iff-imaginary)
                 (:instance imaginary-squares-are-negative))))))
```

Step 9. That means $\sqrt{2}$ is not rational, and neither is it a complex number. The only remaining candidates (in ACL2's universe) are the non-rational reals, so we can prove the main result: the square root of two (if it exists) is irrational.

```
(defthm irrational-sqrt-2
  (implies (equal (* x x) 2)
           (and (realp x)
                (not (rationalp x))))
  :hints (("Goal"
           :cases ((rationalp x) (complexp x))))))
```

Step 10. Next, it would be nice to show that $\sqrt{2}$ actually exists! See the book nonstd/nsa/sqrt.lisp for a proof of that, using non-standard analysis.

Output of lemma-1 *of* even-square-implies-even

```
ACL2(r) !>>>(LOCAL (DEFTHM LEMMA-1
                    (IMPLIES (AND (INTEGERP P)
                                  (<= 0 P)
                                  (EVENP (* P P)))
                             (EVENP P))
                    :HINTS
                    (("Goal" :INDUCT (EVEN-INDUCTION P)))
                    :RULE-CLASSES NIL))
```

[Note: A hint was supplied for our processing of the goal above.
Thanks!]

Name the formula above *1.

We have been told to use induction. One induction scheme is suggested
by the induction hint.

We will induct according to a scheme suggested by (EVEN-INDUCTION P).

If we let (:P P) denote *1 above then the induction scheme we'll use
is
```
(AND (IMPLIES (AND (NOT (OR (ZP P) (EQUAL P 1)))
                   (:P (+ -1 -1 P)))
             (:P P))
     (IMPLIES (OR (ZP P) (EQUAL P 1))
              (:P P))).
```
This induction is justified by the same argument used to admit EVEN-
INDUCTION, namely, the measure (ACL2-COUNT P) is decreasing according
to the relation E0-ORD-< (which is known to be well-founded on the
domain recognized by E0-ORDINALP). When applied to the goal at hand
the above induction scheme produces the following two nontautological
subgoals.

Subgoal *1/2
```
(IMPLIES (AND (NOT (OR (ZP P) (EQUAL P 1)))
              (IMPLIES (AND (INTEGERP (+ -1 -1 P))
                            (<= 0 (+ -1 -1 P))
                            (EVENP (* (+ -1 -1 P) (+ -1 -1 P))))
                       (EVENP (+ -1 -1 P))))
         (IMPLIES (AND (INTEGERP P)
                       (<= 0 P)
                       (EVENP (* P P)))
                  (EVENP P))).
```

By the simple :definition EVENP and the simple :rewrite rules <-+-NEGATIVE-
0-1 and ASSOCIATIVITY-OF-* we reduce the conjecture to

Subgoal *1/2'
```
(IMPLIES (AND (NOT (OR (ZP P) (EQUAL P 1)))
              (OR (NOT (AND (INTEGERP (+ -1 -1 P))
                            (<= 1 (+ -1 P))
                            (INTEGERP (* (+ -1 -1 P) (+ -1 -1 P) 1/2))))
                  (INTEGERP (* (+ -1 -1 P) 1/2)))
              (INTEGERP P)
              (<= 0 P)
              (INTEGERP (* P P 1/2)))
         (INTEGERP (* P 1/2))).
```

This simplifies, using the :definitions FIX, NOT, SYNTAXP and ZP, the
:executable-counterparts of BINARY-*, BINARY-+, CAR, CONSP, EQ, IF,
UNARY-- and ZP, primitive type reasoning, the :rewrite rules ASSOCIATIVITY-
OF-+, COMMUTATIVITY-2-OF-*, COMMUTATIVITY-2-OF-+, COMMUTATIVITY-OF-
, DISTRIBUTIVITY, DISTRIBUTIVITY-OF-MINUS-OVER-+, FOLD-CONSTS-IN-,
FOLD-CONSTS-IN-+, FUNCTIONAL-COMMUTATIVITY-OF-MINUS-*-RIGHT and UNICITY-
OF-1 and the :type-prescription rule NONNEGATIVE-PRODUCT, to the following
two conjectures.

Subgoal *1/2.2
```
(IMPLIES (AND (< 0 P)
              (NOT (EQUAL P 1))
              (< (+ -1 P) 1)
              (INTEGERP P)
              (INTEGERP (* 1/2 P P)))
         (INTEGERP (* 1/2 P))).
```

But simplification reduces this to T, using linear arithmetic and primitive
type reasoning.

```
Subgoal *1/2.1
(IMPLIES (AND (< 0 P)
              (NOT (EQUAL P 1))
              (INTEGERP (+ -1 (* 1/2 P)))
              (INTEGERP P)
              (INTEGERP (* 1/2 P P)))
         (INTEGERP (* 1/2 P))).
```

But simplification reduces this to T, using primitive type reasoning.

```
Subgoal *1/1
(IMPLIES (OR (ZP P) (EQUAL P 1))
         (IMPLIES (AND (INTEGERP P)
                       (<= 0 P)
                       (EVENP (* P P)))
                  (EVENP P))).
```

By the simple :definition EVENP and the simple :rewrite rule ASSOCIATIVITY-OF-* we reduce the conjecture to

```
Subgoal *1/1'
(IMPLIES (AND (OR (ZP P) (EQUAL P 1))
              (INTEGERP P)
              (<= 0 P)
              (INTEGERP (* P P 1/2)))
         (INTEGERP (* P 1/2))).
```

But simplification reduces this to T, using the :definition ZP, the :executable-counterparts of <, BINARY-*, INTEGERP, NOT and ZP and primitive type reasoning.

That completes the proof of *1.

Q.E.D.

```
Summary
Form:  ( DEFTHM LEMMA-1 ...)
Rules: ((:DEFINITION EVENP)
        (:DEFINITION FIX)
        (:DEFINITION IMPLIES)
        (:DEFINITION NOT)
        (:DEFINITION SYNTAXP)
        (:DEFINITION ZP)
        (:EXECUTABLE-COUNTERPART <)
        (:EXECUTABLE-COUNTERPART BINARY-*)
        (:EXECUTABLE-COUNTERPART BINARY-+)
        (:EXECUTABLE-COUNTERPART CAR)
        (:EXECUTABLE-COUNTERPART CONSP)
        (:EXECUTABLE-COUNTERPART EQ)
        (:EXECUTABLE-COUNTERPART IF)
        (:EXECUTABLE-COUNTERPART INTEGERP)
        (:EXECUTABLE-COUNTERPART NOT)
        (:EXECUTABLE-COUNTERPART UNARY--)
        (:EXECUTABLE-COUNTERPART ZP)
        (:FAKE-RUNE-FOR-LINEAR NIL)
        (:FAKE-RUNE-FOR-TYPE-SET NIL)
        (:REWRITE <-+-NEGATIVE-0-1)
        (:REWRITE ASSOCIATIVITY-OF-*)
        (:REWRITE ASSOCIATIVITY-OF-+)
        (:REWRITE COMMUTATIVITY-2-OF-*)
        (:REWRITE COMMUTATIVITY-2-OF-+)
```

```
(:REWRITE COMMUTATIVITY-OF-*)
(:REWRITE DISTRIBUTIVITY)
(:REWRITE DISTRIBUTIVITY-OF-MINUS-OVER-+)
(:REWRITE FOLD-CONSTS-IN-*)
(:REWRITE FOLD-CONSTS-IN-+)
(:REWRITE FUNCTIONAL-COMMUTATIVITY-OF-MINUS-*-RIGHT)
(:REWRITE UNICITY-OF-1)
(:TYPE-PRESCRIPTION NONNEGATIVE-PRODUCT))
Warnings:  None
Time:  0.09 seconds (prove: 0.05, print: 0.02, other: 0.02)
LEMMA-1
```

8.4 System

What is the home page of the system?

<http://www.cs.utexas.edu/users/moore/acl2/>

What are the books about the system?

Computer-Aided Reasoning: An Approach, Matt Kaufmann, Panagiotis Manolios, and J Strother Moore, Kluwer Academic Publishers, June, 2000. (ISBN 0-7923-7744-3)

Computer-Aided Reasoning: ACL2 Case Studies, Matt Kaufmann, Panagiotis Manolios, and J Strother Moore (eds.), Kluwer Academic Publishers, June, 2000. (ISBN 0-7923-7849-0)

See:
<http://www.cs.utexas.edu/users/moore/publications/acl2-books/>.

What is the logic of the system? The logic is based on the theory of recursive functions. It is is a first-order logic with an induction rule of inference. The syntax is that of the applicative subset of Common Lisp, a rich and useful programming language in its own right.

I used to say 'ACL2 is a quantifier-free logic', but that isn't really true. ACL2 has constructs that support quantification (e.g., defchoose that selects an element 'picked' by an existential quantifier). I usually say in my papers 'ACL2 has limited support for quantifiers.' See: <http://www.cs.utexas.edu/users/moore/publications/acl2-papers.html#Foundations>.

What is the implementation architecture of the system? Most of the ACL2 system is written in its own logic. The only exception is a small amount of bootstrapping code, which is implemented in Common Lisp.

The implementation is arranged around a 'waterfall' inference engine . The initial theory as well as theorems already proved are organized as rules. By default rules are stored as rewrite rules, although the user can guide ACL2 to use a theorem in other ways, such as for inferencing types, eliminating destructors, generalizing terms, solving inequalities, and others. Initially, the theorem to be proved is placed in a 'pool' of goals to be solved. The theorem prover proceeds by selecting a goal from the pool and running it through the 'waterfall' of inference methods. Each inference method in the waterfall uses built-in knowledge as well as the appropriate rules to simplify the goal into zero or more subgoals. For example, the conditional rewriter uses rewrite rules to simplify the goal, whereas the cross-fertilizer uses the goal's equality hypothesis to rewrite a term in the goal, the generalizer uses generalization rules to prepare a theorem for induction, and the induction engine converts a goal into base and induction subgoals. If an inference method in the pool is successful, it removes the original goal from the pool and replaces it with the resulting subgoals. Note in particular that once an inference method in the waterfall succeeds, none of the other methods are applied to that goal.

What does working with the system look like? The user interacts with ACL2 by submitting definitions and theorems. ACL2 responds with English text and formulas as its proof attempts progress. The user observes the output from failing proofs and typically formulates lemmas to submit to the system, generally in the form of rewrite rules (though many other rule types are supported), to 'teach' ACL2 additional facts about the function symbols that have been introduced. Alternatively, the user may see a failed proof and decide to give ACL2 a hint (such as enabling or disabling certain rules, specifically requesting that a given instance of a rule be used in the proof, or suggesting a helpful induction scheme) to help it find the proof. The ultimate goal is to use ACL2 to 'certify' a collection of 'books', each of which is a collection of 'events' (typically definitions and theorems).

What is special about the system compared to other systems? ACL2 is being used in at least two industrial settings on relatively large and difficult applications. Its prover heuristics are state-of-the-art for so-called inductive theorem provers, but perhaps more important is its robust engineering and extensive hyperlinked documentation.

A compelling feature is that it is built around a real programming language. This makes it possible to develop a theory in ACL2 and execute it. This allows the user to debug the theory, as might be needed when formalizing a new system from scratch. For example, after formalizing a microprocessor or a virtual machine, it is possible to directly execute (i.e., simulate) a run of the microprocessor or VM, making it easier to find errors created in the modeling step before the (necessarily doomed) verification effort per se gets under way.

What are other versions of the system? Nqthm (aka the Boyer-Moore theorem prover) is a predecessor of ACL2 that uses a simpler, but very similar logic to ACL2. Nqthm pioneered many of the techniques used in ACL2, such as the waterfall design and the automatic discovery of induction schemes.

ACL2(r) is a variant of ACL2 that offers support for reasoning about the irrational real and complex numbers. It modifies the ACL2 logic by introducing notions from non-standard analysis.

Who are the people behind the system? The authors are Matt Kaufmann and
J Moore, but Bob Boyer was also instrumental in the early development of
ACL2. Many people have contributed to the improvement of ACL2, as described in the release notes <http://www.cs.utexas.edu/users/moore/acl2/
v2-6/RELEASE-NOTES.html> and acknowledgments: <http://www.cs.utexas.
edu/users/moore/acl2/v2-6/ACKNOWLEDGMENTS.html>.

What are the main user communities of the system? There is a very active user
community in the University of Texas. In addition, there are active users in
academia all over the world, in Wyoming, Georgia, and Cadiz Spain. ACL2 has
also found use in industrial settings, where it has been used to model, simulate,
and verify various circuits and microprocessors. For example, it is in use at AMD,
IBM, and Rockwell-Collins. Many people in the ACL2 community meet on oc-
casion at ACL2 workshops. See: <http://www.cs.utexas.edu/users/moore/
acl2/workshops.html>.

What large mathematical formalizations have been done in the system? ACL2
has been used to prove a diverse set of results. For example, there are proofs
concerning the validity of micro-processor implementations of floating-point mul-
tipliers and dividers, as well as transcendental functions like the floating-point
square root. There are ACL2 proofs verifying pipeline machines, parallel algorithms, and program translators. There are ACL2 formalizations of finite set theory, graph theory, and the Knuth-Bendix theorem. Other proofs include pieces of
real analysis, such as the fundamental theorem of calculus, and Taylor's theorem.

The results above merely scratch the surface. For a more complete list,
see the ACL2 home page. See: <http://www.cs.utexas.edu/users/moore/
publications/acl2-papers.html>.

What representation of the formalization has been put in this paper? The representation of the proof is direct. The proof is based on the ACL2(r) variant of
ACL2, although ACL2(r) is not needed until the last theorem, which uses the
predicate `realp`. ACL2(r) has built-in types for reals, rationals, integers, and
complex numbers, and these are the only types used in the proof.

What needs to be explained about this specific proof? The last theorem is valid
only in ACL2(r) and not ACL2. I.e., the predicate

```
(realp x)
```

does not exist in ACL2, since ACL2 only supports the rationals. ACL2(r) does
support the reals, so the final statement is actually a theorem of ACL2(r) and
not ACL2. In plain old ACL2, you can prove the stronger result

```
[forall x] (not (equal (* x x) 2))
```

where the [forall x] is implied.

9 PhoX

Christophe Raffalli and Paul Rozière

Formalization by Christophe Raffalli <Christophe.Raffalli@univ-savoie.fr> and Paul Rozière <roziere@logique.jussieu.fr>. Answers by Christophe Raffalli.

9.1 Statement

```
/\m,n : N (m^ N2 = N2 * n^ N2 -> m = N0 & n = N0)
```

9.2 Definitions

Definition of Q

```
def  Q m = m > N0 & \/n:N (m^ N2 = N2 * n^ N2).
```

9.3 Proof

```
Import nat.

flag auto_lvl 1.

theorem minimal.element /\X (\/n:N X n -> \/n:N (X n & /\p:N (X p -> n <= p))).
intro 2.
by_absurd.
rewrite_hyp H0 demorgan1.
use /\n:N ~ X n.
trivial.
intros.
elim well_founded.N with H1.
intros.
intro.
apply H0 with H4.
lefts G $& $\/.
elim H3 with H5.
elim not.lesseq.imply.less.N.
save.

theorem not_odd_and_even.N  /\x,y,z:N (~ (x = N2 * y & x = N1 + N2 * z)).
intro 2.
elim H.
trivial.
intros.
intro.
left H4.
elim H2 with [case].
trivial =H0 H4 H6.
elim H1.
axiom H3.
```

F. Wiedijk (Ed.): The Seventeen Provers of the World, LNAI 3600, pp. 67–71, 2006.
© Springer-Verlag Berlin Heidelberg 2006

```
axiom H6.
intro.
rmh H4.
left H5.
intros.
rmh H5.
left H4.
axiom H4.
intros.
save.

theorem sum_square.N /\x,y:N (x + y)^N2 = x^N2 + N2*x*y + y^N2.
intros.
intro.
save.

fact less.exp.N /\n,x,y:N( x <= y -> x^n <= y^n).
intros.
elim H.
trivial.
rewrite calcul.N.
trivial.
save.

fact less_r.exp.N   /\n,x,y:N( x^n < y^n -> x < y).
intros.
elim lesseq.case1.N with y and x.
apply less.exp.N with n and H3.
elim lesseq.imply.not.greater.N with y^n and x^n ;; Try intros.
save.

fact less.ladd.N /\x,y:N (N0 < y -> x < x + y).
intros.
elim H.
rewrite calcul.N.
trivial.
save.

theorem n.square.pair /\n:N (\/p:N n^N2=N2*p -> \/q:N n=N2*q).
intros.
lefts H0 $\/ $&.
apply odd_or_even.N with H.
lefts G $\/ $& $or.
trivial.
prove   n^N2 = N1 + N2*(N2*y^N2+N2*y).
rewrite H3 sum_square.N.
from N1 + N2 * N2 * y + (N2 * y) ^ N2 = N1 + N4 * y + N2 * N2 * y ^ N2.
intro.
elim not_odd_and_even.N with N (n^N2).
intros.
select 3.
intro.
axiom H1.
axiom G.
axiom H0.
intros.
save.

lem decrease /\m,n : N (m^ N2 = N2 * n^ N2 -> N0 < n -> n < m).
intros.
```

```
elim less_r.exp.N with N2 ;; Try intros.
prove m^N2 = n^N2 + n^N2. axiom H1.
elim less.ladd.N ;; Try intros.
trivial  =H0 H2.
save.

lem sup_zero /\m,n : N (m^ N2 = N2 * n^ N2 -> N0 < m -> N0 < n).
intros.
elim neq.less_or_sup.N with N0 and n ;; Try intros.
rewrite_hyp H1 H3 calcul.N.
trivial.
trivial.
save.

def  Q m = m > N0 & \/n:N (m^ N2 = N2 * n^ N2).

lem dec /\m:N (Q m -> \/m':N (Q m' & m' < m)).
intros.
lefts H0 $Q $\/ $&.
apply sup_zero with H2 and H0.
intro.
instance ?1 n.
intros.
intros.
trivial.
prove \/p:N (m ^ N2 = N2 * p).
intro.
instance ?2  n^N2.
trivial.
apply n.square.pair with G0.
lefts G1 $& $\/.
prove n ^N2 = N2 * q ^N2.
rewrite_hyp H2 H4.
prove N2 * N2 * q ^N2 = N2 * n ^ N2.
from H2.
left G1.
trivial =.
intro.
intros.
intros.
intros.
trivial =H3 G1.
elim decrease.
save.

lem sq2_irrat /\m:N ~Q m.
intros.
intro.
elim minimal.element with Q.
intros $\/ $&.
axiom H.
axiom H0.
lefts H1.
elim dec with H2.
lefts H4.
apply H3 with H5.
elim lesseq.imply.not.greater.N with n and m'.
save.
```

```
theorem square2_irrat /\m,n : N (m^ N2 = N2 * n^ N2 -> m = N0 & n = N0).
intros.
apply sq2_irrat  with H.
elim H with [case].
intro.
intro.
elim H0 with [case].
intro.
rewrite_hyp H1 H2 H4 calcul.N.
left H1;; intros.
prove Q m.
intros $Q $\/ $& ;; Try axiom H1.
trivial.
elim G.
save.
```

The last theorem with LATEX annotations

```
theorem square2_irrat /\m,n : N (m^ N2 = N2 * n^ N2 -> m = N0 & n = N0).
(*! math
\begin{theorem} The square-root of 2 is irrational.
For this we just need to prove the following:
$$ \[ $0 \] $$
\end{theorem}
\begin{proof}
*)
intros.
apply sq2_irrat  with H.
(*! math
We assume \[ $$H1 \].
By the previous lemma we have \[ $$G \].
*)
elim H with [case].
intro.
intro.
(*! math
If \[ $$H2 \] we easily get \[ $0 \].
*)
elim H0 with [case].
intro.
rewrite_hyp H1 H2 H4 calcul.N.
left H1;; intros.
prove Q m.
(*! math
If \[ m > N0 \] then we have \[ Q m \] and a contradiction.
\end{proof}
*)
intros $Q $\/ $& ;; Try axiom H1.
trivial.
elim G.
save.
```

Generated LATEX for the last theorem

Theorem 13. *The square-root of 2 is irrational. For this we just need to prove the following:*

$$\forall m, n : \mathbb{N} \ (m^2 = 2 \cdot n^2 \rightarrow m = 0 \wedge n = 0)$$

Proof. We assume $m^2 = 2 \cdot n^2$. By the previous lemma we have $\neg(Q\,m)$. If $m = 0$ we easily get $n = 0$. If $m > 0$ then we have $Q\,m$ and a contradiction.

9.4   System

What is the home page of the system?

<http://www.lama.univ-savoie.fr/~raffalli/phox.html>

What are the books about the system? There is a section about PhoX and a lot of the exercise in the book are corrected with PhoX in:

Introduction à la logique par David, Nour et Raffalli chez Dunod.

What is the logic of the system? HOL.

What is the implementation architecture of the system? An OCaml main program with ProofGeneral under Emacs or xEmacs.

What does working with the system look like? Nice and easy to learn.

What is special about the system compared to other systems? The small number of extensible tactics making it possible

- not to remember the name of most lemma (they are incorporated in the extension of the existing tactics)
- programming the automated reasonning
- it makes it possible to use the system with first year student!

What are other versions of the system? None.

Who are the people behind the system? Mostly Christophe Raffalli, but also Paul Rozière (Paris VII) for some examples and part of the documentation.

What are the main user communities of the system? Math students from first year to PhD.

What large mathematical formalizations have been done in the system? Very large none, but interesting piece like arithmetic, Zorn and Zermelo from AC, Ramsey infinite theorem (n-uplet and k colors).

What representation of the formalization has been put in this paper? Tactic script, plus example of annotation and generated latex.

10 IMPS

William Farmer

Formalization and answers by William Farmer <wmfarmer@mcmaster.ca>.

10.1 Statement

```
not #(sqrt(2),qq)
```

10.2 Definitions

Definition of `divisor%power`

```
(def-constant divisor%power
  "lambda(d,n:nn,
     iota(m:nn, forsome(w:nn, n = d^m * w and not(d divides w))))"
  (theory h-o-real-arithmetic))
```

Definition of `non%perfect%square`

```
(def-constant non%perfect%square
  "lambda(k:nn,
     forsome(p:nn, positive%prime(p) and odd(divisor%power(p,k))))"
  (theory h-o-real-arithmetic))
```

10.3 Proof

The theorem statement "`not #(sqrt(2),qq)`" says "`sqrt(2)` is not defined in the sort `qq` of rational numbers".

Outline of proof:

1. The notion of the 'divisor power' of d in n is defined for natural numbers d and n. `divisor%power`(d, n) denotes the greatest m such that d^m divides n (provided such an m exists).
2. Some lemmas about `divisor%power` are proved.
3. The notion of a 'non perfect square' is defined as a natural number k for which there is a prime p such `divisor%power`(p, k) is odd.
4. The main theorem, that the square root of a non perfect square is irrational, is then proved as follows. Let k be a natural number for which there is a prime p such `divisor%power`(p, k) is odd. Assume that $\sqrt{k}$ is rational. Then, for some natural numbers m and n, $k \cdot n \cdot n = m \cdot m$. It follows that `divisor%power`$(p, k \cdot n \cdot n)$ is odd and `divisor%power`$(p, m \cdot m)$ is even, which is a contradiction.
5. The irrationality of the square root of 2 is proved as a corollary of the main theorem.

F. Wiedijk (Ed.): The Seventeen Provers of the World, LNAI 3600, pp. 72–87, 2006.
© Springer-Verlag Berlin Heidelberg 2006

```
(include-files
 (files (imps theories/reals/mutual-interp)
        (imps theories/reals/primes)
        (imps theories/reals/polynomials)))

(def-constant divisor%power
  "lambda(d,n:nn,
     iota(m:nn, forsome(w:nn, n = d^m * w and not(d divides w))))"
  (theory h-o-real-arithmetic))

(def-theorem ho-exponent-non-zero-lemma-1
  exponent-non-zero-lemma-1
  ;; "forall(n:zz,x:rr, not(x=0) implies not(x^n = 0))"
  (theory  h-o-real-arithmetic)
  (translation complete-ordered-field-interpretable)
  (proof existing-theorem))

(def-theorem divisor%power-of-d-in-0-is-undefined
  "forall(d:nn, not(#(divisor%power(d,0))))"
  (theory h-o-real-arithmetic)
  (proof
   (

    direct-inference
    (unfold-single-defined-constant (0) divisor%power)
    simplify
    (apply-macete-with-minor-premises eliminate-iota-macete)
    (cut-with-single-formula "0=d or 0<d")
    (block
     (script-comment "'cut-with-single-formula' at (0)")
     (contrapose "with(p:prop,p);")
     (antecedent-inference-strategy (0))
     (contrapose "with(p:prop,forall(j:nn,p));")
     (instantiate-existential ("i+1"))
     (block
      (script-comment "'instantiate-existential' at (0 0)")
      (instantiate-existential ("w"))
      (antecedent-inference "with(p:prop,p implies p);")
      simplify
      (block
       (script-comment "'antecedent-inference' at (1)")
       (apply-macete-with-minor-premises sum-of-exponents-law)
       (block
        (script-comment "'apply-macete-with-minor-premises' at (0)")
        (force-substitution "w*(d^i*d^1)" "(w*d^i)*d^1" (0))
        (block
         (script-comment "'force-substitution' at (0)")
         (backchain-backwards "with(r:rr,0=r);")
         simplify
         )
        (apply-macete-with-minor-premises
         associative-law-for-multiplication-pre-reals
         ) )
       simplify
       ) )
     simplify
     )
    simplify

    )))
```

```
(def-theorem divisor%power-characterization-lemma
  "forall(b,d,m,n,w1,w2:nn,
    b < m and not(d = 0) and n=d^b*w1 and n=d^m*w2 and not(d divides w1)
     implies
    b=m)"
  (theory  h-o-real-arithmetic)
  (proof
   (

    direct-and-antecedent-inference-strategy
    (cut-with-single-formula "d^b*w1 = d^m*w2")
    (cut-with-single-formula "not(d^b = 0)")
    (block
     (script-comment "'cut-with-single-formula' at (0)")
     (contrapose "with(w2,w1:nn,r:rr,r*w1=r*w2);")
     (force-substitution
      "d^b*w1=d^m*w2" "((d^b)^[-1]*d^b)*w1=((d^b)^[-1]*d^m)*w2"
      (0)
      )
     (block
      (script-comment "'force-substitution' at (0)")
      simplify
      (contrapose "with(w1,d:nn,not(d divides w1));")
      (apply-macete-with-minor-premises divisibility-lemma)
      (instantiate-existential ("w2*d^(m-b-1)"))
      simplify
      (block
       (script-comment "'instantiate-existential' at (1 0)")
       (apply-macete-with-minor-premises zz-*-closed)
       (cut-with-single-formula "0=[-1]+[-1]*b+m or 0<[-1]+[-1]*b+m")
       (block
        (script-comment "'cut-with-single-formula' at (0)")
        (antecedent-inference "with(p:prop,p or p);")
        simplify
        (block
         (script-comment "'antecedent-inference' at (1)")
         (apply-macete-with-minor-premises
          integer-exponentiation-definedness)
         simplify
         ) )
       simplify
       ) )
     (block
      (script-comment "'force-substitution' at (1)")
      direct-inference
      (force-substitution  "(d^b)^[-1]*d^b*w1=(d^b)^[-1]*d^m*w2"
                           "(d^b)^[-1]*(d^b*w1)=(d^b)^[-1]*(d^m*w2)" (0)
                           )
      (block
       (script-comment "'force-substitution' at (0)")
       (backchain "with(w2,w1:nn,r:rr,r*w1=r*w2);")
       simplify
       )
      (block
       (script-comment "'force-substitution' at (1)")
       (weaken (7 6 5 4 3 2 1 0))
```

```
           (apply-macete-with-minor-premises
            associative-law-for-multiplication-pre-reals
            ) ) ) )
        (apply-macete-with-minor-premises ho-exponent-non-zero-lemma-1)
        )))
(def-theorem divisor%power-characterization
   "forall(d,n,m:nn,
      not(d = 0)
        implies
      (m = divisor%power(d,n)
         iff
       forsome(w:nn, n = d^m * w and not(d divides w))))"
   reverse
   (theory h-o-real-arithmetic)
   (proof
    (

     (unfold-single-defined-constant (0) divisor%power)
     (apply-macete-with-minor-premises eliminate-iota-macete)
     direct-and-antecedent-inference-strategy
     (cut-with-single-formula "b<m or b=m or b>m")
     (block
      (script-comment "'cut-with-single-formula' at (0)")
      (antecedent-inference "with(p:prop,p or p or p);")
      (block
       (script-comment "'antecedent-inference' at (0)")
       (apply-macete-with-minor-premises
        divisor%power-characterization-lemma)
       auto-instantiate-existential
       )
      (block
       (script-comment "'antecedent-inference' at (2)")
       (force-substitution "b=m" "m=b" (0))
       (block
        (script-comment "'force-substitution' at (0)")
        (apply-macete-with-minor-premises
         divisor%power-characterization-lemma)
        auto-instantiate-existential
        (incorporate-antecedent "with(m,b:nn,b>m);")
        (unfold-single-defined-constant (0) >)
        )
       simplify
       ) )
      simplify

     )))
(def-theorem divisor%power-is-almost-total-aux
   "forall(d:nn,
      2<=d
        implies
      forall(n:zz, 1<=n implies lambda(n1:zz, #(divisor%power(d,n1)))(n)))"
   (theory h-o-real-arithmetic)
   (proof
    (

     (apply-macete-with-minor-premises complete-induction-schema)
     simplify
```

```
direct-and-antecedent-inference-strategy
(cut-with-single-formula "d divides m or not(d divides m)")
(block
 (script-comment "'cut-with-single-formula' at (0)")
 (antecedent-inference "with(p:prop,p or p);")
 (block
  (script-comment "'antecedent-inference' at (0)")
  (incorporate-antecedent "with(m:zz,d:nn,d divides m);")
  (apply-macete-with-minor-premises divisibility-lemma)
  direct-and-antecedent-inference-strategy
  (backchain "with(r:rr,m:zz,m=r);")
  (cut-with-single-formula "1<=k and k<m")
  (block
   (script-comment "'cut-with-single-formula' at (0)")
   (instantiate-universal-antecedent "with(p:prop,forall(k:zz,p));" ("k"))
   (incorporate-antecedent "with(n:nn,#(n));")
   (force-substitution "#(divisor%power(d,k))"
                       "forsome(m1:nn, m1=divisor%power(d,k))" (0)
                       )
   (block
    (script-comment "'force-substitution' at (0)")
    (force-substitution "#(divisor%power(d,k*d))"
                        "forsome(m2:nn, m2=divisor%power(d,k*d))" (0)
                        )
    (block
     (script-comment "'force-substitution' at (0)")
     (apply-macete-with-minor-premises divisor%power-characterization)
     direct-and-antecedent-inference-strategy
     (instantiate-existential ("m1+1"))
     auto-instantiate-existential
     (backchain "with(w,m1,d:nn,k:zz,k=d^m1*w);")
     (force-substitution "d^m1*w*d" "d^m1*d*w" (0))
     simplify
     (block
      (script-comment "'force-substitution' at (1)")
      (force-substitution "d^m1*w*d" "d^m1*(w*d)" (0))
      (block
       (script-comment "'force-substitution' at (0)")
       (apply-macete-locally-with-minor-premises
        commutative-law-for-multiplication-pre-reals (0) "w*d"
        )
       (apply-macete-with-minor-premises
        associative-law-for-multiplication-pre-reals
        ) )
      (apply-macete-with-minor-premises
       associative-law-for-multiplication-pre-reals
       ) ) )
     simplify
     )
    simplify
    )
   (block
    (script-comment "'cut-with-single-formula' at (1)")
    direct-inference
    (block
     (script-comment "'direct-inference' at (0)")
     (cut-with-single-formula "0<k or 0=k or k<0")
```

```
  (block
   (script-comment "'cut-with-single-formula' at (0)")
   (antecedent-inference "with(p:prop,p or p or p);")
   simplify
   (block
    (script-comment "'antecedent-inference' at (1)")
    (contrapose "with(d:nn,k,m:zz,m=k*d);")
    simplify
    )
   (block
    (script-comment "'antecedent-inference' at (2)")
    (cut-with-single-formula "k*d<0")
    (block
     (script-comment "'cut-with-single-formula' at (0)")
     (contrapose "with(r:rr,m:zz,m=r);")
     simplify
     )
    (block
     (script-comment "'cut-with-single-formula' at (1)")
     (force-substitution "k*d" "d*k" (0))
     (block
      (script-comment "'force-substitution' at (0)")
      (apply-macete-with-minor-premises
       strict-negativity-for-products
       )
      simplify
      )
     simplify
     ) ) )
   simplify
   )
  (block
   (script-comment "'direct-inference' at (1)")
   (backchain "with(r:rr,m:zz,m=r);")
   (force-substitution "k*d" "d*k" (0))
   simplify
   simplify
   ) ) )
 (block
  (script-comment "'antecedent-inference' at (1 1 (1 . 0))")
  (force-substitution "#(divisor%power(d,m))"
                      "forsome(m1:nn, m1=divisor%power(d,m))" (0)
                      )
  (block
   (script-comment "'force-substitution' at (0)")
   (apply-macete-with-minor-premises divisor%power-characterization)
   (instantiate-existential ("0"))
   (instantiate-existential ("m"))
   simplify
   )
  (block
   (script-comment "'force-substitution' at nil")
   (weaken (3 2 1 0))
   simplify
   ) ) )
 simplify

)))
```

```
(def-theorem divisor%power-is-almost-total
  "forall(d,n:nn, 2 <= d and 1 <= n implies #(divisor%power(d,n)))"
  (theory h-o-real-arithmetic)
  (proof
   (

    direct-and-antecedent-inference-strategy
    (instantiate-theorem divisor%power-is-almost-total-aux ("d"))
    (incorporate-antecedent "with(p:prop,forall(n:zz,p));")
    simplify

    )))
(def-theorem divisor%power-sum-law
  "forall(p,a,b:nn,
     positive%prime(p) and 1 <= a and 1 <= b
      implies
     divisor%power(p,a*b) = divisor%power(p,a) + divisor%power(p,b))"
  (theory h-o-real-arithmetic)
  (proof
   (

    direct-and-antecedent-inference-strategy
    (cut-with-single-formula "2<=p")
    (block
     (script-comment "'cut-with-single-formula' at (0)")
     (cut-with-single-formula
      "#(divisor%power(p,a)) and #(divisor%power(p,b))")
     (block
      (script-comment "'cut-with-single-formula' at (0)")
      (antecedent-inference "with(p:prop,p and p);")
      (cut-with-single-formula
       "forsome(m1:nn,m1=divisor%power(p,a)) and
        forsome(m2:nn,m2=divisor%power(p,b))"
       )
      (block
       (script-comment "'cut-with-single-formula' at (0)")
       (antecedent-inference-strategy (0))
       (backchain-backwards "with(a,p,m1:nn,m1=divisor%power(p,a));")
       (backchain-backwards "with(b,p,m2:nn,m2=divisor%power(p,b));")
       (incorporate-antecedent "with(a,p,m1:nn,m1=divisor%power(p,a));")
       (incorporate-antecedent "with(n,m2:nn,m2=n);")
       (apply-macete-with-minor-premises divisor%power-characterization)
       direct-and-antecedent-inference-strategy
       (cut-with-single-formula "a*b=p^(m1+m2)*w*w_$0")
       (block
        (script-comment "'cut-with-single-formula' at (0)")
        (cut-with-single-formula "not(p divides w*w_$0)")
        (block
         (script-comment "'cut-with-single-formula' at (0)")
         (cut-with-single-formula
          "forsome(w:nn, a*b = p^(m1+m2) * w and not(p divides w))"
          )
         (block
          (script-comment "'cut-with-single-formula' at (0)")
          (incorporate-antecedent "with(p:prop,forsome(w:nn,p));")
          (apply-macete-with-minor-premises
           rev%divisor%power-characterization
           )
```

```
            direct-inference
            )
          (block
           (script-comment "'cut-with-single-formula' at (1)")
           (instantiate-existential ("w*w_$0"))
           simplify
           ) )
          (instantiate-theorem prime-divisor-of-a-product ("p" "w" "w_$0"))
          )
        (block
         (script-comment "'cut-with-single-formula' at (1)")
         (backchain "with(w_$0,m2,p,b:nn,b=p^m2*w_$0);")
         (backchain "with(w,m1,p,a:nn,a=p^m1*w);")
         (force-substitution "p^m1*w*(p^m2*w_$0)" "p^m1*(p^m2*w)*w_$0" (0))
         simplify
         (block
          (script-comment "'force-substitution' at (1)")
          (apply-macete-locally-with-minor-premises
           commutative-law-for-multiplication-pre-reals (0) "p^m2*w"
           )
          (apply-macete-with-minor-premises
           associative-law-for-multiplication-pre-reals
           )
          (apply-macete-with-minor-premises
           associative-law-for-multiplication-pre-reals
           ) ) ) )
       simplify
       )
      (block
       (script-comment "'cut-with-single-formula' at (1)")
       (apply-macete-with-minor-premises divisor%power-is-almost-total)
       simplify
       ) )
      (block
       (script-comment "'cut-with-single-formula' at (1)")
       (incorporate-antecedent "with(p:nn,positive%prime(p));")
       (unfold-single-defined-constant (0) positive%prime)
       direct-and-antecedent-inference-strategy
       simplify
       )

      )))

(def-constant non%perfect%square
  "lambda(k:nn,
      forsome(p:nn, positive%prime(p) and odd(divisor%power(p,k))))"
  (theory h-o-real-arithmetic))

(def-theorem non-perfect-squares-are-positive
  "forall(k:nn, non%perfect%square(k) implies 1 <= k)"
  (theory h-o-real-arithmetic)
  (proof
   (

    (unfold-single-defined-constant (0) non%perfect%square)
    direct-and-antecedent-inference-strategy
    (cut-with-single-formula "#(divisor%power(p,k))")
    (cut-with-single-formula "0=k or 0<k")
```

```
  (block
   (script-comment "'cut-with-single-formula' at (0)")
   (antecedent-inference "with(p:prop,p or p);")
   (block
    (script-comment "'antecedent-inference' at (0)")
    (contrapose "with(n:nn,#(n));")
    (backchain-backwards "with(k:nn,0=k);")
    (apply-macete-with-minor-premises
     divisor%power-of-d-in-0-is-undefined)
    )
   simplify
   )
  simplify

  )))
(def-theorem sqrt-positive-is-positive
  "forall(x:rr, 0 < x implies 0 < sqrt(x))"
  (theory h-o-real-arithmetic)
  (proof
   (
    (force-substitution "sqrt(x)" "nth%root(2,x)" (0))
    (block
     (script-comment "'force-substitution' at (0)")
     (apply-macete-with-minor-premises nth%root-positive-for-positive)
     simplify
     )
    (block
     (script-comment "'force-substitution' at (1)")
     unfold-defined-constants
     simplify
     )

    )))
(def-theorem square-of-inequality-of-nonnegatives
  "forall(x,y:rr, 0 <= x and 0 <= y implies x <= y iff x^2 <= y^2)"
  (theory h-o-real-arithmetic)
  (proof
   (
    (force-substitution "x^2<=y^2" "(x-y)*(x+y)<=0" (0))
    (block
     (script-comment "'force-substitution' at (0)")
     direct-and-antecedent-inference-strategy
     (block
      (script-comment
       "'direct-and-antecedent-inference-strategy' at (0 0 0 0)")
      (apply-macete-with-minor-premises bifurcate-product-<=-inequality)
      simplify
      )
     (block
      (script-comment
       "'direct-and-antecedent-inference-strategy' at (0 0 1 0)")
      (contrapose "with(r:rr,r<=0);")
      simplify
      ) )
    simplify

    )))
```

```
(def-theorem square-of-equation-of-nonnegatives
  "forall(x,y:rr, 0 <= x and 0 <= y implies x = y iff x^2 = y^2)"
  (theory h-o-real-arithmetic)
  (proof
   (

    (force-substitution "x=y iff x^2=y^2"
                        "(x<=y and y<=x) iff (x^2<=y^2 and y^2<=x^2)" (0)
                        )
    (block
     (script-comment "'force-substitution' at (0)")
     (apply-macete-locally square-of-inequality-of-nonnegatives (0) "x<=y")
     (apply-macete-locally square-of-inequality-of-nonnegatives (0) "y<=x")
     )
    (prove-by-logic-and-simplification 0)

    )))

(def-theorem square-of-sqrt-positive
  "forall(x:rr, 0 < x implies sqrt(x)^2 = x)"
  (theory h-o-real-arithmetic)
  (proof
   (

    direct-and-antecedent-inference-strategy
    (instantiate-theorem sqrt-positive-is-positive ("x"))
    (incorporate-antecedent "with(x:rr,0<sqrt(x));")
    (unfold-single-defined-constant-globally sqrt)
    direct-inference
    (eliminate-defined-iota-expression 0 w)
    (force-substitution "x" "w*w" (0))
    (weaken (3 2 1 0))
    simplify

    )))

(def-theorem sqrt-nps-is-irrational-lemma-1
  "forall(a,b,c:nn, odd(a) implies not(a + 2*b = 2*c))"
  (theory h-o-real-arithmetic)
  (proof
   (

    direct-and-antecedent-inference-strategy
    (cut-with-single-formula "odd(a +2*b)")
    (block
     (script-comment "'cut-with-single-formula' at (0)")
     (cut-with-single-formula "even(2*c)")
     (block
      (script-comment "'cut-with-single-formula' at (0)")
      (instantiate-theorem even-and-odd-natural-numbers-are-disjoint ("a+2*b"))
      (contrapose "with(p:prop,not(p));")
      (backchain "with(r:rr,r=r);")
      )
     (block
      (script-comment "'cut-with-single-formula' at (1)")
      (unfold-single-defined-constant (0) even)
      (instantiate-existential ("c"))
      ) )
    (block
     (script-comment "'cut-with-single-formula' at (1)")
```

```
      (incorporate-antecedent "with(p:prop,p);")
      (unfold-single-defined-constant-globally odd)
      direct-and-antecedent-inference-strategy
      (instantiate-existential ("j+b"))
      (backchain "with(p:prop,p);")
      simplify
      )

   )))

(def-theorem sqrt-nps-is-irrational-lemma-2
  "forall(n:nn, 1 <= n implies 1 <= n^2)"
  (theory h-o-real-arithmetic)
  (proof
   (

    direct-and-antecedent-inference-strategy
    (force-substitution "1<=n^2" "0<=(n-1)*(n+1)" (0))
    simplify
    simplify

    )))

(def-theorem sqrt-nps-is-irrational-lemma-3
  "forall(p,k,m,n:nn,
     1<=k and 1<=m and 1<=n and positive%prime(p) and odd(divisor%power(p,k))
       implies
     not(divisor%power(p,k*n^2)=divisor%power(p,m^2)))"
  (theory h-o-real-arithmetic)
  (proof
   (

    direct-and-antecedent-inference-strategy
    (apply-macete-with-minor-premises divisor%power-sum-law)
    (block
     (script-comment "'apply-macete-with-minor-premises' at (0)")
     (force-substitution "n^2" "n*n" (0))
     (block
      (script-comment "'force-substitution' at (0)")
      (force-substitution "m^2" "m*m" (0))
      (block
       (script-comment "'force-substitution' at (0)")
       (apply-macete-with-minor-premises divisor%power-sum-law)
       simplify
       (apply-macete-with-minor-premises sqrt-nps-is-irrational-lemma-1)
       (block
        (script-comment "'apply-macete-with-minor-premises' at (1)")
        (apply-macete-with-minor-premises divisor%power-is-almost-total)
        simplify
        (apply-macete-with-minor-premises divisor%power-is-almost-total)
        simplify (incorporate-antecedent "with(p:nn,positive%prime(p));")
        (unfold-single-defined-constant (0) positive%prime)
        simplify
        )
       (block
        (script-comment "'apply-macete-with-minor-premises' at (2)")
        (apply-macete-with-minor-premises divisor%power-is-almost-total)
        simplify
        ) )
```

```
      simplify
      )
     simplify
     )
    (apply-macete-with-minor-premises sqrt-nps-is-irrational-lemma-2)

    )))

;;; The Main Theorem: The square root of a non perfect square is
;;; irrational.

(def-theorem sqrt-nps-is-irrational
  "forall(k:nn, non%perfect%square(k) implies not(#(sqrt(k),qq)))"
  (theory h-o-real-arithmetic)
  (proof
   (

    direct-and-antecedent-inference-strategy
    (cut-with-single-formula "1<=k")
    (block
     (script-comment "'cut-with-single-formula' at (0)")
     (incorporate-antecedent "with(k:nn,non%perfect%square(k));")
     (unfold-single-defined-constant (0) non%perfect%square)
     direct-and-antecedent-inference-strategy
     (cut-with-single-formula "2<=p")
     (block
      (script-comment "'cut-with-single-formula' at (0)")
      (instantiate-theorem sqrt-positive-is-positive ("k"))
      (block
       (script-comment "'instantiate-theorem' at (0 0)")
       (contrapose "with(p:prop,not(p));")
       simplify
       )
      (block
       (script-comment "'instantiate-theorem' at (0 1)")
       (cut-with-single-formula "0=0")
       (contrapose "0=0;")
       (instantiate-theorem positive-rational-characterization ("sqrt(k)"))
       (contrapose "with(r:rr,r=r);")
       (apply-macete-with-minor-premises square-of-equation-of-nonnegatives)
       (block
        (script-comment "'apply-macete-with-minor-premises' at (0)")
        (apply-macete-with-minor-premises square-of-sqrt-positive)
        (apply-macete-with-minor-premises exponents-of-fractions)
        (apply-macete-with-minor-premises
         right-denominator-removal-for-equalities
         )
        (contrapose "0=0;")
        (antecedent-inference "with(p:prop,p and p);")
        (cut-with-single-formula "divisor%power(p,k*n^2)=divisor%power(p,m^2)")
        (block
         (script-comment "'cut-with-single-formula' at (0)")
         (contrapose "with(r:rr,p:nn,divisor%power(p,r)=divisor%power(p,r));")
         (apply-macete-with-minor-premises sqrt-nps-is-irrational-lemma-3)
         direct-and-antecedent-inference-strategy
         simplify
         simplify
         )
```

```
    (block
     (script-comment "'cut-with-single-formula' at (1)")
     (backchain "with(r:rr,r=r);")
     simplify
     (apply-macete-with-minor-premises divisor%power-is-almost-total)
     (block
      (script-comment "'apply-macete-with-minor-premises' at (0)")
      simplify
      (apply-macete-with-minor-premises sqrt-nps-is-irrational-lemma-2)
      simplify
      )
     simplify
     ) )
    (block
     (script-comment "'apply-macete-with-minor-premises' at (1)")
     (weaken (8 7 6 5 4 3 1 0))
     (apply-macete-with-minor-premises fractional-expression-manipulation)
     simplify
     (block
      (script-comment "'apply-macete-with-minor-premises' at (1)")
      (contrapose "with(p:prop,p);")
      simplify
      ) ) ) )
   (block
    (script-comment "'cut-with-single-formula' at (1)")
    (incorporate-antecedent "with(p:nn,positive%prime(p));")
    (unfold-single-defined-constant (0) positive%prime)
    simplify
    ) )
   (apply-macete-with-minor-premises non-perfect-squares-are-positive)

   )))
(def-theorem sqrt-2-is-irrational
  "not #(sqrt(2),qq)"
  (theory h-o-real-arithmetic)
  (proof
   (
    (apply-macete-with-minor-premises sqrt-nps-is-irrational)
    (unfold-single-defined-constant (0) non%perfect%square)
    (instantiate-existential ("2"))
    (instantiate-theorem primality-test-refinement ("2"))
    (block
     (script-comment "'instantiate-existential' at (0 1)")
     (force-substitution "divisor%power(2,2)" "1" (0))
     (block
      (script-comment "'force-substitution' at (0)")
      (unfold-single-defined-constant (0) odd)
      (instantiate-existential ("0"))
      simplify
      )
     (block
      (script-comment "'force-substitution' at (1)")
      (force-substitution "divisor%power(2,2)==1" "1=divisor%power(2,2)" (0))
      (block
       (script-comment "'force-substitution' at (0)")
       (apply-macete-with-minor-premises divisor%power-characterization)
       (instantiate-existential ("1"))
```

```
 simplify
 (block
  (script-comment "'instantiate-existential' at (0 1)")
  (unfold-single-defined-constant (0) divides)
  simplify
  ) )
 simplify
 ) )

)))
```

10.4   System

What is the home page of the system?

$$\text{http://imps.mcmaster.ca/}$$

What are the books about the system? The best references for IMPS are:

J. D. Guttman, and F. J. Thayer, 'IMPS: An Interactive Mathematical Proof System', *Journal of Automated Reasoning*, 11:213-248, 1993.

W. M. Farmer, J. D. Guttman, and F. J. Thayer, *The IMPS User's Manual*, Technical Report M-93B138, 289 pp., The MITRE Corporation, November 1993. Available at <http://imps.mcmaster.ca/manual/> or <http://imps.mcmaster.ca/doc/manual.pdf>.

What is the logic of the system? The logic of IMPS is LUTINS, a version of Church's simple theory of types that admits undefined terms, partial functions, and subtypes. The following three papers collectively present the logic:

W. M. Farmer, 'A Partial Functions Version of Church's Simple Theory of Types', *Journal of Symbolic Logic*, 55:1269-1291, 1990.

W. M. Farmer, 'A Simple Type Theory with Partial Functions and Subtypes', *Annals of Pure and Applied Logic*, 64:211-240, 1993.

W. M. Farmer, 'Theory Interpretation in Simple Type Theory', in: J. Heering et al., eds., *Higher-Order Algebra, Logic, and Term Rewriting*, Lecture Notes in Computer Science, vol. 816, pp. 96-123, Springer-Verlag, 1994.

What is the implementation architecture of the system? A running IMPS system is composed of two intercommunicating processes: a Common Lisp IMPS process and an XEmacs user interface process. IMPS was originally written in the T programming language. The original T code is executed in Common Lisp using a partial macro/emulation of T.

What does working with the system look like? A running IMPS system consists of an XEmacs window for interacting with IMPS and an Xdvi window for viewing expressions and proofs. There are XEmacs buffers that show the Common Lisp read-eval-print loop, the current deduction graph, the current subgoals, and the IMPS theory files in use.

What is special about the system compared to other systems? IMPS has several unique characteristics:

- The logic admits undefined terms and partial functions but formulas are always true or false. (References: See LUTINS papers above.)
- Proofs are a blend of computation and deduction. There are two main computation devices: (1) The IMPS simplifier performs automatic simplification using rewrite rules, algebraic simplification, and definedness checking. (2) The IMPS macete mechanism semiautomatically applies theorems to subgoals. (References: See IMPS references above.)
- Mathematics is organized using the little theories version of the axiomatic method. In the little theories approach, reasoning is distributed over a network of theories linked by theory interpretations. The interpretations serve as conduits for passing information (in the form of theorems, definitions, etc.) from one theory to another. (References: W. M. Farmer, J. D. Guttman, and F. J. Thayer, 'Little Theories', in: D. Kapur, ed., Automated Deduction – CADE-11, Lecture Notes in Computer Science, Vol. 607, pp. 567-581, Springer-Verlag, 1992.)
- A partial function may be defined by recursion as the least fixed point of a monotone functional. A list of partial functions can be defined by mutual recursion via a list of monotone functions. (Reference: W. M. Farmer, 'A Scheme for Defining Partial Higher-Order Functions by Recursion', in: A. Butterfield, ed., *3rd Irish Workshop on Formal Methods*, 13 pp., electronic Workshops in Computing, Springer-Verlag, <http://ewic.org.uk/ewic/workshop/view.cfm/IWFM-99>, 1999.)
- The IMPS logic LUTINS includes a definite description operator (instead of a choice operator as found in other systems). Definite descriptions are quite useful for defining functions and other mathematical objects. (Reference: See IMPS User's Manual above.)
- Proofs are represented as deduction graphs. Deduction graphs may contain cycles and parallel attempts to solve a subgoal. (Reference: See IMPS User's Manual above.)
- IMPS employs a unique, pragmatic style of proof script for storing deduction graphs, building tactics, and reusing parts of a deduction graph construction. (Reference: W. M. Farmer, J. D. Guttman, M. E. Nadel, and F. J. Thayer, 'Proof script pragmatics in IMPS', in: A. Bundy, ed., *Automated Deduction – CADE-12*, Lecture Notes in Computer Science, Vol. 814, pp. 356 -370, Springer-Verlag, 1994.)

What are other versions of the system? Version 2.0 is currently the only supported version of IMPS.

Who are the people behind the system? The developers of IMPS are William M. Farmer (McMaster), Joshua D. Guttman (MITRE), and F. Javier Thayer (MITRE).

What are the main user communities of the system? The two main user communities of IMPS are researchers at The MITRE Corporation and students at McMaster University.

What large mathematical formalizations have been done in the system? The IMPS theory library contains a large amount and variety of basic mathematics including formalizations of the real number system and objects like sets and sequences; theories of abstract mathematical structures such as groups and metric spaces; and theories to support specific applications of IMPS in computer science. Some example theorems proved in IMPS are:

- Banach contractive mapping fixed point theorem
- Knaster fixed point theorem
- Fundamental theorem of calculus
- Fundamental counting theorem for group theory
- Fundamental theorem of arithmetic

What representation of the formalization has been put in this paper? A formalization in IMPS consists of one or more IMPS library files. Each file contains a list of 'def-forms' for defining and modifying IMPS objects and for loading sections of the IMPS library as well as individual library files. There are about 30 kinds of def-forms. For example, there are def-forms for creating theories and interpretations, installing definitions and theorems, and specifying the parse and print syntax of formal symbols.

A user can create an IMPS library file by simply typing the desired def-forms. In practice, however, a user will usually add a def-form to a library file as follows. The user will select a location in the file and then select the desired kind of def-form to place there from a menu. The IMPS user interface will place a template of the selected def-form at the selected location in the file. Finally, the user will fill in the template as desired. The def-form for installing a theorem contains a proof script, which is a list of proof command and control statements that, when executed, will create a proof in the form of an IMPS deduction graph. The proof script in a theorem def-form is normally generated automatically from a deduction graph that the user has created interactively.

What needs to be explained about this specific proof?

- `divisor%power` is defined using `iota`, the IMPS definite description operator.
- `sqrt` and `divisor%power` are strictly partial functions.
- The irrationality of the square root of a non perfect square is expressed as a sort definedness statement.
- Some theorems from the theory `complete-ordered-field` are used in the theory `h-o-real-arithmetic` via an interpretation from `complete-ordered-field` to `h-o-real-arithmetic`.

11 Metamath

Formalization and answers by Norman Megill <nm@alum.mit.edu>.

11.1   Statement

```
$p |- ( sqr ' 2 ) e/ QQ
```

11.2   Definitions

Definition of `sqr`

```
${
  $d x y z $.
  $( Define a function whose value is the square root of a nonnegative
     real number. The square root of x is the supremum of all reals
     whose square is less than x. See sqrcl for its closure,
     sqrval for its value, sqrsqe and sqsqr for its relationship to
     squares, and sqr11 for uniqueness. $)
  df-sqr $a |- sqr = { <. x , y >. | ( ( x e. RR /\ 0 <_ x ) /\
    y = sup ( { z e. RR | ( 0 <_ z /\ ( z x. z ) <_ x ) } , RR , < ) ) } $.
$}
```

Definition of `QQ`

```
${
  $d x y z $.
  $( Define the set of rationals. Definition of rational numbers in
     [Apostol] p. 22. $)
  df-q $a |- QQ = { x | E. y e. ZZ E. z e. NN x = ( y / z ) } $.
$}
```

11.3   Proof

Irrationality of square root of 2

```
${
  sqr2irrlem1.1 $e |- A e. NN $.
  sqr2irrlem1.2 $e |- B e. NN $.
  $( Lemma for irrationality of square root of 2. Technical lemma used
     to simplify the main induction step. $)
  sqr2irrlem1 $p |- ( ( A ^ 2 ) = ( 2 x. ( B ^ 2 ) ) ->
                     ( ( B < A /\ ( A / 2 ) e. NN ) /\
                     ( B ^ 2 ) = ( 2 x. ( ( A / 2 ) ^ 2 ) ) ) ) $=
    ( c2 cexp co cmulc wceq clt wbr cdiv cn wcel wa c1 nnre sqrecl recn
    mulid2 caddc ax1re ltplus1 df-2 breqtrr 2re nnsqcl nngt0 ltmul1i mpbi
    eqbrtrr breq2 mpbiri cc0 cle wb ax0re ltlei lt2sqe mp2an sylibr 2cn 2pos
    gt0ne0i divmul eleq1 nnesq sylbir eqcoms jca redivcl remulcl mulcan nncn
```

```
sqdiv sqval opreq2i eqtr mulass mulcl muln0 divcan2 3eqtr3 eqeq1i bitr3
biimpr eqcomd ) AEFGZEBEFGZHGZIZBAJKZAELGZMNZOWIEWMEFGZHGZIWKWLWNWKWIWHJK
ZWLWKWQWIWJJKPWIHGZWIWJJWIWIBBDQZRZSZTPEJKWRWJJKPPPUAGEJPUBUCUDUEPEWIUBUF
WTWIBDUGZUHUIUJUKWHWJWIJULUMUNBUOKUNAUOKWLWQUPUNBUQWSBDUHURUNAUQACQZACUHU
RBAWSXCUSUTVAWNWJWHWJWHIWHELGZWIIZWNWHEWIWHAXCRSZVBXAEUFVCVDZVEXEXDMNZWNX
EXHWIMNXBXDWIMVFUMACVGVAVHVIVJWKWPWIWPWIIZWKXIEWPHGZWJIWKEWPWIVBWPEWOUFWM
AEXCUFXGVKRZVLSXAXGVMXJWHWJEEHGZWOHGXLWHXLLGZHGXJWHWOXMXLHWOWHEEFGZLGXMAE
ACVNVBXGVOXNXLWHLEVBVPVQVRVQEEWOVBVBWOXKSVSXLWHEEVBVBVTXFEEVBVBXGXGWAWBWC
WDWEWFWGVJ $.
    $( [20-Aug-01] $)
$}
```

$(Lemma for irrationality of square root of 2. Eliminates hypotheses with
   weak deduction theorem. $)
```
sqr2irrlem2 $p |- ( ( A e. NN /\ B e. NN ) ->
                    ( ( A ^ 2 ) = ( 2 x. ( B ^ 2 ) ) ->
                    ( ( B < A /\ ( A / 2 ) e. NN ) /\
                    ( B ^ 2 ) = ( 2 x. ( ( A / 2 ) ^ 2 ) ) ) ) ) $=
  ( cn wcel c2 cexp co cmulc wceq clt wbr cdiv wa wi cif opreq1 eqeq1d breq2
  eleq1d anbi12d opreq1d opreq2d eqeq2d imbi12d breq1 anbi1d 2nn elimel
  sqr2irrlem1 dedth2h ) ACDZBCDZAEFGZEBEFGZHGZIZBAJKZAELGZCDZMZMZUNEUREFGZHGZIZ
  MZNUKAEOZEFGZUOIZBVEJKZVEELGZCDZMZUNEVIEFGZHGZIZMZNVFEULBEOZEFGZHGZIZVPVEJK
  ZVJMZVQVMIZMZMZNABEEEAVEIZUPVGVDVOWDUMVFUOAVEEFPQWDUTVKVCVNWDUQVHUSVJAVEBJRWDU
  RVICAVEELPZSTWDVBVMUNWDVAVLEHWDURVIEFWEUAUBUCTUDBVPIZVGVSVOWCWFUOVRVFWFUNVQ
  EHBVPEFPZUBUCWFVKWAVNWBWFVHVTVJBVPVEJUEUFWFUNVQVMWGQTUDVEVPAECUGUHBECUGUHUI
  UJ $.
    $( [20-Aug-01] $)
```

```
${
  $d x y z w $.
```
$(Main theorem for irrationality of square root of 2. There are no
   natural numbers such that the square of one is twice the square of the
   other. Uses strong induction. $)
```
sqr2irrlem3 $p |- -. E. x e. NN E. y e. NN
                 ( x ^ 2 ) = ( 2 x. ( y ^ 2 ) ) $=
  ( vz vw cv c2 cexp co cmulc wceq cn wrex wn wral wcel weq opreq1 eqeq1d
  negbid biraldv opreq2d eqeq2d cbvralv syl6bb clt wbr wi wa cdiv breq1
  imbi12d rcla4v imp syl6 imp3a imnan sylib adantll sqr2irrlem2 adantlr
  mtod exp31 r19.21adv indstr ralnex rgen mpbi ) AEZFGHZFBEZFGHZIHZJZBKLZMZ
  AKNVNAKLMVOAKVHKOZVMMZBKNZVOVRCEZFGHZFDEZFGHZIHZJZMZDKNZACACPZVRVTVLJZMZB
  KNWFWGVQWIBKWGVMWHWGVIVTVLVHVSFGQRSTWIWEBDKBDPZWHWDWJVLWCVTWJVKWBFIVJWAFG
  QUAUBSUCUDVPVSVHUEUFZWFUGZCKNZVQBKVPWMVJKOZVQVPWMUHWNUHVMVJVHUEUFZVHFUIHZ
  KOZUHZVKFWPFGHZIHZJZUHZWMWNXBMZVPWMWNUHZWRXAMZUGXCXDWOWQXEXDWOVKWCJZMZDKN
  ZWQXEUGWMWNWOXHUGZWLXICVJKCBPZWKWOWFXHVSVJVHUEUJXJWEXGDKXJWDXFXJVTVKWCVSV
  JFGQRSTUKULUMXGXEDWPKWAWPJZXFXAXKWCWTVKXKWBWSFIWAWPFGQUAUBSULUNUOWRXAUPUQ
  URVPWNVMXBUGWMVHVJUSUTVAVBVCVDVMBKVEUQVFVNAKVEVG $.
    $( [20-Aug-01] $)
$}
```

```
${
  sqr2irrlem4.1 $e |- A e. NN $.
  sqr2irrlem4.2 $e |- B e. NN $.
```
$(Lemma for irrationality of square root of 2. $)
```
sqr2irrlem4 $p |- ( ( sqr ` 2 ) = ( A / B ) <->
                  ( A ^ 2 ) = ( 2 x. ( B ^ 2 ) ) ) $=
  ( c2 cexp co cmulc wceq csqr cfv cdiv nncn nnne0 sqdiv eqcomi nnsqcl 2cn
  divcan4 eqeq12i nnre sqrecl recn 2re remulcl divl1 eqcom 3bitr3 cc0 cle
  wbr wb ax0re 2pos ltlei redivcl sqege0 sqr11 mp2an bitr4 nngt0 divgt0i
  sqrsqe ax-mp eqeq2i bitr2 ) AEFGZEBEFGZHGZIZEJKZABLGZCEFGZEFGZJKZIZVKVLIVJEVMI
```

```
ZVOVGVHLGZVIVHLGZIVMEIVJVPVQVMVREVMVQABACMBDMBDNZOPVHEVHBDQZMZRVHVTNZSTVG
VIVHVGAACUAZUBUCVIEVHUDVHVTUAUEUCWAWBUFVMEUGUHUIEUJUKUIVMUJUKVOVPULUIEUMU
DUNUOVLABWCBDUAZVSUPZUQEVMUDVLWEUBURUSUTVNVLVKUIVLUJUKVNVLIUIVLUMWEABWCWD
ACVABDVAVBUOVLWEVCVDVEVF $.
  $( [20-Aug-01] $)
$}
```

$(Lemma for irrationality of square root of 2. Eliminates hypotheses with
  weak deduction theorem. $)
```
sqr2irrlem5 $p |- ( ( A e. NN /\ B e. NN ) -> ( ( sqr ' 2 ) = ( A / B )
                  <-> ( A ^ 2 ) = ( 2 x. ( B ^ 2 ) ) ) ) $=
  ( cn wcel c2 csqr cfv cdiv co wceq cexp cmulc wb cif opreq1 eqeq2d eqeq1d
  bibi12d opreq2 opreq2d 2nn elimel sqr2irrlem4 dedth2h ) ACDZBCDZEFGZABHIZJZ
  AEKIZEBEKIZLIZJZMUGUEAENZBHIZJZUNEKIZULJZMUGUNUFBENZHIZJZUQEUSEKIZLIZJZMABE
  EAUNJZUIUPUMURVEUHUOUGAUNBHOPVEUJUQULAUNEKOQRBUSJZUPVAURVDVFUOUTUGBUSUNHSPV
  FULVCUQVFUKVBELBUSEKOTPRUNUSAECUAUBBECUAUBUCUD $.
  $( [20-Aug-01] $)
```

```
${
  $d x y $.
  $( The square root of 2 is irrational. $)
  sqr2irr $p |- ( sqr ' 2 ) e/ QQ $=
    ( vx vy c2 csqr cfv cq wnel wcel wn cv cdiv co wceq cn wrex cz cexp
    cmulc sqr2irrlem3 sqr2irrlem5 bi2rexa mtbir cc0 clt wbr wa wi wb nngt0t
    adantr cr ax0re ltmuldivt mp3an1 nnret zret syl2an mpd ancoms 2re 2pos
    sqrgt0i breq2 mpbii syl5bir cc nncnt mulzer2t syl breq1d adantl sylibd
    exp r19.23adv anc2li elnnz syl6ibr impac r19.22i2 mto elq df-nel mpbir )
    CDEZFGWDFHZIWEWDAJZBJZKLZMZBNOZAPOZWKWJANOZWLWFCQLCWGCQLRLMZBNOANOABSWIWM
    ABNNWFWGTUAUBWJWJAPNWFPHZWJWFNHZWNWJWNUCWFUDUEZUFWOWNWJWPWNWIWPBNWNWGNHZW
    IWPUGWNWQUFZWIUCWGRLZWFUDUEZWPWRWTUCWHUDUEZWIWQWNWTXAUHZWQWNUFUCWGUDUEZXB
    WQXCWNWGUIUJWGUKHZWFUKHZXCXBUGZWQWNUCUKHXDXEXFULUCWGWFUMUNWGUOWFUPUQURUSW
    IUCWDUDUEXACUTVAVBWDWHUCUDVCVDVEWQWTWPUHWNWQWSUCWFUDWQWGVFHWSUCMWGVGWGVHV
    IVJVKVLVMVNVOWFVPVQVRVSVTABWDWAUBWDFWBWC $.
    $( [8-Jan-02] $)
$}
```

Steps in the proof of the last theorem

51	mtbir.1=sqr2irrlem3	$p |- -. E. x e. NN E. y e. NN (x ^ 2) = (2 x. (y ^ 2))
60	bi2rexa.1=sqr2irrlem5	$p |- ((x e. NN /\ y e. NN) -> ((sqr ' 2) = (x / y) <-> (x ^ 2) = (2 x. (y ^ 2))))
61	mtbir.2=bi2rexa	$p |- (E. x e. NN E. y e. NN (sqr ' 2) = (x / y) <-> E. x e. NN E. y e. NN (x ^ 2) = (2 x. (y ^ 2)))
62	mto.1=mtbir	$p |- -. E. x e. NN E. y e. NN (sqr ' 2) = (x / y)
135	adantr.1=nngt0t	$p |- (y e. NN -> 0 < y)
136	mpd.1=adantr	$p |- ((y e. NN /\ x e. ZZ) -> 0 < y)
154	mp3an1.1=ax0re	$p |- 0 e. RR
158	mp3an1.2=ltmuldivt	$p |- ((0 e. RR /\ y e. RR /\ x e. RR) -> (0 < y -> ((0 x. y) < x <-> 0 < (x / y))))
159	syl2an.1=mp3an1	$p |- ((y e. RR /\ x e. RR) -> (0 < y -> ((0 x. y) < x <-> 0 < (x / y))))

161	syl2an.2=nnret	$p |- (y e. NN -> y e. RR)
163	syl2an.3=zret	$p |- (x e. ZZ -> x e. RR)
164	mpd.2=syl2an	$p |- ((y e. NN /\ x e. ZZ) -> (0 < y -> ((0 x. y) < x <-> 0 < (x / y))))
165	ancoms.1=mpd	$p |- ((y e. NN /\ x e. ZZ) -> ((0 x. y) < x <-> 0 < (x / y)))
166	syl5bir.1=ancoms	$p |- ((x e. ZZ /\ y e. NN) -> ((0 x. y) < x <-> 0 < (x / y)))
174	sqrlem1.1=2re	$p |- 2 e. RR
175	sqrlem1.2=2pos	$p |- 0 < 2
176	mpbii.min=sqrgt0i	$p |- 0 < (sqr ' 2)
181	mpbii.maj=breq2	$p |- ((sqr ' 2) = (x / y) -> (0 < (sqr ' 2) <-> 0 < (x / y)))
182	syl5bir.2=mpbii	$p |- ((sqr ' 2) = (x / y) -> 0 < (x / y))
183	sylibd.1=syl5bir	$p |- ((x e. ZZ /\ y e. NN) -> ((sqr ' 2) = (x / y) -> (0 x. y) < x))
202	syl.1=nncnt	$p |- (y e. NN -> y e. CC)
204	syl.2=mulzer2t	$p |- (y e. CC -> (0 x. y) = 0)
205	breq1d.1=syl	$p |- (y e. NN -> (0 x. y) = 0)
206	adantl.1=breq1d	$p |- (y e. NN -> ((0 x. y) < x <-> 0 < x))
207	sylibd.2=adantl	$p |- ((x e. ZZ /\ y e. NN) -> ((0 x. y) < x <-> 0 < x))
208	exp.1=sylibd	$p |- ((x e. ZZ /\ y e. NN) -> ((sqr ' 2) = (x / y) -> 0 < x))
209	r19.23adv.1=exp	$p |- (x e. ZZ -> (y e. NN -> ((sqr ' 2) = (x / y) -> 0 < x)))
210	anc2li.1=r19.23adv	$p |- (x e. ZZ -> (E. y e. NN (sqr ' 2) = (x / y) -> 0 < x))
211	syl6ibr.1=anc2li	$p |- (x e. ZZ -> (E. y e. NN (sqr ' 2) = (x / y) -> (x e. ZZ /\ 0 < x)))
213	syl6ibr.2=elnnz	$p |- (x e. NN <-> (x e. ZZ /\ 0 < x))
214	impac.1=syl6ibr	$p |- (x e. ZZ -> (E. y e. NN (sqr ' 2) = (x / y) -> x e. NN))
215	r19.22i2.1=impac	$p |- ((x e. ZZ /\ E. y e. NN (sqr ' 2) = (x / y)) -> (x e. NN /\ E. y e. NN (sqr ' 2) = (x / y)))
216	mto.2=r19.22i2	$p |- (E. x e. ZZ E. y e. NN (sqr ' 2) = (x / y) -> E. x e. NN E. y e. NN (sqr ' 2) = (x / y))
217	mtbir.1=mto	$p |- -. E. x e. ZZ E. y e. NN (sqr ' 2) = (x / y)
221	mtbir.2=elq	$p |- ((sqr ' 2) e. QQ <-> E. x e. ZZ E. y e. NN (sqr ' 2) = (x / y))
222	mpbir.min=mtbir	$p |- -. (sqr ' 2) e. QQ
225	mpbir.maj=df-nel	$a |- ((sqr ' 2) e/ QQ <-> -. (sqr ' 2) e. QQ)
226	sqr2irr=mpbir	$p |- (sqr ' 2) e/ QQ

Generated page for the last theorem

Theorem sqr2irr 4859

Description: The square root of 2 is irrational.

Assertion
sqr2irr $\vdash (\sqrt{\,}{}'2) \notin \mathbb{Q}$

Proof of Theorem sqr2irr

Step	Hyp	Ref	Expression
1		sqr2irrlem3 4856	$5 \vdash \neg\exists x \in \mathbb{N}\,\exists y \in \mathbb{N}\,(x \uparrow 2) = (2 \cdot (y \uparrow 2))$
2		sqr2irrlem5 4858	$6 \vdash ((x \in \mathbb{N} \wedge y \in \mathbb{N}) \to ((\sqrt{\,}{}'2) = (x/y) \leftrightarrow (x \uparrow 2) = (2 \cdot (y \uparrow 2))))$
3	2	bi2rexa 1266	$5 \vdash (\exists x \in \mathbb{N}\,\exists y \in \mathbb{N}\,(\sqrt{\,}{}'2) = (x/y) \leftrightarrow \exists x \in \mathbb{N}\,\exists y \in \mathbb{N}\,(x \uparrow 2) = (2 \cdot (y \uparrow 2)))$
4	1,3	mtbir 178	$4 \vdash \neg\exists x \in \mathbb{N}\,\exists y \in \mathbb{N}\,(\sqrt{\,}{}'2) = (x/y)$
5		nngt0t 4514	$15 \vdash (y \in \mathbb{N} \to 0 < y)$
6	5	adantr 320	$14 \vdash ((y \in \mathbb{N} \wedge x \in \mathbb{Z}) \to 0 < y)$
7		ax0re 4131	$16 \vdash 0 \in \mathbb{R}$
8		ltmuldivt 4479	$16 \vdash ((0 \in \mathbb{R} \wedge y \in \mathbb{R} \wedge x \in \mathbb{R}) \to (0 < y \to ((0 \cdot y) < x \leftrightarrow 0 < (x/y))))$
9	7,8	mp3an1 662	$15 \vdash ((y \in \mathbb{R} \wedge x \in \mathbb{R}) \to (0 < y \to ((0 \cdot y) < x \leftrightarrow 0 < (x/y))))$
10		nnret 4500	$15 \vdash (y \in \mathbb{N} \to y \in \mathbb{R})$
11		zret 4640	$15 \vdash (x \in \mathbb{Z} \to x \in \mathbb{R})$
12	9,10,11	syl2an 365	$14 \vdash ((y \in \mathbb{N} \wedge x \in \mathbb{Z}) \to (0 < y \to ((0 \cdot y) < x \leftrightarrow 0 < (x/y))))$
13	6,12	mpd 47	$13 \vdash ((y \in \mathbb{N} \wedge x \in \mathbb{Z}) \to ((0 \cdot y) < x \leftrightarrow 0 < (x/y)))$
14	13	ancoms 349	$12 \vdash ((x \in \mathbb{Z} \wedge y \in \mathbb{N}) \to ((0 \cdot y) < x \leftrightarrow 0 < (x/y)))$
15		2re 4543	$14 \vdash 2 \in \mathbb{R}$
16		2pos 4552	$14 \vdash 0 < 2$
17	15,16	sqrgt0i 4832	$13 \vdash 0 < (\sqrt{\,}{}'2)$
18		breq2 2110	$13 \vdash ((\sqrt{\,}{}'2) = (x/y) \to (0 < (\sqrt{\,}{}'2) \leftrightarrow 0 < (x/y)))$
19	17,18	mpbii 179	$12 \vdash ((\sqrt{\,}{}'2) = (x/y) \to 0 < (x/y))$
20	14,19	syl5bir 195	$11 \vdash ((x \in \mathbb{Z} \wedge y \in \mathbb{N}) \to ((\sqrt{\,}{}'2) = (x/y) \to (0 \cdot y) < x))$
21		nncnt 4501	$14 \vdash (y \in \mathbb{N} \to y \in \mathbb{C})$
22		mulzer2t 4261	$14 \vdash (y \in \mathbb{C} \to (0 \cdot y) = 0)$
23	21,22	syl 12	$13 \vdash (y \in \mathbb{N} \to (0 \cdot y) = 0)$
24	23	breq1d 2115	$12 \vdash (y \in \mathbb{N} \to ((0 \cdot y) < x \leftrightarrow 0 < x))$
25	24	adant1 319	$11 \vdash ((x \in \mathbb{Z} \wedge y \in \mathbb{N}) \to ((0 \cdot y) < x \leftrightarrow 0 < x))$
26	20,25	sylibd 188	$10 \vdash ((x \in \mathbb{Z} \wedge y \in \mathbb{N}) \to ((\sqrt{\,}{}'2) = (x/y) \to 0 < x))$
27	26	exp 305	$9 \vdash (x \in \mathbb{Z} \to (y \in \mathbb{N} \to ((\sqrt{\,}{}'2) = (x/y) \to 0 < x)))$
28	27	r19.23adv 1322	$8 \vdash (x \in \mathbb{Z} \to (\exists y \in \mathbb{N}\,(\sqrt{\,}{}'2) = (x/y) \to 0 < x))$
29	28	anc2li 264	$7 \vdash (x \in \mathbb{Z} \to (\exists y \in \mathbb{N}\,(\sqrt{\,}{}'2) = (x/y) \to (x \in \mathbb{Z} \wedge 0 < x)))$
30		elnnz 4645	$7 \vdash (x \in \mathbb{N} \leftrightarrow (x \in \mathbb{Z} \wedge 0 < x))$
31	29,30	syl6ibr 197	$6 \vdash (x \in \mathbb{Z} \to (\exists y \in \mathbb{N}\,(\sqrt{\,}{}'2) = (x/y) \to x \in \mathbb{N}))$
32	31	impac 318	$5 \vdash ((x \in \mathbb{Z} \wedge \exists y \in \mathbb{N}\,(\sqrt{\,}{}'2) = (x/y)) \to (x \in \mathbb{N} \wedge \exists y \in \mathbb{N}\,(\sqrt{\,}{}'2) = (x/y)))$
33	32	r19.22i2 1310	$4 \vdash (\exists x \in \mathbb{Z}\,\exists y \in \mathbb{N}\,(\sqrt{\,}{}'2) = (x/y) \to \exists x \in \mathbb{N}\,\exists y \in \mathbb{N}\,(\sqrt{\,}{}'2) = (x/y))$
34	4,33	mto 100	$3 \vdash \neg\exists x \in \mathbb{Z}\,\exists y \in \mathbb{N}\,(\sqrt{\,}{}'2) = (x/y)$
35		elq 4705	$3 \vdash ((\sqrt{\,}{}'2) \in \mathbb{Q} \leftrightarrow \exists x \in \mathbb{Z}\,\exists y \in \mathbb{N}\,(\sqrt{\,}{}'2) = (x/y))$
36	34,35	mtbir 178	$2 \vdash \neg(\sqrt{\,}{}'2) \in \mathbb{Q}$
37		df-nel 1229	$2 \vdash ((\sqrt{\,}{}'2) \notin \mathbb{Q} \leftrightarrow \neg(\sqrt{\,}{}'2) \in \mathbb{Q})$
38	36,37	mpbir 176	$1 \vdash (\sqrt{\,}{}'2) \notin \mathbb{Q}$

11.4 System

What is the home page of the system?

<http://metamath.org/>

What are the books about the system?

Megill, Norman D., *Metamath, A Computer Language for Pure Mathematics*, 1997.

available as a PDF file from the home page, describes the basic system. The Metamath program itself incorporates up-to-date help describing its current features, such as the generation hyperlinked web pages with its proofs.

What is the logic of the system? The logic is a Hilbert-style system of standard first-order logic and ZFC set theory, with modus ponens and generalization as the rules of inference. However, Metamath works with schemes and never with the actual logic. For example, the `wff` metavariable in the Axiom of Replacement is an ordinary variable for Metamath. Its axioms of logic are an unusual set of schemes (equivalent to those of the standard 'textbook' or Herbrand formalization) which are devised to allow all possible theorem schemes to be derived directly within the constraints of a 'simple metalogic' defined for its language. With roots in simplified formalizations of first-order logic devised by Tarski and colleagues in the 1960s, the precise formalization used is system S3′ in Remark 9.6 of:

> Megill, Norman D., 'A Finitely Axiomatized Formalization of Predicate Calculus with Equality,' *Notre Dame Journal of Formal Logic*, 36:435-453, 1995.

What is the implementation architecture of the system? The Metamath program is written in strict ANSI C. It will compile on any platform with a `gcc` compiler. The user interacts with it through a command-line interface. Originally written on a VAX VMS system, the command-line syntax has a VMS 'feel' to it.

What does working with the system look like? Except possibly for simple theorems in propositional logic, it is not a system for the casual user to build proofs with. On the one hand, its command-line interface is reasonably user-friendly, with extensive help and clear and detailed error messages. On the other hand, many small theorems or lemmas are needed to build up a framework suitable, for example, for proving the irrationality of the square root of 2. Although here this was proved with half a dozen lemmas on top of previously proved results, over 2000 lemmas are ultimately involved in proving it all the way back to the ZFC axioms. An intimate familiarity with the database is needed to build new proofs efficiently.

Once a theorem is proved, there are extensive tools for displaying and analyzing its proof. For example, there is a command to trace back the axioms that were involved in proving a given theorem, so it is easy to determine whether say the Axiom of Choice was used. Mechanically following any proof is trivial, since the metalogical rules of inference are so simple.

What is special about the system compared to other systems?

1. It is a proof verifier, not an automated prover. The proof verification is fast; the verification of the construction of real numbers (thousands of lemmas) takes a couple of seconds on a modern computer.

2. The proof verification engine makes no assumptions about the underlying logic; instead all axioms, including those of propositional calculus, are placed in the database. Weaker systems of logic, such as intuitionistic or quantum logic, can be handled with different sets of axioms.
3. There is no explicit deduction theorem and it is rarely used even implicitly. In set theory, an interesting use of the Axiom of Extensionality provides nearly the same power, but without the exponential explosion of Hilbert-style steps that results from an application of the standard deduction theorem.
4. The core verification algorithm is very simple, being essentially nothing more than substitution of expressions for variables, enhanced with checking for conflicts of variables that should be distinct.

What are other versions of the system? A demo Java applet, 'Metamath Solitaire,' incorporates Metamath's ZFC axiom system (as well as a few other systems of logic). In this version, a unification algorithm lets the user know exactly what possibilities are available at any point in a proof, making it impossible to make a 'mistake.' The applet is not practical for larger proofs.

In its present form, Metamath treats definitions as additional axioms added to the system, and an unsound definition can result in inconsistency. Raph Levien is developing a new language called Ghilbert (`ghilbert.org`) that has its roots in Metamath but guarantees the soundness of definitions and provides features useful for collaborative work. He has written translators from Metamath to Ghilbert and vice-versa. One of his long-term goals is an HOL to Ghilbert translator.

Who are the people behind the system? Norman Megill.

What are the main user communities of the system? The only users who have built significant proofs are its author and Raph Levien. Several users have contributed shorter proofs of some propositional calculus theorems.

The 'consumers' of the system are the visitors to its web pages, where the proofs are displayed. The site, in existence since 1997, currently has around 10000 visitors per year.

What large mathematical formalizations have been done in the system? The largest projects have been the construction of real and complex numbers, the development of Hilbert space from this foundation, and as a separate database a large collection of theorems of quantum logic (orthomodular lattices).

The Hilbert space and quantum logic projects were used to verify a number of new results in these fields that have resulted in several papers. The papers present their proofs in the traditional informal fashion; the Metamath verifications were done simply to provide confidence that no errors were made in the proofs.

What representation of the formalization has been put in this paper? The axioms of classical first-order logic and ZFC set theory.

What needs to be explained about this specific proof? In the source code, the user places the assertion to be proved but omits the proof. The user builds the proof within the program in an interactive fashion, which is then written to the source by the program. The native format of the proofs is a reverse-Polish list of previous assertions that are unified to construct the proof, and they can be stored or converted to that representation if desired, but they tend to be very long. The ones shown here are in a compressed format that is not human-readable but is efficient in terms of storage space.

12 Theorema

Wolfgang Windsteiger, Bruno Buchberger, and Markus Rozenkranz

Formalization and answers by Wolfgang Windsteiger <Wolfgang.
Windsteiger@risc.uni-linz.ac.at>, Bruno Buchberger <Bruno.
Buchberger@risc.uni-linz.ac.at> and Markus Rosenkranz <Markus.
Rosenkranz@risc.uni-linz.ac.at>.

12.1 Statement

Theorem["sqrt[2] irrational", $\neg$ rat$[\sqrt{2}]$]

12.2 Definitions

Definition["rational", any$[r]$,

$\quad$ rat$[r] :\Leftrightarrow \underset{a,b}{\exists} (\text{nat}[a] \wedge \text{nat}[b] \wedge r = \frac{a}{b} \wedge \text{coprime}[a,b])$]

Definition["sqrt", any$[x]$,

$\quad \sqrt{x} := \underset{y}{\exists!} (y^2 = x)$]

12.3 Proof

Load Theorema and Set Preferences

Needs["Theorema'"]

SetOptions[Prove, transformBy $\rightarrow$ ProofSimplifier,

$\quad$ TransformerOptions $\rightarrow$ {brances $\rightarrow$ Proved, steps $\rightarrow$ Essential}];

The Proof of the Main Theorem

Theorem["sqrt[2] irrational", $\neg$ rat$[\sqrt{2}]$]

Definition["rational", any$[r]$,

$\quad$ rat$[r] :\Leftrightarrow \underset{a,b}{\exists} (\text{nat}[a] \wedge \text{nat}[b] \wedge r = \frac{a}{b} \wedge \text{coprime}[a,b])$]

Definition["sqrt", any$[x]$,

$\quad \sqrt{x} := \underset{y}{\exists!} (y^2 = x)$]

Lemma["coprime", any$[a,b]$, with$[\text{nat}[a] \wedge \text{nat}[b]]$,

$\quad (2b^2 = a^2) \Rightarrow \neg$ coprime$[a,b]$]

F. Wiedijk (Ed.): The Seventeen Provers of the World, LNAI 3600, pp. 96–107, 2006.
© Springer-Verlag Berlin Heidelberg 2006

Prove[Theorem["sqrt[2] irrational"],
    using → ⟨Lemma["coprime"], Definition["rational"], Definition["sqrt"]⟩,
    built-in → Built-in["Rational Numbers"], by → ElementaryReasoner,
    ProverOptions → {SimplifyFormula → True, RWCombine → True}];

Prove:

    (Theorem (sqrt[2] irrational)) $\neg$ rat[$\sqrt{2}$],

under the assumptions:

    (Lemma (coprime)) $\underset{a,b}{\forall}$ (nat[a] $\wedge$ nat[b] $\Rightarrow$ ((2∗b^2 = a^2) $\Rightarrow$ $\neg$ coprime[a, b])),

    (Definition (rational)) $\underset{r}{\forall}$ rat[r] :$\Leftrightarrow$ $\underset{a,b}{\exists}$ ((nat[a] $\wedge$ nat[b])$\wedge$
                                        (r = $\frac{a}{b}$ $\wedge$ coprime[a, b])),

    (Definition (sqrt)) $\underset{x}{\forall}$ $\sqrt{x}$:= $\underset{y}{\exists!}$ y^2 = x.

From what we already know follows:
From (Definition (sqrt)) we can infer by expansion of the "such that"-quantifier

    (1) $\underset{x,y}{\forall}$ ($\sqrt{x}$ = y $\Leftrightarrow$ y^2 = x).

We prove (Theorem (sqrt[2] irrational)) by contradiction.
We assume

    (3)   rat[$\sqrt{2}$],

and show a contradiction.
Formula (3), by (Definition (rational)), implies:

    (4) $\underset{a,b}{\exists}$ (coprime[a, b] $\wedge$ nat[a] $\wedge$ nat[b] $\wedge$ $\sqrt{2}$ = $\frac{a}{b}$).

By (4) we can take appropriate values such that:

    (5)   coprime[a_0, b_0] $\wedge$ nat[a_0] $\wedge$ nat[b_0] $\wedge$ $\sqrt{2}$ = $\frac{a_0}{b_0}$.

By modus ponens, from (5.2), (5.3) and an appropriate instance of (Lemma (coprime)) follows:

    (6)   2 ∗ $b_0{}^2$ = $a_0{}^2$ $\Rightarrow$ $\neg$ coprime[a_0, b_0],

Formula (5.4), by (1), implies:

    (7) $\left(\dfrac{a_0}{b_0}\right)^2$ = 2.

Using built-in simplification rules we can simplify the knowledge base:
Formula (7) simplifies to

(8) $2 * b_0{}^2 = a_0{}^2$.

From (8) and (6) we obtain by modus ponens

(9) $\neg \, \text{coprime}[a_0, b_0]$.

Now, (9) and (5.1) are contradictory.

The Proof of the Auxiliary Lemma

The auxiliary Lemma "coprime" is a statement essentially about natural numbers. In the spirit of theory exploration we assume this lemma to be proven during an (earlier) exploration of the notion "coprime" within the universe of natural numbers. In this section, we show this phase of exploration of the natural numbers.

Lemma["coprime", any[a, b],
  $(2b^2 = a^2) \Rightarrow \neg \, \text{coprime}[a, b]$]

Definition["even", any[a],
  is-even[a] $:\Leftrightarrow \exists_m (a = 2m)$]

Proposition["even numbers", any[a, b],
  $(2b = a) \Rightarrow$ is-even[a]   "characteristic"
  is-even[a^2] $\Rightarrow$ is-even[a] "even square"   ]

Proposition["common factor", any[a, b],
  $\neg \, \text{coprime}[2a, 2b]$]

Prove[Lemma["coprime"], using $\rightarrow$ ⟨Proposition["even numbers"],
       Proposition["common factor"], Definition["even"]⟩,
    built-in $\rightarrow$ Built-in["Natural Numbers"], by $\rightarrow$ ElementaryReasoner,
    ProverOptions $\rightarrow$ {SimplifyFormula $\rightarrow$ True}, SearchDepth $\rightarrow$ 40];

Prove:

  (Lemma (coprime)) $\forall_{a,b} ((2 * b^2 = a^2) \Rightarrow \neg \, \text{coprime}[a, b])$,

under the assumptions:

  (Proposition (even numbers): characteristic) $\forall_{a,b} ((2 * b = a) \Rightarrow$ is-even[a]),

  (Proposition (even numbers): even square) $\forall_a ($is-even[a^2] $\Rightarrow$ is-even[a]),

(Proposition (common factor)) $\underset{a,b}{\forall} \neg$ coprime$[2 * a, 2 * b]$,

(Definition (even)) $\underset{a}{\forall}$ is-even$[a] :\Leftrightarrow \underset{m}{\exists} (a = 2 * m)$.

We assume

(1) $2 * b_0^2 = a_0^2$,

and show

(2) $\neg$ coprime$[a_0, b_0]$.

We prove (2) by contradiction.
We assume

(3)   coprime$[a_0, b_0]$,

and show a contradiction.
Formula (1), by (Proposition (even numbers): characteristic), implies:

is-even$[a_0^2]$,

which, by (Proposition (even numbers): even square), implies:

is-even$[a_0]$,

which, by (Definition (even)), implies:

(4) $\underset{m}{\exists} (a_0 = 2 * m)$.

By (4) we can take appropriate values such that:

(5) $a_0 = 2 * m_0$.

Formula (3), by (5), implies:

(6)   coprime$[2 * m_0, b_0]$.

Formula (1), by (5), implies:

(7) $2 * b_0^2 = (2 * m_0)^2$.

Using available computation rules we can simplify the knowledge base:
Formula (7) simplifies to

(8) $2 * m_0^2 = b_0^2$.

Formula (8), by (Proposition (even numbers): characteristic), implies:

is-even$[b_0^2]$,

which, by (Proposition (even numbers): even square), implies:

is-even$[b_0]$,

which, by (Definition (even)), implies:

(9) $\underset{m}{\exists} (b_0 = 2 * m)$.

By (9) we can take appropriate values such that:

(10) $b_0 = 2 * m_1$.

Formula (6), by (10), implies:

(15)   coprime$[2 * m_0, 2 * m_1]$.

Now, (15) and (Proposition (common factor)) are contradictory.

12.4   System

What is the home page of the system?

<http://www.theorema.org/>

What are the books about the system? The essential theoretical ideas involved in the *Theorema* system can be found already in [5]. A comprehensive description of the basic design of a computer-system based on these ideas is then given in [1]. For a more elaborate exposition and for concrete design principles of the current *Theorema* system, we refer to the survey papers [[3,4]].

Most of the system components are described in all detail in journal papers, conference proceedings articles, or technical reports. All downloadable material can be found on the *Theorema* homepage.

What is the logic of the system? The logic frame of *Theorema* is higher order predicate logic, which is extended by the language construct "sequence variables". Sequence variables are variables for which an arbitrary finite number of terms can be substituted. Sequence variables are a convenient construct for the formulation of algorithms in terms of pattern matching within logic. Thus, the *Theorema* language is also particularly suited for expressing logic algorithms like theorem provers etc. A logical study of sequence variables is given in [6].

In fact, the *Theorema* system is a (growing) collection of various general purpose and special theorem provers. The general purpose provers (like the first order predicate logic natural deduction prover) are valid only for special fragments of predicate logic (e.g. first order predicate logic). The special provers are valid only under the additional assumption that special knowledge is available that characterizes the underlying special theory. For example, the (various versions) of the induction prover assume that, for certain functions, an induction principle holds; the geometry prover based on the Gröbner bases method assumes that the universe of discourse is the field of complex numbers and the basic properties of complex numbers are available; the set theory prover assumes that the axioms and basic properties of set theory are valid. We do not yet have a prover for a general version of higher order logic. Of course, this approach to building a theorem proving system supposes that the correctness of special theorem provers is (automatically) proved w.r.t. to more general provers. So far, this research program is only partially carried out. For example, Gröbner bases theory is proved correct in a fairly formal way. A complete formal proof within *Theorema* is planned for the near future.

What is the implementation architecture of the system? All *Theorema* 'reasoners' (provers, solvers, and simplifiers) are written in the programming language of Mathematica. *Theorema* does *not* use the Mathematica algorithm library or any implicit mathematical knowledge presupposed in Mathematica algorithms. The *Theorema* language is a version of higher order predicate logic. The currently available reasoners comprise *general purpose reasoners* (several methods for proving in first order predicate logic, a prover for equational reasoning, or a general simplification prover based on equality rewriting) and special purpose reasoners (like Collins' decision procedure for the theory of real closed fields, a special prover for geometry based on algebraic techniques like Gröbner bases, or the simplification prover for number domains used in the proofs shown in Section 12.3) that are valid only in particular theories. Various external provers like e.g. Otter can be accessed through *Theorema* by translating *Theorema* formulae to the specific input format for these provers and getting the results back. Reasoners available in Mathematica can also be accessed by *Theorema* upon explicit request by the user. The *Theorema* language includes a programming language as a natural sub-language.

Theorema provers have a modular structure, i.e. every *Theorema* prover is composed from smaller units, so-called 'special prover modules'. These prover modules are separate units, and can therefore be combined in arbitrary way. In the current status, the access to special prover modules is restricted to the system developers, but a mechanism for users to compose their own provers from available special prover modules is planned for future versions of the system. *Theorema* uses a general proof search procedure that maintains a global proof object. The proof object has a tree-structure where each node in the tree represents a *proof situation* made up basically from the proof goal and the current assumptions. In each step, the proof search procedure tries to apply a special prover module in order to simplify the current proof situation. A special prover module can be applied to a proof situation if one of its inference rules can be applied to the proof situation. Inference rules in the prover modules are implemented as Mathematica programs that take a proof situation as parameter and return a new proof situation. Applicability of an inference rule is tested by pattern matching on the parameters of the Mathematica program against the current proof situation. When applying a special prover module to a proof situation the proof search procedure inserts the result of the first applicable rule as a new node into the global proof object. The proof search continues until a trivial proof situation (e.g. the goal is identical to one of the assumptions) appears on one branch of the tree, in which case the proof succeeds, or until the maximal search depth is exceeded on all branches, in which case the proof attempt fails.

What does working with the system look like? The current version of *Theorema* is implemented as an extension package to Mathematica, thus, the standard way of working with *Theorema* is an interactive user-system-dialog in the well-known Mathematica notebook FrontEnd. The Mathematica notebook FrontEnd supports configurable two-dimensional mathematical notation both in input and output. The examples in Section 12.3 demonstrate a typical *Theorema* session. Two categories of commands are available for the user:

Organization of Knowledge: The *Theorema* Formal Text Language allows the user to enter arbitrary definitions, axioms, propositions, algorithms, etc. to the system and combine such formulae into theories in a nested way so that hierarchies of mathematical knowledge bases (theories) can be built up. All formulae may receive key words and labels for easy reference. Labels, however, carry no logical meaning. Declaration of free variables and conditions on these variables are specified using the keywords 'any' and 'with'. The individual formulae can be entered in a two-dimensional syntax very close to how formulae are written in mathematical textbooks. The actual input of arbitrary two-dimensional notation and special mathematical symbols is supported by the standard Mathematica notebook FrontEnd through input palettes and keyboard shortcuts. The input of *Theorema*-specific notation, like e.g. a formal text entity containing labelled formulae as used in Proposition "even numbers", is taken care of by additional input palettes. The definitions, theorems, lemmata, and propositions as they display in Section 12.3 illustrate some of the features of the Formal Text Language.

Note that the *Theorema* language also supports several notational variants for mathematical syntax in order to accommodate to the preferences of the user. As an example, we used the standard form of the existential quantifier

$$\underset{a,b}{\exists}\, (\mathrm{nat}[a] \wedge \mathrm{nat}[b] \wedge r = \frac{a}{b} \wedge \mathrm{coprime}[a,b])$$

in Definition "rational" as given in Section 12.2. Supported notational variants, which would all be interpreted by all *Theorema* provers in exactly the same way, are:

$$\underset{\mathrm{nat}[a],\mathrm{nat}[b]}{\exists}\, (r = \frac{a}{b} \wedge \mathrm{coprime}[a,b]),$$

$$\underset{\mathrm{nat}[a,b]}{\exists}\, (r = \frac{a}{b} \wedge \mathrm{coprime}[a,b]), \text{ or}$$

$$\underset{\mathrm{nat}[a]\wedge\mathrm{nat}[b]}{\exists}\, (r = \frac{a}{b} \wedge \mathrm{coprime}[a,b]).$$

Mathematical Activities: Mathematical knowledge can then be processed in various ways using the *Theorema* User Language. Currently, the User Language supports 'proving', 'solving', and 'simplifying', see the commands `Prove[...]` in Section 12.3 for typical examples. These examples also exhibit, how knowledge specified in the Formal Text Language can be referred to in the User Language. Note also, that the keywords such as 'any' or 'with' are processed when formulae are passed to a prover: Compare the formulae as they are echoed at the beginning of the proof to how they appear in the Formal Text Language.

Proofs (or traces of solving or simplifying) are generated completely automatically and display very much in the form as they would be written in mathematical textbooks including intermediate explanatory text in natural language. Alternatively, *Theorema* also offers an interactive mode, where user-interaction *during proof generation* is supported. Mathematical formulae are displayed in two-dimensional syntax. The proofs appear in the *Theorema* system almost exactly as they are typeset in Section 12.3.

However, some of the features of the *Theorema* user interface cannot be modelled in the style of this paper:

– Proof branches are organized in hierarchically nested cells, which can be opened or closed by double-clicking the cell bracket on the right margin of the window. This allows the user to hide (or display) certain parts of a proof easily by mouse-click.
– Formula labels are active elements, such that clicking a formula reference in the running text shows the full formula in a separate pop-up window.
– Goal formulae, assumptions, labels, and explanatory text use different colors.

Also, there are means in *Theorema* to design and implement one's own syntax including the design of new mathematical symbols of arbitrary complexity ('logicographic symbols').

What is special about the system compared to other systems?

– *Theorema* is both a logic language and a programming language. This means that, for example, within the same language and system, a formula that describes an algorithm can be proved correct and can then be executed on concrete input.
– The three fundamental mathematical activities proving, solving, and simplifying can be done in one uniform language and logic frame.
– *Theorema* is a multi-method system: instead of using one uniform proof method for all of mathematics *Theorema* provides sophisticated special provers for certain mathematical theories. These special provers are partly based on powerful computer algebra methods, which were the research focus of the working group in earlier years.
– *Theorema* has an attractive two-dimensional, extensible syntax.
– Most of the *Theorema* provers generate proofs in a natural, human-readable style with intermediate explanatory text and various tools that help to get various (contracted and expanded) views of proofs.
– *Theorema* has various structuring mechanisms for large mathematical knowledge bases, notably the recursive 'Theory' construct and a functor construct, which is similar to but more general than the functor construct of SML.

What are other versions of the system? There are no other versions of the system. The current version is free for download from the *Theorema* webpage under "software".

Who are the people behind the system? The development of *Theorema* has been initiated by Bruno Buchberger, who also implemented first prototypes in the mid 1990's and directs the project since then in cooperation with Tudor Jebelean and Wolfgang Windsteiger. Current senior *Theorema* researchers are, in addition, Temur Kutsia, Florina Piroi, and Markus Rosenkranz. Former *Theorema* PhD students, who contributed to the system, are Daniela Vasaru-Dupre, Mircea Marin, Koji Nakagawa, Judit Robu, and Elena Tomuta. For a complete (and always up-to-date) listing of persons involved in the *Theorema* project we refer to the *Theorema* webpage.

What are the main user communities of the system? There is a small community of alpha testers, mainly math researchers and math teachers. A major didactic case study in undergraduate math education at the Johannes Kepler University of Linz and the Polytechnic University Hagenberg is under way.

What large mathematical formalizations have been done in the system? Elementary analysis (with the typical epsilon/delta proofs), equivalence relations and partitions based on set theory, polynomial interpolation, the theory of lists with verified list algorithms like sorting, and the automated synthesis of the Gröbner bases algorithm.

What representation of the formalization has been put in this paper? The formalization in Section 12.3 should be self-explanatory. In fact, it is a main design principle of *Theorema* that formalizations using the *Theorema* language constructs should be self-explanatory and easy to read. The theorem is formulated as a statement over the positive real numbers. The first part shown in Section 12.3 contains the main proof that reduces the problem over the positive reals to a lemma over the natural numbers. Section 12.3 shows the second part that contains the proof of the auxiliary lemma over the naturals.

What needs to be explained about this specific proof? In the proof of the main theorem, we assume that all variables range over the *positive real numbers*, i.e. all formulae in the knowledge base should be true statements in the domain of positive real numbers.

The proof of the theorem as shown in Section 12.3 is generated completely automatically within *Theorema*. The only user-interactions required are

- to choose an appropriate prover from the *Theorema* prover library (in the example the "Elementary Reasoner"),
- to specify appropriate prover options for the chosen prover, and
- to provide the auxiliary Lemma "coprime" necessary in the proof.

In the spirit of the layered approach of *Theorema*, the auxiliary lemma can then be proved in a separate proving session as shown in Section 12.3. Again, auxiliary knowledge needed in this proof (in the example the Propositions "even numbers" and "common factor") can be proved in separate phases of exploring a theory.

However, we do not present the proofs of these propositions here, because when investigating the irrationality of $\sqrt{2}$ one would usually consider these propositions to be *known properties of natural numbers*. Phases of theory exploration can be structured bottom-up or top-down just like human mathematicians build up hierarchically structured mathematical knowledge.

Typically, different phases of theory exploration are characterized by using different proving techniques. In the case of *automated theory exploration* using *Theorema* this means that switching from one exploration phase to another would be reflected in changing the prover that is used in the Prove-calls. In this example, in fact, we use the Elementary Reasoner in both phases, but we allow the prover to access different portions of built-in computational knowledge in either phase.

The special feature of the Elementary Reasoner used for generating the proofs shown in Section 12.3 is the smooth integration of 'proving' and 'simplifying' ('computing') within one system. 'Simplifying', here, means 'simplifying expressions (to canonical form) based on the *algorithmic semantics* of the language'. The algorithmic semantics of the *Theorema* language consists of computation rules for the *algorithmic part of the language*[1], i.e. finite sets, finite tuples, quantifiers with a finite range, and basic arithmetic on numbers. Sets, tuples, and quantifiers are represented as special data structures and the operations on these entities are implemented in the *Theorema* language semantics using the programming language of Mathematica. Only for arithmetic on natural numbers, integers, and rational numbers the *Theorema* semantics may access the arithmetic rules from the underlying Mathematica system.

In the example, the option built-in→Built-in["Rational Numbers"] allows the Elementary Reasoner explicitly to use built-in computation rules for operations on rational numbers. Arithmetic on numbers is, in fact, the only case, where *Theorema* silently relies on the mathematical algorithm library available from Mathematica[2]. On explicit user request, however, the interface allows this prover to even access special simplification algorithms from Mathematica when performing computational simplification. Specifying the prover option SimplifyFormula→True (default value is False) tells the prover to post-process any formula obtained from a computation by Mathematica's FullSimplify function. FullSimplify is a black-box simplifier for Mathematica expressions, which uses powerful simplification rules, in particular for arithmetic expressions. Moreover, the prover performs additional simplification of equalities involving arithmetic expressions, such that certain equalities are turned into equalities that are more likely to be usable for rewriting. In our context, the correctness of the built-in simplifier is based exclusively on the field axioms (for proofs over the reals) and the ring axioms (for proofs over the naturals[3]), respectively. In

---

[1] In contrast, the semantics of the *non-algorithmic part of the language* is coded into inference rules that make up the *Theorema* special prover modules.

[2] Apart from that, Mathematica is used just as a programming environment!

[3] To be precise: the simplifier for the naturals uses the ring axioms without the axiom ensuring the existence of additive inverses.

other words, the 'hidden knowledge' used by the simplifier are only the field or ring axioms[3], respectively. All other knowledge, e.g. Lemma "coprime", Proposition "even numbers", and Proposition "common factor", must be mentioned explicitly in the call of the prover.

A combination of these capabilities is used in the main proof when simplifying formula

(7) $\quad \left(\dfrac{a_0}{b_0}\right)^2 = 2$

to

(8) $\quad 2b_0{}^2 = a_0{}^2$

and in the proof of the auxiliary lemma when simplifying

(7) $\quad 2b_0{}^2 = (2m_0)^2$

to

(8) $\quad 2m_0{}^2 = b_0{}^2.$

Definition "sqrt" uses a convenient language construct available in *Theorema*: The 'the-unique'-quantifier $\underset{y}{\exists!}\, P_y$ denotes 'the unique y satisfying P_y'. The expression $f[x] := \underset{y}{\exists!}\, P_{x,y}$ is a means to express an implicit definition for the function f, for which, of course, we need to verify $\underset{x}{\forall}\,\underset{y}{\exists!}\, P_{x,y}$ beforehand. In the concrete example of Definition "sqrt", we assume that $\underset{x}{\forall}\,\underset{y}{\exists!}\, y^2 = x$ holds over the positive real numbers. Based on this convention the prover applies an inference rule for the 'the-unique'-quantifier in order to rewrite Definition "sqrt" in the main proof into

(2) $\quad \underset{x,y}{\forall}\, (\sqrt{x} = y \Leftrightarrow y^2 = x).$

All other steps in the proofs are basic predicate logic and therefore require no further explanation.

References

1. B. Buchberger. Symbolic Computation: Computer Algebra and Logic. In K. Schulz, editor, *FroCoS: Frontiers of Combined Systems*, 1996.
2. B. Buchberger. Algorithm Supported Mathematical Theory Exploration. In B. Buchberger and John Campbell, editors, *Proceedings of AISC 2004 (7th International Conference on Artificial Intelligence and Symbolic Computation*, volume 3249 of *Springer Lecture Notes in Artificial Intelligence*, RISC, Johannes Kepler University, Austria, September 22-24 2004. Springer Berlin Heidelberg. ISSN 0302-9743, ISBN 3-540-23212-5.

3. B. Buchberger, C. Dupre, T. Jebelean, F. Kriftner, K. Nakagawa, D. Vasaru, and W. Windsteiger. The Theorema Project: A Progress Report. In M. Kerber and M. Kohlhase, editors, *Symbolic Computation and Automated Reasoning (Proceedings of CALCULEMUS 2000, Symposium on the Integration of Symbolic Computation and Mechanized Reasoning)*, pages 98–113. St. Andrews, Scotland, Copyright: A.K. Peters, Natick, Massachusetts, 6-7 August 2000.

4. B. Buchberger, T. Jebelean, F. Kriftner, M. Marin, E. Tomuta, and D. Vasaru. A Survey of the Theorema project. In W. Kuechlin, editor, *Proceedings of ISSAC'97 (International Symposium on Symbolic and Algebraic Computation, Maui, Hawaii, July 21-23, 1997), ACM Press 1997*, pages 384–391, 1997.

5. B. Buchberger and F. Lichtenberger. *Mathematik für Informatiker I.* Springer Verlag, 2nd edition, 1981.

6. T. Kutsia and B. Buchberger. Predicate Logic with Sequence Variables and Sequence Function Symbols. In Andrea Asperti, Grzegorz Bancerek, and Andrzej Trybulec, editors, *Proceedings of the 3rd International Conference on Mathematical Knowledge Management, MKM'04*, volume 3119 of *Lecture Notes in Computer Science*, pages 205–219, Bialowieza, Poland, Sep 19–21 2004. Springer Verlag.

13 Lego

Conor McBride

Formalization by Conor McBride <ctm@cs.nott.ac.uk>. Answers by
Conor McBride and Robert Pollack <rap@dcs.ed.ac.uk>.

13.1 Statement

```
{b|nat}{a|nat}(Eq (times two (times a a)) (times b b))->
      (Eq a zero /\ Eq b zero)
```

13.2 Definitions

Definition of Prime

```
[Prime = [p:nat]
        {a|NAT}{b,x|Nat}{Phi|Prop}
        {q:Eq (times p x) (times a b)}
        {phiL:{a':nat}
              (Eq a (times p a'))->(Eq x (times a' b))->Phi}
        {phiR:{b':nat}
              (Eq b (times p b'))->(Eq x (times a b'))->Phi}
        Phi
];
```

13.3 Proof

Conor's proof that 2 has no rational root.

This proof is accepted by LEGO version 1.3.1 with its standard library.

`Make lib_nat;` (* loading basic logic, nat, plus, times etc *)

(* note, plus and times are defined by recursion on their first arg *)

Alternative eliminators for nat

LEGO's induction tactic figures out which induction principle to use by looking
at the type of the variable on which we're doing induction. Consequently, we can
persuade the tactic to use an alternative induction principle if we alias the type.

Nat_elim is just the case analysis principle for natural numbers—the same
as the induction principle except that there's no inductive hypothesis in the step
case. It's intended to be used in combination with...

...NAT_elim, which performs no case analysis but says you can have an
inductive hypothesis for any smaller value, where y is smaller than suc (plus
x y). This is 'well-founded induction' for the < relation, but expressed more
concretely.

The effect is very similar to that of 'Case' and 'Fix' in Coq.

F. Wiedijk (Ed.): The Seventeen Provers of the World, LNAI 3600, pp. 108–115, 2006.
© Springer-Verlag Berlin Heidelberg 2006

```
[Nat = nat];
[NAT = Nat];

(* case analysis: just a weakening of induction *)

Goal Nat_elim : {Phi:nat->Type}
                {phiz:Phi zero}
                {phis:{n:Nat}Phi (suc n)}
                {n:Nat}Phi n;
intros ___;
  Expand Nat; Induction n;
    Immed;
    intros; Immed;
Save;

(* suc-plus guarded induction: the usual proof *)

Goal NAT_elim :
    {Phi:nat->Type}
    {phi:{n:Nat}
        {ih:{x,y|Nat}(Eq n (suc (plus x y)))->Phi y}
        Phi n}
    {n:NAT}Phi n;
intros Phi phi n';
(* claim that we can build the hypothesis collector for each n *)
Claim {n:nat}{x,y|Nat}(Eq n (suc (plus x y)))->Phi y;
(* use phi on the claimed collector *)
Refine phi n' (?+1 n');
(* now build the collector by one-step induction *)
  Induction n;
    Qnify; (* nothing to collect for zero *)
    intros n nhyp;
      Induction x; (* case analysis on the slack *)
        Qnify;
          Refine phi;   (* if the bound is tight, use phi to *)
            Immed;      (* generate the new member of the collection *)
        Qnify;
          Refine nhyp; (* otherwise, we've already collected it *)
            Immed;
Save;
```

Equational laws governing plus *and* times: some of these are doubtless in the library, but it takes longer to remember their names than to prove them again.

```
Goal plusZero : {x:nat}Eq (plus x zero) x;
Induction x;
  Refine Eq_refl;
  intros;
    Refine Eq_resp suc;
      Immed;
Save;

Goal plusSuc : {x,y:nat}Eq (plus x (suc y)) (suc (plus x y));
Induction x;
  intros; Refine Eq_refl;
  intros;
    Refine Eq_resp suc;
      Immed;
Save;
```

```
Goal plusAssoc : {x,y,z:nat}Eq (plus (plus x y) z) (plus x (plus y z));
Induction x;
  intros; Refine Eq_refl;
  intros;
    Refine Eq_resp suc;
      Immed;
Save;

Goal plusComm : {x,y:nat}Eq (plus x y) (plus y x);
Induction y;
  Refine plusZero;
  intros y yh x;
    Refine Eq_trans (plusSuc x y);
      Refine Eq_resp suc;
        Immed;
Save;

Goal plusCommA : {x,y,z:nat}Eq (plus x (plus y z)) (plus y (plus x z));
intros;
  Refine Eq_trans ? (plusAssoc ???);
    Refine Eq_trans (Eq_sym (plusAssoc ???));
      Refine Eq_resp ([w:nat]plus w z);
        Refine plusComm;
Save;

Goal timesZero : {x:nat}Eq (times x zero) zero;
Induction x;
  Refine Eq_refl;
    intros;
      Immed;
Save;

Goal timesSuc : {x,y:nat}Eq (times x (suc y)) (plus x (times x y));
Induction x;
  intros; Refine Eq_refl;
  intros x xh y;
    Equiv Eq (suc (plus y (times x (suc y)))) ?;
      Equiv Eq ? (suc (plus x (plus y (times x y))));
        Refine Eq_resp;
          Qrepl xh y;
            Refine plusCommA;
Save;

Goal timesComm : {x,y:nat}Eq (times x y) (times y x);
Induction y;
  Refine timesZero;
  intros y yh x;
    Refine Eq_trans (timesSuc ??);
      Refine Eq_resp (plus x);
        Immed;
Save;

Goal timesDistL : {x,y,z:nat}Eq (times (plus x y) z)
                                (plus (times x z) (times y z));
Induction x;
  intros; Refine Eq_refl;
    intros x xh y z;
      Refine Eq_trans (Eq_resp (plus z) (xh y z));
        Refine Eq_sym (plusAssoc ???);
Save;
```

```
Goal timesAssoc : {x,y,z:nat}Eq (times (times x y) z) (times x (times y z));
Induction x;
  intros; Refine Eq_refl;
  intros x xh y z;
    Refine Eq_trans (timesDistL ???);
      Refine Eq_resp (plus (times y z));
        Immed;
Save;
```

Inversion principles for equations governing plus and times: these aren't in the library, at least not in this form.

```
[Phi|Type]; (* Inversion principles are polymorphic in any goal *)

Goal plusCancelL : {y,z|nat}{phi:{q':Eq y z}Phi}{x|nat}
                   {q:Eq (plus x y) (plus x z)}Phi;
intros ___;
Induction x;
  intros;
    Refine phi q;
  intros x xh; Qnify;
    Refine xh;
      Immed;
Save;

Goal timesToZero : {a,b|Nat}
                   {phiL:(Eq a zero)->Phi}
                   {phiR:(Eq b zero)->Phi}
                   {tz:Eq (times a b) zero}
                   Phi;
Induction a;
  intros; Refine phiL (Eq_refl ?);
  intros a;
    Induction b;
      intros; Refine phiR (Eq_refl ?);
      Qnify;
Save;

Goal timesToNonZero : {x,y|nat}
                      {phi:{x',y'|nat}(Eq x (suc x'))->(Eq y (suc y'))->Phi}
                      {z|nat}{q:Eq (times x y) (suc z)}Phi;
Induction x;
  Qnify;
  intros x xh;
    Induction y;
      intros __; Qrepl timesZero (suc x); Qnify;
      intros;
        [EQR=Eq_refl]; Refine phi Then Immed;
Save;
```

(* I actually want plusDivisionL, but plusDivisionR is easier to prove, because here we do induction where times does computation. *)
```
Goal plusDivisionR : {b|nat}{a,x,c|Nat}
                     {phi:{c'|nat}(Eq (times c' (suc x)) c)->
                                  (Eq a (plus b c'))->Phi}
                     {q:Eq (times a (suc x)) (plus (times b (suc x)) c)}
                     Phi;
```

```
Induction b;
  intros _____; Refine phi;
    Immed;
    Refine Eq_refl;
  intros b bh;
    Induction a;
      Qnify;
      intros a x c phi;
        Qrepl plusAssoc (suc x) (times b (suc x)) c;
          Refine plusCancelL;
            Refine bh;
              intros c q1 q2; Refine phi q1;
                Refine Eq_resp ? q2;
Save;

(* A bit of timesComm gives us the one we really need. *)
Goal plusDivisionL : {b|nat}{a,x,c|Nat}
                     {phi:{c'|nat}(Eq (times (suc x) c') c)->
                                  (Eq a (plus b c'))->Phi}
                     {q:Eq (times (suc x) a) (plus (times (suc x) b) c)}
                     Phi;
intros _____;
  Qrepl timesComm (suc x) a; Qrepl timesComm (suc x) b;
    Refine plusDivisionR;
      intros c'; Qrepl timesComm c' (suc x);
        Immed;
Save;

Discharge Phi;
```

Definition of primality:

This choice of definition makes primality easy to exploit (especially as it's presented as an inversion principle), but hard to establish.

```
[Prime = [p:nat]
         {a|NAT}{b,x|Nat}{Phi|Prop}
         {q:Eq (times p x) (times a b)}
         {phiL:{a':nat}
               (Eq a (times p a'))->(Eq x (times a' b))->Phi}
         {phiR:{b':nat}
               (Eq b (times p b'))->(Eq x (times a b'))->Phi}
         Phi
];
```

Proof that 2 is Prime. Nontrivial because of the above definition. Manageable because 1 is the only number between 0 and 2.

```
Goal doublePlusGood : {x,y:nat}Eq (times (suc (suc x)) y)
                                  (plus (times two y) (times x y));
intros __;
  Refine Eq_trans ? (Eq_sym (plusAssoc ???));
    Refine Eq_resp (plus y);
      Refine Eq_trans ? (Eq_sym (plusAssoc ???));
        Refine Eq_refl;
Save;
```

```
Goal twoPrime : Prime two;
Expand Prime;
  Induction a;
    Induction n;
      intros useless b x _;
        Refine timesToZero Then Expand Nat Then Qnify;
                             (* Qnify needs to know it's a nat *)
          intros; Refine phiL;
            Refine +1 (Eq_sym (timesZero ?));
            Refine Eq_refl;
      Induction n;
        intros useless b x _;
          Qrepl plusZero b;
            intros; Refine phiR;
              Refine +1 Eq_sym q;
              Refine Eq_sym (plusZero x);
          intros n nhyp b x _;
            Qrepl doublePlusGood n b;
              Refine plusDivisionL;
                intros c q1 q2; Qrepl q2; intros __;
                  Refine nhyp|one (Eq_refl ?) q1;
                    intros a' q3 q4; Refine phiL (suc a');
                      Refine Eq_resp suc;
                        Refine Eq_trans ? (Eq_sym (plusSuc ??));
                          Refine Eq_resp ? q3;
                      Refine Eq_resp (plus b) q4;
                    intros b' q3 q4; Refine phiR b';
                      Immed;
                      Qrepl q3; Qrepl q4;
                        Refine Eq_sym (doublePlusGood ??);
Save;
```

Now the proof that primes ($\geq$ 2) have no rational root. It's the classic 'minimal counterexample' proof unwound as an induction: we apply the inductive hypothesis to the smaller counterexample we construct.

```
[pm2:nat]
[p=suc (suc pm2)] (* p is at least 2 *)
[Pp:Prime p];

Goal noRatRoot : {b|NAT}{a|Nat}{q:Eq (times p (times a a)) (times b b)}
                      and (Eq a zero) (Eq b zero);
Induction b;
  Induction n; (* if b is zero, so is a, and the result holds *)
    intros useless;
      intros a;
        Refine timesToZero;
          Expand Nat; Qnify;
          Refine timesToZero; Refine ?+1;
            intros; Refine pair; Immed; Refine Eq_refl;
  intros b hyp a q; (* otherwise, build a smaller counterexample *)
    Refine Pp q; (* use primality once *)
      Refine cut ?+1; (* standard technique for exploiting symmetry *)
        intros H a' aq1 aq2; Refine H;
          Immed;
          Refine Eq_trans aq2;
            Refine timesComm;
```

```
      intros c bq; Qrepl bq; Qrepl timesAssoc p c c;
    Refine timesToNonZero ? (Eq_sym bq); (* need c to be nonzero *)
      intros p' c' dull cq; Qrepl cq; intros q2;
        Refine Pp (Eq_sym q2); (* use primality twice *)
        Refine cut ?+1; (* symmetry again *)
          intros H a' aq1 aq2; Refine H;
            Immed;
            Refine Eq_trans aq2;
              Refine timesComm;
          intros d aq; Qrepl aq; Qrepl timesAssoc p d d;
            intros q3;
              Refine hyp ? (Eq_sym q3); (* now use ind hyp *)
                Next +2; Expand NAT Nat; Qnify; (* trivial solution *)
                Next +1; (* show induction was properly guarded *)
                  Refine Eq_trans bq; Expand p; Qrepl cq;
                    Refine plusComm;
Save;

Discharge pm2;
```

Putting it all together

```
[noRatRootTwo = noRatRoot zero twoPrime
  : {b|nat}{a|nat}(Eq (times two (times a a)) (times b b))->
    (Eq a zero /\ Eq b zero)];
```

13.4   System

What is the home page of the system?

<http://www.dcs.ed.ac.uk/home/lego/>

What are the books about the system? The manuals for the Lego system and the Lego library are:

Zhaohui Luo and Robert Pollack, *LEGO Proof Development System: User's Manual*, May 1992, 79 pp.

The LEGO Library – Version 1.3, November 1998, 71 pp.

both available from the Lego home page. There's also a *LEGO 1.3.1 Reference Card* there.

What is the logic of the system? Constructive type theory. The logic is Luo's ECC (Extended Calculus of Constructions) with inductive definitions. It is very close to what's called UTT in:

Zhaohui Luo, *Computation and Reasoning: A Type Theory for Computer Science*, International Series of Monographs on Computer Science, 11, Oxford University Press, 1994, ISBN 0-19-853835-9.

What is the implementation architecture of the system? The constructive engine is described in:

> Gérard Huet, 'The Constructive Engine', in: R. Narasimhan (ed.), *A Perspective in Theoretical Computer Science*, World Scientific Publishing, 1989.

What does working with the system look like? Interactive top-level. User gives commands to change the system state. Refinement proof.

What is special about the system compared to other systems? Stable, large scale constructive type theory proof tool. A bit long in the tooth, but still has better existential variables and better argument synthesis than Coq.

What are other versions of the system? Anthony Bailey's has made a coercive subtyping version of Lego. Conor McBride has modified Lego into a system called Oleg.

Who are the people behind the system? Robert Pollack, Zhaohui Luo, many other workers.

What are the main user communities of the system? Researchers and students: many MSc and PhD theses. The main universities involved were: Edinburgh (PhD's: me, James McKinna, Thorsten Altenkirch, Thomas Schreiber, Martin Hoffman, Conor McBride, maybe more). At KUN there was Mark Ruys. At Munich LMU there was Bernhard Reus. At Manchester there was Anthony Bailey. At Ulm there was Bernhard Reuss.

What large mathematical formalizations have been done in the system? The meta theory of PTS, as described in:

> Robert Pollack, *The Theory of LEGO: a proof checker for the Extended Calculus of Constructions*, PhD thesis, University of Edinburgh, 1994, x+143 pp.

What representation of the formalization has been put in this paper? Script file with Lego input. The explanations originally were comments in the script.

14 Nuprl

Paul Jackson

Formalization and answers by Paul Jackson <pbj@dcs.ed.ac.uk>.

14.1 Statement

$\neg(\exists u:\mathbb{Q}.\ u\ *_q\ u\ =\ 2\ /\ 1)$

14.2 Definitions

Definition of $\mathbb{Q}$

*D rat_df	Rat== rat
*A rat	Rat == $\mathbb{Z} \times \mathbb{Z}^{-0}$
*T rat_wf	Rat $\in \mathbb{U}_1$
*D qnumer_df	<q:Q:*>.num== qnumer(<q>)
*A qnumer	q.num == q.1
*T qnumer_wf	$\forall$q:Rat. q.num $\in \mathbb{Z}$
*D qdenom_df	<q:Q:*>.den== qdenom(<q>)
*A qdenom	q.den == q.2
*T qdenom_wf	$\forall$q:Rat. q.den $\in \mathbb{Z}^{-0}$
*D qequiv_df	<x:x:*> $\equiv$q <y:y:*>== qequiv(<x>; <y>)
*A qequiv	x $\equiv$q y == x.num * y.den = y.num * x.den
*T qequiv_wf	$\forall$x,y:Rat. x $\equiv$q y $\in \mathbb{U}_1$
*D qrat_df	Q== qrat
*A qrat	$\mathbb{Q}$ == x,y:Rat//x $\equiv$q y
*T qrat_wf	$\mathbb{Q} \in \mathbb{U}_1$

14.3 Proof

%[

Theory Descriptions:

- rat_1
  Definition of rationals as pair of ints. Slight alteration of **rat_1** theory from standard distribution.
- quot_2
  Extension of **quot_1**. Further support for use of quotient type, where all injections into type are explicitly tagged.
- rat_2
  Definition of rationals using quotient type, building on **rat_1**.

F. Wiedijk (Ed.): The Seventeen Provers of the World, LNAI 3600, pp. 116–126, 2006.
© Springer-Verlag Berlin Heidelberg 2006

- num_thy_2
  Additions to num_thy_1.
- root_2_irrat
  The main proofs, over the integers and over the rationals.

]%

```
set_theory_filenames wdir ["rat_1"] ;;
set_theory_filenames wdir ["quot_2"] ;;
set_theory_filenames wdir ["rat_2"] ;;
set_theory_filenames wdir ["num_thy_2"] ;;
set_theory_filenames wdir ["root_2_irrat"] ;;

set_theory_ancestors "rat_1" ["STD"];;
set_theory_ancestors "quot_2" ["STD"];;
set_theory_ancestors "num_thy_2" ["STD"];;
set_theory_ancestors "rat_2" ["rat_1";"quot_2"];;
set_theory_ancestors "root_2_irrat" ["rat_2";"num_thy_2"];;
```

File root_2_irrat.prl:

```
*C root_2_irrat_begin       *********** ROOT_2_IRRAT ***********
*T qrat_irreduc_witness     ∀u:ℚ. ↓(∃n:ℤ. ∃d:ℤ⁻⁰. u = n / d ∧ CoPrime(n,d))
*T exists_zero_one_elim     ∀P:ℕ2 → ℙ. (∃i:ℕ2. P[i]) ⟺ P[0] ∨ P[1]
*T two_div_square           ∀n:ℤ. 2 | n * n ⟹ 2 | n
*T root_2_irrat_over_int    ¬(∃m,n:ℤ. CoPrime(m,n) ∧ m * m = 2 * n * n)
*T root_2_irrat             ¬(∃u:ℚ. u *_q u = 2 / 1)
*C root_2_irrat_end         ************************************
```

Proof of qrat_irreduc_witness:

```
⊢ ∀u:ℚ. ↓(∃n:ℤ. ∃d:ℤ⁻⁰. u = n / d ∈ ℚ ∧ CoPrime(n,d))
|
BY (D 0 THENM InstLemma 'qrat_witness' [⌜u⌝]
|    THENM D 2 THENM D 0 THENM ExRepD ...a)
|
1. u: ℚ
2. n: ℤ
3. d: ℤ⁻⁰
4. u = n / d ∈ ℚ
⊢ ∃n:ℤ. ∃d:ℤ⁻⁰. u = n / d ∈ ℚ ∧ CoPrime(n,d)
|
BY % Facts to help type-checking %
|
|  (Assert ⌜gcd(n;d) ≠ 0⌝ THENA
|    (D 0 THENM Sel (-1) (FLemma 'gcd_zero_result' [5]) ...))
|  THEN
|  (Assert ⌜d ÷ gcd(n;d) ≠ 0⌝ THENA
|    (Backchain ''div_zero_a gcd_is_divisor_2'' ...))
|
5. gcd(n;d) ≠ 0
6. d ÷ gcd(n;d) ≠ 0
|
BY (Inst [⌜n ÷ gcd(n;d)⌝;⌜d ÷ gcd(n;d)⌝] 0 ...a)
|\
```

```
| ⊢ u = (n ÷ gcd(n;d)) / (d ÷ gcd(n;d)) ∈ ℚ
| |
| BY (RWH (RevLemmaWithC ['n',⌜gcd(n;d)⌝] 'numq_factor_cancel') 0 ...a)
| |
| ⊢ u = (gcd(n;d) * (n ÷ gcd(n;d))) / (gcd(n;d) * (d ÷ gcd(n;d))) ∈ ℚ
| |
| BY RWH (LemmaC 'mul_com') 0
| |  THENM RWH (GenLemmaC 1 'divides_iff_div_exact') 0
| |  THENA Repeat
| |    (Progress Auto
| |     ORELSE (RemoveLabel THEN EqTypeCD)
| |     ORELSE Backchain ''gcd_is_divisor_1 gcd_is_divisor_2 int_entire_a'')
| |
| ⊢ u = n / d ∈ ℚ
| |
| BY Auto
 \
  ⊢ CoPrime(n ÷ gcd(n;d),d ÷ gcd(n;d))
  |
  BY Unfold 'coprime' 0
  |
  ⊢ GCD(n ÷ gcd(n;d);d ÷ gcd(n;d);1)
  |
  BY (Using ['n',⌜gcd(n;d)⌝] (BLemma 'gcd_p_mul_elim')
  |   THENM RWH IntSimpC 0  ...a)
  |
  ⊢ GCD((n ÷ gcd(n;d)) * gcd(n;d);(d ÷ gcd(n;d)) * gcd(n;d);gcd(n;d))
  |
  BY (RWH (GenLemmaC 1 'divides_iff_div_exact') 0
      THEN Backchain ''gcd_is_divisor_1 gcd_is_divisor_2 gcd_sat_gcd_p'' ...)
```

Proof of exists_zero_one_elim:

```
⊢ ∀P:ℕ2 → ℙ. (∃i:ℕ2. P[i]) ⟺ P[0] ∨ P[1]
|
BY GenExRepD THENA Auto
|\
| 1. P: ℕ2 → ℙ
| 2. i: ℕ2
| 3. P[i]
| ⊢ P[0] ∨ P[1]
| |
| BY (Assert ⌜i = 0 ∨ i = 1⌝ ...a)
| |\
| | ⊢ i = 0 ∨ i = 1
| | |
| | BY SIAuto
|  \
|   4. i = 0 ∨ i = 1
|   |
|   BY D 4
|   |\
|   | 4. i = 0
|   | |
|   | BY HypSubst 4 3 THENA Auto
|   | |
|   | 3. P[0]
```

```
|   | |
|   | BY ProveProp THENA Auto
|   \
|     4. i = 1
|     |
|     BY HypSubst 4 3 THENA Auto
|     |
|     3. P[1]
|     |
|     BY (ProveProp ...)
|\
| 1. P: ℕ2 → ℙ
| 2. P[0]
| ⊢ ∃i:ℕ2. P[i]
| |
| BY (Inst [⌜0⌝] 0 ...)
 \
   1. P: ℕ2 → ℙ
   2. P[1]
   ⊢ ∃i:ℕ2. P[i]
   |
   BY (Inst [⌜1⌝] 0 ...)
```

Proof of two_div_square*:*

```
⊢ ∀n:ℤ. 2 | n * n ⇒ 2 | n
|
BY (D 0 ...a)
|
1. n: ℤ
⊢ 2 | n * n ⇒ 2 | n
|
BY Assert ⌜n * n = 0 mod 2 ⇒ n = 0 mod 2⌝
|\
| ⊢ n * n = 0 mod 2 ⇒ n = 0 mod 2
| |
| BY (D 0 ...a)
| |
| 2. n * n = 0 mod 2
| ⊢ n = 0 mod 2
| |
| BY (InstLemma 'eqmod_exists' [⌜2⌝;⌜n⌝] ...a)
| |
| 3. ∃b:ℕ2. n = b mod 2
| |
| BY (RWH (LemmaC 'exists_zero_one_elim') 3 ...a)
| |
| 3. n = 0 mod 2 ∨ n = 1 mod 2
| |
| BY D 3 THEN Auto
| |
| 3. n = 1 mod 2
| |
| BY (FLemma 'multiply_functionality_wrt_eqmod' [3;3]
| |    THENM ArithSimp 4 ...a)
| |
| 4. n * n = 1 mod 2
```

```
| |
| BY (FLemma 'eqmod_unique' [2;4] ...a)
| |
| 5. 0 = 1
| |
| BY Auto
 \
  2. n * n = 0 mod 2 ⇒ n = 0 mod 2
  |
  BY (Unfold 'eqmod' 2 THEN ArithSimp 2 ...)
```

Proof of `root_2_irrat_over_int`:

```
⊢ ¬(∃m:ℤ. ∃n:ℤ. CoPrime(m,n) ∧ m * m = 2 * n * n)
|
BY (D 0 THENM ExRepD ...a)
|
1. m: ℤ
2. n: ℤ
3. CoPrime(m,n)
4. m * m = 2 * n * n
⊢ False
|
BY Assert ⌈2 | m⌉
|\
| ⊢ 2 | m
| |
| BY (BLemma 'two_div_square' THENM Unfold 'divides' 0
|     THENM AutoInstConcl [] ...a)
 \
  5. 2 | m
  |
  BY Assert ⌈2 | n⌉
  |\
  | ⊢ 2 | n
  | |
  | BY (BLemma 'two_div_square' THENM All (Unfold 'divides')
  |     THENM ExRepD THENM Inst [⌈c * c⌉] 0
  |     THENM RWO "6" 4 ...)
   \
    6. 2 | n
    |
    BY (RWO "coprime_elim" 3 THENM FHyp 3 [5;6] ...a)
    |
    3. ∀c:ℤ. c | m ⇒ c | n ⇒ c ∼ 1
    7. 2 ∼ 1
    |
    BY (RWO "assoced_elim" 7 THENM D (-1) ...)
```

Proof of `root_2_irrat`:

```
⊢ ¬(∃u:ℚ. u *_q u = 2 / 1 ∈ ℚ)
|
BY (D 0 THENM D (-1) ...a)
|
1. u: ℚ
2. u *_q u = 2 / 1 ∈ ℚ
```

```
⊢ False
|
BY (InstLemma 'qrat_irreduc_witness' [⌜u⌝]
|    THENM D (-1) THENM ExRepD
|    THENM RWW "5" 2 THENM On [4;1] Thin ...a)
|
1. n: ℤ
2. d: ℤ⁻⁰
3. CoPrime(n,d)
4. (n / d) *_q (n / d) = 2 / 1 ∈ ℚ
|
BY (Unfolds ''mulq numq'' 4 THENM AbReduce 4
|    THENM RWO "eq_qrat_elim" 4
|    THENM Unfolds ''qmul qequiv'' 4 THENM AbReduce 4
|    THENM RWH IntSimpC 4 ...a)
|
4. n * n = 2 * d * d
|
BY AssertLemma 'root_2_irrat_over_int' [] THENM D (-1)
|
⊢ ∃m:ℤ. ∃n:ℤ. CoPrime(m,n) ∧ m * m = 2 * n * n
|
BY (AutoInstConcl [] ...)
```

Script of root_2_irrat:

```
TACTIC  top :
  (D 0 THENM D (-1) ...a)
SUBTREES
  TACTIC  top 1 :
    (InstLemma 'qrat_irreduc_witness' [⌜u⌝]
     THENM D (-1) THENM ExRepD
     THENM RWW "5" 2 THENM On [4;1] Thin ...a)
  SUBTREES
    TACTIC  top 1 1 :
      (Unfolds ''mulq numq'' 4 THENM AbReduce 4
       THENM RWO "eq_qrat_elim" 4
       THENM Unfolds ''qmul qequiv'' 4 THENM AbReduce 4
       THENM RWH IntSimpC 4 ...a)
    SUBTREES
      TACTIC  top 1 1 1 :
        AssertLemma 'root_2_irrat_over_int' [] THENM D (-1)
      SUBTREES
        TACTIC  top 1 1 1 1 :
          (AutoInstConcl [] ...)
        SUBTREES
          "<no subterms>"
        END
      END
    END
  END
END
```

S-expression of root_2_irrat *in file* root_2_irrat.thy:

```
(|root_2_irrat| THM NIL ((|not|) (NIL (|exists|) (NIL (|qrat|)) (("u") (
|equal|) (NIL (|qrat|)) (NIL (|mulq|) (NIL . "u") (NIL . "u")) (NIL (|nu
```

mq|) (NIL (|natural_number| ("2" . |natural|))) (NIL (|natural_number| (
"1" . |natural|))))))) (COMPLETE (((|!ml_text_cons|) (NIL (|!text| ("" .
|string|))) (NIL (|!ml_text_cons|) (NIL (|aux_auto|) (NIL (|!text| ("D
0 THENM D (-1)" . |string|)))) (NIL (|!text| ("" . |string|))))) (((|!ml
_text_cons|) (NIL (|!text| ("" . |string|))) (NIL (|!ml_text_cons|) (NIL
(|aux_auto|) (NIL (|!text_cons|) (NIL (|!text| ("InstLemma ‘qrat_irredu
c_witness‘ [" . |string|))) (NIL (|!text_cons|) (NIL (|!prl_term|) (NIL
. "u")) (NIL (|!text_cons|) (NIL (|!text| ("]" . |string|))) (NIL (|!tex
t_cons|) (NIL (|!newline|)) (NIL (|!text_cons|) (NIL (|!text| ("THENM D
(-1) THENM ExRepD" . |string|))) (NIL (|!text_cons|) (NIL (|!newline|))
(NIL (|!text| ("THENM RWW \"5\" 2 THENM On [4;1] Thin" . |string|)))))))))
))) (NIL (|!text| ("" . |string|))))) (((|!ml_text_cons|) (NIL (|!text|
("" . |string|))) (NIL (|!ml_text_cons|) (NIL (|aux_auto|) (NIL (|!text_
cons|) (NIL (|!text| ("Unfolds ‘‘mulq numq‘‘ 4 THENM AbReduce 4 " . |str
ing|))) (NIL (|!text_cons|) (NIL (|!newline|)) (NIL (|!text_cons|) (NIL
(|!text| ("THENM RWO \"eq_qrat_elim\" 4 " . |string|))) (NIL (|!text_con
s|) (NIL (|!newline|)) (NIL (|!text_cons|) (NIL (|!text| ("THENM Unfolds
‘‘qmul qequiv‘‘ 4 THENM AbReduce 4" . |string|))) (NIL (|!text_cons|) (
NIL (|!newline|)) (NIL (|!text| ("THENM RWH IntSimpC 4" . |string|)))))))
)))) (NIL (|!text| ("" . |string|))))) (((|!text| ("AssertLemma ‘root_2_
irrat_over_int‘ [] THENM D (-1)" . |string|))) (((|!ml_text_cons|) (NIL
(|!text| ("" . |string|))) (NIL (|!ml_text_cons|) (NIL (|auto|) (NIL (|!
text| ("AutoInstConcl []" . |string|)))) (NIL (|!text| ("" . |string|)))
)))))))) (((|lambda|) (("%") (|spread|) (NIL . "%") (("u" "%1") (|apply|)
(NIL (|lambda|) (("%2") (|apply|) (NIL (|lambda|) (("%2") (|axiom|))) (N
IL (|apply|) (NIL . "%2") (NIL . "u")))) (NIL (|qrat_irreduc_witness| (N
UPRL-PARAMETER-VARS::|\\v| . |level-expression|)))))) (REFS (|coprime_wf
| |auto| |root_2_irrat_over_int| |qnum_wf| |qmul_wf| |qnum| |pi2| |pi1|
|qdenom| |qnumer| |qequiv| |qmul| |eq_qrat_elim| |quot_inj| |qrat_inj| |
quot_let| |qrat_proj| |mulq| |numq| |true| |comb_for_mulq_wf| |rev_impli
es| |iff| |and| |squash| |qrat_irreduc_witness| |prl_term| |inewline| |
itext_cons| |nequal_wf| |false| |nequal| |int_nzero| |subtype| |numq_wf|
 |mulq_wf| |all| |qrat_wf| |prop| |member| |exists| |implies| |not| |aux
_auto| |iml_text_cons|) (|root_2_irrat_over_int| |eq_qrat_elim| |comb_fo
r_mulq_wf| |qrat_irreduc_witness|))) NIL)

14.4 System

What is the home page of the system?

> <http://www.cs.cornell.edu/Info/Projects/NuPrl/nuprl.html>

What are the books about the system? The Nuprl book:

> Robert L. Constable, et al., *Implementing Mathematics with the Nuprl
> Proof Development System*, Prentice Hall, Engelwood Cliffs, New Jersey,
> April 1986, x+299 pp, ISBN 0134518322.

is the standard reference. However the system has changed sufficiently that none
of the tutorials given in the book will work in the current system. The manual
of version 4.2:

> Paul B. Jackson, *The Nuprl Proof Development System, Version 4.2.
> Reference Manual and User's Guide*, July 1995.

and the manual of version 5:

Nuprl 5 Manual (Draft).

both are available from the Nuprl home page.

The Nuprl home page also provides access to the Nuprl *Math Library* which showcases a selection of recent developments in Nuprl.

What is the logic of the system? Nuprl uses a constructive type theory based on that of Martin-Löf as described in his paper *Constructive Mathematics and Computer Programming*, in proceedings of Sixth International Congress for Logic, Methodology, and Philosophy of Science, North Holland, 1982, pp. 153–175. Some particular features of the type theory are commented on below in the section on distinguishing features of Nuprl.

Witnesses of inhabitation of a type do not contain sufficient information to guide proofs of inhabitation, as they do in systems such as Coq and Lego. This is partly because the presence of subtypes in the type theory. These witnesses therefore do not function as 'proof objects'.

What is the implementation architecture of the system? Nuprl has an LCF architecture based on an abstract data type of proofs. This proof datatype maintains the structure of both incomplete and complete proofs, down to the level of primitive inferences if desired. The implementation of the datatype is not as small as in HOL or Isabelle. For example, it has primitive rules for arithmetic simplification and deciding linear arithmetic problems.

Nuprl has an extensive tactic collection covering operations such as typechecking, rewriting, forward and backward chaining, arithmetic reasoning and inequality reasoning. Tactics are written in Edinburgh ML.

Nuprl 4.2 is implemented in Common Lisp and the 1979 Edinburgh ML.

What does working with the system look like? Proofs are developed interactively by running tactics in a proof tree editor. With this editor, one focuses on one node of the proof tree at a time. The editor presents the user with the full sequent for the node, together with, if any, the tactic run on that node and the children proof nodes generated by the tactic. The Nuprl Math Library presents proofs using views similar to those generated by this proof tree editor.

All Nuprl expressions are entered using a structure editor and presented on the screen and in print using syntax chosen for brevity and clarity. There are no requirements that display syntax be parsable. The structure editor is also used for the ML tactics: for example, the ... notation is used in display forms for invocations of Nuprl's typechecking and basic-reasoning tactic.

With Nuprl 4.2 one typically has

- 1 scrollable library window, listing loaded theorems, definitions, display forms, comments, and ML objects.
- 1 ML top loop window

- For each proof (many proofs can be open simultaneously)
  1 proof tree editor window as described above.
  The proof refinement window is read only.
- To enter main goals of theorems, or enter tactics when developing proofs, one pops up temporary 'term editor' windows which permit structure editing.
  Term editor windows are also used for displaying and editing definitions and display forms, and for the ML top loop (one needs to be able to enter Nuprl term arguments to tactics).

Proofs are saved to files in the form of proof scripts, recording the tactics used to generate the proofs.

Definitions, theorems, ML code and comments are grouped together in *theories*. Each theory is saved in a single .thy file using Lisp S-expression syntax. This syntax is verbose and low-level, and users rarely view or edit these files directly with a text editor.

What is special about the system compared to other systems?

- The type theory includes less-common *subtype* and *quotient type* type constructors, and, since 1995, *very-dependent* function types, where the type of the value of the function on some argument can depend on its value on other arguments smaller in some well-founded order.
- Having subtypes defined by arbitrary predicates makes type checking undecidable, and all type checking is done by proof. This contrasts with PVS where a type-checking algorithm automates all simpler type-checking tasks. Caching of type-checking obligations improves the efficiency of type-checking by proof.
- The computation language is untyped, enabling the expression of polymorphic functions without dummy type arguments and the definition of general recursive functions with the Y combinator.
- Structure editors are used for all interaction with the system. This permits the use of rich syntaxes for terms, proofs and theories that don't have to be mechanically parsable. Any ambiguities in syntax are easily resolved by interaction with the editors.
- Proofs are edited and viewed as proof trees, rather than, for example, goal stacks.

What are other versions of the system? The proofs described here have been carried out in Nuprl 4.2 which dates from about 1995. There are more recent versions of Nuprl (Nuprl 5, MetaPrl) with significant developments in the user interface, type theory, and performance, but the level of automation in these versions is mostly not much different from that shown above. Further details can be found from the Nuprl home page.

The Nuprl Math Library pages accessible from the home page illustrate ongoing work in producing readable presentations of formal mathematics.

Who are the people behind the system? The principal people involved in the design and implementation of Nuprl 4 were Bob Constable, Stuart Allen, Richard Eaton, Jason Hickey, Doug Howe and Paul Jackson. Many others were involved in previous versions.

What are the main user communities of the system? The main users of Nuprl are virtually all existing or former members of the Nuprl group at Cornell.

What large mathematical formalizations have been done in the system? Specific developments, roughly ordered from more purely mathematical to more applied include:

- Constructive real analysis: the intermediate value theorem (Howe, Chirimar 1991, Forester 1993)
- Computational abstract algebra: multivariate polynomial arithmetic, unique factorisation domains (Jackson 1995)
- Girard's paradox (Howe 1987)
- Metatheory of propositional logics (Caldwell, Gent, Underwood 1990-2001)
- Computational metatheory (Howe 1988)
- Extracting constructive content from classical proofs: Higman's Lemma (Murthy 1991)
- Automata theory, Turing machines (Bickford, Constable, Kreitz, Nogin, Naumov, Jackson, Uribe 1986-2001)

See the Nuprl home pages (both publications and Math Library pages) for full citations and further details.

What representation of the formalization has been put in this paper? Proofs are shown above in one of the formats commonly used for full proofs. For brevity, each sequent in the tree is shown only with those hypotheses and conclusion formulae and types that have changed from ancestor sequents in the tree.

Proofs are saved to files in the form of proof scripts. As an example, the proof section shows the usual display of the proof script for root_2_irrat. This is how scripts are displayed interactively when one wants to edit directly an existing script. The 'top 1 2 3' addresses are automatically filled in. These aren't saved when scripts are saved.

What needs to be explained about this specific proof? The proof follows the traditional approach that is ascribed to Pythagoras and that Lamport chose for his 1993 DEC SRC report *How to Write a Proof*.

This Nuprl V4.2 development relies on slight modifications and extensions of standard V4.2 theories concerning number theory and the rationals. In particular, whereas the standard theory stops with a definition of the rationals as pairs of integers, here we take here the extra step of using Nuprl's quotient type to construct a more abstract and elegant rational type:

```
rat:
  Rat ==  ℤ × ℤ⁻⁰
qequiv:
  x ≡q y ==  x.num * y.den = y.num * x.den
qrat:
  ℚ ==  x,y:Rat//x ≡q y
```

For constructivity reasons, elements of quotient types in Nuprl are single representatives of equivalence classes rather than the equivalence classes themselves. When functions are typed with $\mathbb{Q}$ rather than Rat, the type theory requires the functions to respect the standard equality on rationals. For example, the typing lemma for the function $\mathbb{Q}$ is:

```
mulq_wf:
  ∀u:ℚ. ∀v:ℚ.  u *q v ∈ ℚ
```

Any proof of this typing lemma must not only show that the function returns an element of $\mathbb{Q}$ for arguments in $\mathbb{Q}$, but also that it returns equivalent rationals for equivalent arguments.

The proofs presented above are revisions of the proofs as originally entered: steps have been combined to reduce the lengths of the proofs and emphasize the main steps of the proofs. For comparison, the two_div_square proof has not been revised.

The proof of qrat_irreduc_witness is complicated by the fact that Nuprl V4.2's tactics don't handle subtypes as well as, for example, PVS. Integer division (the $\div$ operation) is only well-formed for non-zero second arguments, and the tactics need explicit help from the user to prove this.

The $\downarrow$ operator in

```
qrat_irreduc_witness:
  ∀u:ℚ. ↓(∃n:ℤ. ∃d:ℤ⁻⁰. u = n / d ∈ ℚ ∧ CoPrime(n,d))
```

is called *squash*. The type $\downarrow T$ is a singleton type if T is inhabited, otherwise it is an empty type. The lemma is slightly simpler to prove with the squash operation included than without. Without, the proof must exhibit a function, implicitly or explicitly, that computes the same numerator n and denominator d for any pair of equal rational numbers u. In other words, the proof must involve computing canonical forms of rational numbers and showing these forms are unique.

The full Nuprl theory and ML files for this work are available online at <http://www.dcs.ed.ac.uk/home/pbj/nuprl>.

The Nuprl Math Library contains an alternate proof of the irrationality of $\sqrt{2}$ produced by Stuart Allen. This alternate proof does not involve the rationals, but does show the irrationality of square roots of arbitrary primes.

15 Ωmega

Christoph Benzmüller, Armin Fiedler, Andreas Meier, Martin Pollet, and
Jörg Siekmann

Formalization[1] and answers by Christoph Benzmüller <chris@ags.
uni-sb.de>, Armin Fiedler <afiedler@ags.uni-sb.de>, Andreas Meier
<ameier@ags.uni-sb.de>, Martin Pollet <pollet@ags.uni-sb.de> and
Jörg Siekmann <siekmann@ags.uni-sb.de>.

15.1 Statement

```
(not (rat (sqrt 2)))
```

15.2 Definitions

Definition of rat

```
(th~defdef rat
        (in rational)
        (definition
          (lam (x num)
               (exists-sort (lam (y num)
                (exists-sort (lam (z num)
                 (= x (frac y z))) int\0)) int)))
          (sort)
          (help "The set of rationals, constructed as fractions a/b of integers."))
```

Definition of sqrt

```
(th~defdef sqrt
        (in real)
        (definition
          (lam (x num) (that (lam (y num) (= (power y 2) x)))))
          (help "Definition of square root."))
```

15.3 Proof

Some definitions from the Ωmega library

```
(th~deftheorem rat-criterion
        (in real)
        (conclusion
          (forall-sort (lam (x num)
            (exists-sort (lam (y num)
              (exists-sort (lam (z num)
                (and (= (times x y) z)
```

---

[1] This paper represents the work as submitted in 2002. Publication has been delayed
and in the meantime we have better and far more advanced results (see Section 15.4)
on this problem.

F. Wiedijk (Ed.): The Seventeen Provers of the World, LNAI 3600, pp. 127–141, 2006.

```
            (not (exists-sort (lam (d num)
                      (common-divisor y z d))
                  int))))
        int))
      int))
    rat))
  (help "x rational implies there exist integers y, z which have no common divisor
        and furthermore z = x · y."))
```

```
(th~deftheorem even-on-integers
      (in real)
      (conclusion
       (forall-sort (lam (x num)
         (equiv (evenp x)
               (exists-sort (lam (y num)
                 (= x (times 2 y))) int))) int))
      (help "An integer x is even, iff an integer y exists so that x = 2y."))
```

```
(th~deftheorem square-even
      (in real)
      (conclusion
       (forall-sort (lam (x num)
         (equiv (evenp (power x 2)) (evenp x)))
        int))
      (help "x is even, iff x^2 is even."))
```

```
(th~deftheorem even-common-divisor
      (in real)
      (conclusion
       (forall-sort (lam (x num)
         (forall-sort (lam (y num)
           (implies (and (evenp x) (evenp y))
                    (common-divisor x y 2)))
          int))
        int))
      (help "If x and y are even, then they have '2' as a common divisor."))
```

```
(th~deftheorem power-int-closed
          (in real)
          (conclusion
           (forall-sort (lam (x num)
            (forall-sort (lam (y num)
             (int (power y x)))
            int))
           int))
          (termdecl)
          (help "The set of integers is closed under power."))
```

```
(th~defproblem sqrt2-not-rat
          (in real)
          (conclusion (not (rat (sqrt 2))))
          (help "√2 is not a rational number."))
```

Proof script for sqrt2-not-rat

```
DECLARATION DECLARE ((CONSTANTS (M NUM) (N NUM) (K NUM)))
RULES NOTI default default
MBASE IMPORT-ASS (RAT-CRITERION)
TACTICS FORALLE-SORT default default ((SQRT 2)) default
```

```
TACTICS EXISTSE-SORT default default (N) default
TACTICS ANDE default default default
TACTICS EXISTSE-SORT (L7) default (M) default
TACTICS ANDE* (L8) (NIL)
OMEGA-BASIC LEMMA default ((= (POWER M 2) (TIMES 2 (POWER N 2))))
TACTICS BY-COMPUTATION (L13) ((L11))
OMEGA-BASIC LEMMA (L9) ((EVENP (POWER M 2)))
RULES DEFN-CONTRACT default default default
OMEGA-BASIC LEMMA (L9) ((INT (POWER N 2)))
TACTICS WELLSORTED default default
TACTICS EXISTSI-SORT (L15) ((POWER N 2)) (L13) (L16) default
MBASE IMPORT-ASS (SQUARE-EVEN)
TACTICS ASSERT ((EVENP M)) ((SQUARE-EVEN L10 L14)) (NIL)
RULES DEFN-EXPAND (L17) default default
TACTICS EXISTSE-SORT default default (K) default
TACTICS ANDE (L19) default default
OMEGA-BASIC LEMMA default ((= (POWER N 2) (TIMES 2 (POWER K 2))))
TACTICS BY-COMPUTATION (L23) ((L13 L22))
OMEGA-BASIC LEMMA default ((EVENP (POWER N 2)))
RULES DEFN-CONTRACT default default default
OMEGA-BASIC LEMMA (L20) ((INT (POWER K 2)))
TACTICS WELLSORTED (L26) ((L21))
TACTICS EXISTSI-SORT default ((POWER K 2)) (L23) default default
TACTICS ASSERT ((EVENP N)) ((SQUARE-EVEN L6 L24)) (NIL)
MBASE IMPORT-ASS (EVEN-COMMON-DIVISOR)
OMEGA-BASIC LEMMA (L20) ((INT 2))
TACTICS WELLSORTED (L28) (NIL)
TACTICS ASSERT (FALSE) ((EVEN-COMMON-DIVISOR L10 L6 L12 L17 L27 L28)) (NIL)
RULES WEAKEN default default
```

First ten steps of Emacs session corresponding to the proof script

We load the theory **Real**, in which the problem is defined.

```
OMEGA: load-problems

THEORY-NAME (EXISTING-THEORY) The name of a theory whose problems ar to be loaded: [REAL]real
;;; Rules loaded for theory REAL.
;;; Theorems loaded for theory REAL.
;;; Tactics loaded for theory REAL.
;;; Methods loaded for theory REAL.
;;; Rules loaded for theory REAL.
;;; Theorems loaded for theory REAL.
;;; Tactics loaded for theory REAL.
;;; Methods loaded for theory REAL.
;;; Rules loaded for theory REAL.
;;; Theorems loaded for theory REAL.
;;; Tactics loaded for theory REAL.
;;; Methods loaded for theory REAL.
;;; Rules loaded for theory REAL.
;;; Theorems loaded for theory REAL.
;;; Tactics loaded for theory REAL.
;;; Methods loaded for theory REAL.
;;; Rules loaded for theory REAL.
;;; Theorems loaded for theory REAL.
;;; Tactics loaded for theory REAL.
;;; Methods loaded for theory REAL.
;;; Rules loaded for theory REAL.
;;; Theorems loaded for theory REAL.
;;; Tactics loaded for theory REAL.
;;; Methods loaded for theory REAL.
```

Step: 1. First we load the problem from the Ωmega database and declare some constant symbols which we will later employ.

```
OMEGA: prove

PROOF-PLAN (PROOF-PLAN) A natural deduction proof or a problem: sqrt2-not-rat
```

```
Changing to proof plan SQRT2-NOT-RAT-21

OMEGA: show-pds

        ...

SQRT2-NOT-RAT ()              ! (NOT (RAT (SQRT 2)))                                OPEN

OMEGA: declare (constants (m num) (n num) (k num))
```

Step: 2. We prove the goal indirectly.

```
OMEGA: noti

NEGATION (NDLINE) A negated line: [SQRT2-NOT-RAT]

FALSITY (NDLINE) A falsity line: [()]
;;;CSM Arbitrary [2]: 0 provers have to be killed

OMEGA: show-pds

L1              (L1)         ! (RAT (SQRT 2))                                       HYP
        ...

L2              (L1)         ! FALSE                                                OPEN

SQRT2-NOT-RAT ()             ! (NOT (RAT (SQRT 2)))                            NOTI: (L2)
```

Step: 3. We load the theorem `RAT-CRITERION` from the database.

```
OMEGA: import-ass

ASS-NAME (THY-ASSUMPTION) A name of an assumption to be imported from the problem theory: rat-criterion

OMEGA: show-pds

L1              (L1)         ! (RAT (SQRT 2))                                       HYP
        ...

L2              (L1)         ! FALSE                                                OPEN

RAT-CRITERION (RAT-CRITERION) ! (FORALL-SORT ([X].                                  THM
                                  (EXISTS-SORT ([Y].
                                   (EXISTS-SORT ([Z].
                                    (AND (= (TIMES X Y) Z)
                                         (NOT (EXISTS-SORT ([D]. (COMMON-DIVISOR Y Z D))
                                                           INT))))
                                   INT))
                                  INT))
                                 RAT)

SQRT2-NOT-RAT ()             ! (NOT (RAT (SQRT 2)))                            NOTI: (L2)
```

Step: 4. We instantiate the (sorted) universal quantifier of `RAT-CRITERION` with term (`sqrt 2`). Thereby we employ the information in `L1` saying that (`SQRT 2`) is of sort `RAT`.

```
OMEGA: foralle-sort

UNIV-LINE (NDLINE) Universal line: [RAT-CRITERION]

LINE (NDLINE) A line: [()]

TERM (TERM) Term to substitute: (sqrt 2)

SO-LINE (NDLINE) A line with sort: [L1];;;CSM Arbitrary [2]: 0 provers have to be killed

OMEGA: show-line* (rat-criterion 13)

RAT-CRITERION (RAT-CRITERION) ! (FORALL-SORT ([X].                                  THM
                                  (EXISTS-SORT ([Y].
                                   (EXISTS-SORT ([Z].
                                    (AND (= (TIMES X Y) Z)
                                         (NOT (EXISTS-SORT ([D]. (COMMON-DIVISOR Y Z D))
                                                           INT))))
                                   INT))
                                  INT))
                                 RAT)

L3              (L1)         ! (EXISTS-SORT ([DC-4248].       FORALLE-SORT: ((SQRT 2)) (RAT-CRITERION L1)
                                 (EXISTS-SORT ([DC-4251].
                                  (AND (= (TIMES (SQRT 2) DC-4248)
                                          DC-4251)
                                       (NOT (EXISTS-SORT ([DC-4255]. (COMMON-DIVISOR DC-4248 DC-4251 DC-4255))
                                                         INT))))
                                 INT))
                                INT)
```

Step: 5. We eliminate the first (sorted) existential quantifier by introducing constant **n**. This generates the additional information that **n** is of sort integer in line **L4**.

```
OMEGA: existse-sort

EX-LINE (NDLINE) An existential line: [L3]

LINE (NDLINE) A line to be proved: [L2]

PARAM (TERMSYM) A term: [dc-42481]n

PREM (NDLINE) The second premise line: [()]
;;;CSM Arbitrary [2]: 0 provers have to be killed


OMEGA: show-line* (12 13 14 15)
```

```
L2      (L1)          ! FALSE                                                          EXISTSE-SORT: (N) (L3 L5)

L3      (L1)          ! (EXISTS-SORT ([DC-4248].                          FORALLE-SORT: ((SQRT 2)) (RAT-CRITERION L1)
                         (EXISTS-SORT ([DC-4251].
                           (AND (= (TIMES (SQRT 2) DC-4248)
                                   DC-4251)
                             (NOT (EXISTS-SORT ([DC-4255]. (COMMON-DIVISOR DC-4248 DC-4251 DC-4255))
                                               INT))))
                         INT))
                       INT)

L4      (L4)          ! (AND (INT N)                                                               HYP
                         (EXISTS-SORT ([DC-4260].
                           (AND (= (TIMES (SQRT 2) N)
                                   DC-4260)
                             (NOT (EXISTS-SORT ([DC-4264]. (COMMON-DIVISOR N DC-4260 DC-4264))
                                               INT))))
                         INT))

L5      (L4 L1)       ! FALSE                                                                      OPEN
```

Step: 6. We split the obtained conjunction in **L4** in its conjuncts.

```
OMEGA: ande

CONJUNCTION (NDLINE) Conjunction to split: [L4]

LCONJ (NDLINE) Left conjunct: [()]

RCONJ (NDLINE) Right conjunct: [()]
;;;CSM Arbitrary [2]: 0 provers have to be killed


OMEGA: show-line* (16 17)
```

```
L6      (L4)          ! (INT N)                                                          ANDE: (L4)

L7      (L4)          ! (EXISTS-SORT ([DC-4260].                                          ANDE: (L4)
                         (AND (= (TIMES (SQRT 2) N)
                                 DC-4260)
                           (NOT (EXISTS-SORT ([DC-4264]. (COMMON-DIVISOR N DC-4260 DC-4264))
                                             INT))))
                       INT)
```

Step: 7. We eliminate the second (sorted) existential quantifier by introducing constant **m**. This introduces the conjunction in line **L8**.

```
OMEGA: existse-sort

EX-LINE (NDLINE) An existential line: [L3]17

LINE (NDLINE) A line to be proved: [L5]

PARAM (TERMSYM) A term: [dc-42601]m

PREM (NDLINE) The second premise line: [()]
;;;CSM Arbitrary [2]: 0 provers have to be killed


OMEGA: show-line* (17 15 18 19)
```

```
L7        (L4)          ! (EXISTS-SORT ([DC-4260].                                          ANDE: (L4)
                          (AND (= (TIMES (SQRT 2) N)
                                  DC-4260)
                               (NOT (EXISTS-SORT ([DC-4264]. (COMMON-DIVISOR N DC-4260 DC-4264))
                                                 INT))))
                          INT)

L5        (L4 L1)       ! FALSE                                            EXISTSE-SORT: (M) (L7 L9)

L8        (L8)          ! (AND (INT M)                                                      HYP
                          (AND (= (TIMES (SQRT 2) N)
                                  M)
                               (NOT (EXISTS-SORT ([DC-4270]. (COMMON-DIVISOR N M DC-4270))
                                                 INT))))

L9        (L8 L4 L1)    ! FALSE                                                            OPEN
```

Step: 8. We split the conjunction in line L8 in its multiple conjuncts.

```
OMEGA: ande*

CONJUNCT-LIST (NDLINE) Premises to split: 18

CONJUNCTION (NDLINE-LIST) List of conjuncts: ()
;;;CSM Arbitrary [2]: 0 provers have to be killed


OMEGA:
OMEGA: show-line* (110 111 112)

L10       (L8)          ! (INT M)                                                    ANDE*: (L8)

L11       (L8)          ! (= (TIMES (SQRT 2) N) M)                                    ANDE*: (L8)

L12       (L8)      ! (NOT (EXISTS-SORT ([DC-4270]. (COMMON-DIVISOR N M DC-4270))     ANDE*: (L8)
                                        INT))
```

Step: 9. We want to infer from (= (TIMES (SQRT 2) N) M) in L11 that (= (POWER M 2) (TIMES 2 (POWER N 2))). For this we anticpate the later formula by introducing it as a lemma for the current open subgoal L9. Thereby the support nodes of L9 become automatically available as support lines for the introduced lemma.

```
OMEGA: lemma

NODE (NDPLANLINE) An open node: [L9]

FORMULA (FORMULA) Formula to be proved as lemma: (= (power m 2) (times 2 (power n 2)))

OMEGA: show-line* (113)

L13       (L8 L4 L1)      ! (= (POWER M 2) (TIMES 2 (POWER N 2)))                           OPEN
```

Step: 10. The lemma is proven by applying the computer algebra system Maple; the command for this is BY-COMPUTATION. The computation problem is passed from Ωmega to the mathematical software bus MathWeb, which in turn passes the problem to an available instance of Maple.

```
OMEGA: by-computation

LINE1 (NDLINE) A line an arithmetic term to justify.: 113

LINE2 (NDLINE-LIST) A list containing premises to be used.: (111)

OMEGA:
OMEGA: ;;;CSM Arbitrary [2]: 0 provers have to be killed


OMEGA: show-line* (111 113)

L11       (L8)          ! (= (TIMES (SQRT 2) N) M)                                    ANDE*: (L8)

L13       (L8 L4 L1)    ! (= (POWER M 2) (TIMES 2 (POWER N 2)))              BY-COMPUTATION: (L11)
```

LATEX presentation of unexpanded proof of `sqrt2-not-rat`

L19.	L19	$\vdash [\mathbb{Z}_{[\nu \to o]}(K_{[\nu]}) \wedge M_{[\nu]} = (2 \cdot_{[(\nu,\nu) \to \nu]} K)]$	(Hyp)
L22.	ECD, L19	$\vdash M = (2 \cdot K)$	($\wedge E$ L19)
L21.	ECD, L19	$\vdash \mathbb{Z}(K)$	($\wedge E$ L19)
L8.	L8	$\vdash [\mathbb{Z}(M) \wedge [(\sqrt{_{[\nu \to \nu]}2} \cdot N_{[\nu]}) = M \wedge \neg \exists X_{359[\nu]} :$ $\mathbb{Z}_{[\nu \to o]} \bullet \text{Common-Divisor}_{[(\nu,\nu,\nu) \to o]}(N, M, X_{359})]]$	(Hyp)
L12.	$\mathcal{H}_1$	$\vdash \neg \exists X_{359[\nu]} : \mathbb{Z} \bullet \text{Common-Divisor}(N, M, X_{359})$	($\wedge E*$ L8)
L11.	$\mathcal{H}_1$	$\vdash (\sqrt{2} \cdot N) = M$	($\wedge E*$ L8)
L10.	$\mathcal{H}_1$	$\vdash \mathbb{Z}(M)$	($\wedge E*$ L8)
L4.	L4	$\vdash [\mathbb{Z}(N) \wedge \exists X_{2[\nu]} : \mathbb{Z} \bullet [(\sqrt{2} \cdot N) = X_2 \wedge \neg \exists X_{3[\nu]} :$ $\mathbb{Z} \bullet \text{Common-Divisor}(N, X_2, X_3)]]$	(Hyp)
L7.	$\mathcal{H}_2$	$\vdash \exists X_{2[\nu]} : \mathbb{Z} \bullet [(\sqrt{2} \cdot N) = X_2 \wedge \neg \exists X_{3[\nu]} :$ $\mathbb{Z} \bullet \text{Common-Divisor}(N, X_2, X_3)]$	($\wedge E$ L4)
L6.	$\mathcal{H}_2$	$\vdash \mathbb{Z}(N)$	($\wedge E$ L4)
L1.	L1	$\vdash \mathbb{Q}_{[\nu \to o]}(\sqrt{2})$	(Hyp)
L2.	$\mathcal{H}_3$	$\vdash \perp_{[o]}$	(Existse-Sort L3,L5)
RC.	RC	$\vdash \forall X_{4[\nu]} : \mathbb{Q}_{[\nu \to o]} \bullet \exists X_{5[\nu]} : \mathbb{Z}, X_{6[\nu]} : \mathbb{Z} \bullet [(X_4 \cdot X_5) =$ $X_6 \wedge \neg \exists X_{7[\nu]} : \mathbb{Z} \bullet \text{Common-Divisor}(X_5, X_6, X_7)]$	(Thm)
L9.	$\mathcal{H}_4$	$\vdash \perp$	(Existse-Sort L18,L20)
L5.	$\mathcal{H}_5$	$\vdash \perp$	(Existse-Sort L7,L9)
L3.	$\mathcal{H}_3$	$\vdash \exists X_{8[\nu]} : \mathbb{Z}, X_{9[\nu]} : \mathbb{Z} \bullet [(\sqrt{2} \cdot X_8) = X_9 \wedge \neg \exists X_{10[\nu]} :$ $\mathbb{Z} \bullet \text{Common-Divisor}(X_8, X_9, X_{10})]$	(Foralle-Sort RC,L1)
L13.	$\mathcal{H}_4$	$\vdash (M \hat{\ }_{[(\nu,\nu) \to \nu]} 2) = (2 \cdot (N \hat{\ } 2))$	(By-Computation L11)
L15.	$\mathcal{H}_4$	$\vdash \exists X_{11[\nu]} : \mathbb{Z} \bullet (M \hat{\ } 2) = (2 \cdot X_{11})$	(Existsi-Sort L13,L16)
L14.	$\mathcal{H}_4$	$\vdash \text{Evenp}_{[\nu \to o]}((M \hat{\ } 2))$	(Defni L15)
L16.	$\mathcal{H}_4$	$\vdash \mathbb{Z}((N \hat{\ } 2))$	(Wellsorted L6)
SE.	SE	$\vdash \forall X_{12[\nu]} : \mathbb{Z} \bullet [\text{Evenp}((X_{12} \hat{\ } 2)) \Leftrightarrow \text{Evenp}(X_{12})]$	(Thm)
L20.	$\mathcal{H}_6$	$\vdash \perp$	(Weaken L29)
L17.	$\mathcal{H}_4$	$\vdash \text{Evenp}(M)$	(Assert SE,L10,L14)
L18.	$\mathcal{H}_4$	$\vdash \exists X_{13[\nu]} : \mathbb{Z} \bullet M = (2 \cdot X_{13})$	(Defne L17)
L23.	$\mathcal{H}_6$	$\vdash (N \hat{\ } 2) = (2 \cdot (K \hat{\ } 2))$	(By-Computation L13, L22)
L25.	$\mathcal{H}_6$	$\vdash \exists X_{14[\nu]} : \mathbb{Z} \bullet (N \hat{\ } 2) = (2 \cdot X_{14})$	(Existsi-Sort L23,L26)
L24.	$\mathcal{H}_6$	$\vdash \text{Evenp}((N \hat{\ } 2))$	(Defni L25)
L27.	$\mathcal{H}_6$	$\vdash \text{Evenp}(N)$	(Assert SE,L6,L24)
L26.	$\mathcal{H}_6$	$\vdash \mathbb{Z}((K \hat{\ } 2))$	(Wellsorted L21)
ECD.	ECD	$\vdash \forall X_{15[\nu]} : \mathbb{Z}, X_{16[\nu]} : \mathbb{Z} \bullet [[\text{Evenp}(X_{15}) \wedge$ $\text{Evenp}(X_{16})] \Rightarrow \text{Common-Divisor}(X_{15}, X_{16}, 2)]$	(Thm)
L28.	$\mathcal{H}_6$	$\vdash \mathbb{Z}(2)$	(Wellsorted)
L29.	$\mathcal{H}_6$	$\vdash \perp$	(Assert ECD,L10,L6, L12,L17,L27,L28)
S2NR.	$\mathcal{H}_7$	$\vdash \neg \mathbb{Q}(\sqrt{2})$	($\neg I$ L2)

S2NR = Sqrt2-Not-Rat; ECD = Even-Common-Divisor; SE = Square-Even; RC = Rat-Criterion;
$\mathcal{H}_1$ = ECD, SE, L8; $\mathcal{H}_2$ = ECD, SE, L4; $\mathcal{H}_3$ = ECD, RC, SE, L1; $\mathcal{H}_4$ = ECD, RC, SE, L1, L4, L8;
$\mathcal{H}_5$ = ECD, RC, SE, L1, L4; $\mathcal{H}_6$ = ECD, RC, SE, L1, L4, L8, L19; $\mathcal{H}_7$ = ECD, RC, SE

P.rex natural language presentation of unexpanded proof of `sqrt2-not-rat`

Theorem 1. *Let 2 be a common divisor of x and y if x is even and y is even for all $y \in \mathbb{Z}$ for all $x \in \mathbb{Z}$. Let x be even if and only if x^2 is even for all $x \in \mathbb{Z}$. Let there be a $y \in \mathbb{Z}$ such that there exists a $z \in \mathbb{Z}$ such that $x \cdot y = z$ and there is no $d \in \mathbb{Z}$ such that d is a common divisor of y and z for all $x \in \mathbb{Q}$. Then $\sqrt{2}$ isn't rational.*

Proof. Let 2 be a common divisor of x and y if x is even and y is even for all $y \in \mathbb{Z}$ for all $x \in \mathbb{Z}$. Let x be even if and only if x^2 is even for all $x \in \mathbb{Z}$. Let there be a $y \in \mathbb{Z}$ such that there is a $z \in \mathbb{Z}$ such that $x \cdot y = z$ and there is no $d \in \mathbb{Z}$ such that d is a common divisor of y and z for all $x \in \mathbb{Q}$.

We prove that $\sqrt{2}$ isn't rational by a contradiction. Let $\sqrt{2}$ be rational.

Let $n \in \mathbb{Z}$ and let there be a $dc_{269} \in \mathbb{Z}$ such that $\sqrt{2} \cdot n = dc_{269}$ and there doesn't exist a $dc_{273} \in \mathbb{Z}$ such that dc_{273} is a common divisor of n and dc_{269}.

Let $m \in \mathbb{Z}$, let $\sqrt{2} \cdot n = m$ and let there be no $dc_{279} \in \mathbb{Z}$ such that dc_{279} is a common divisor of n and m.

We prove that $m^2 = 2 \cdot n^2$ in order to prove that there exists a $dc_{287} \in \mathbb{Z}$ such that $m^2 = 2 \cdot dc_{287}$. $m^2 = 2 \cdot n^2$ since $\sqrt{2} \cdot n = m$.

Therefore m^2 is even. That implies that m is even because $m \in \mathbb{Z}$. That leads to the existence of a $dc_{343} \in \mathbb{Z}$ such that $m = 2 \cdot dc_{343}$.

Let $k \in \mathbb{Z}$ and let $m = 2 \cdot k$. $2 \in \mathbb{Z}$.

We prove that $n^2 = 2 \cdot k^2$ in order to prove that there is a $dc_{353} \in \mathbb{Z}$ such that $n^2 = 2 \cdot dc_{353}$. $n^2 = 2 \cdot k^2$ since $m^2 = 2 \cdot n^2$ and $m = 2 \cdot k$.

That implies that n^2 is even. That implies that n is even since $n \in \mathbb{Z}$. Therefore we have a contradiction since $m \in \mathbb{Z}$, $n \in \mathbb{Z}$, there doesn't exist a $dc_{279} \in \mathbb{Z}$ such that dc_{279} is a common divisor of n and m, m is even and $2 \in \mathbb{Z}$.

PDS proof object of unexpanded proof of `sqrt2-not-rat`

```
(PDS (problem SQRT2-NOT-RAT)
  (in REAL)
  (declarations (type-variables )(type-constants )
    (constants  (K NUM) (N NUM) (M NUM))(meta-variables )(variables ))
  (conclusion SQRT2-NOT-RAT)
  (assumptions)
  (open-nodes)
  (support-nodes EVEN-COMMON-DIVISOR SQUARE-EVEN RAT-CRITERION)
  (nodes
    (L19 (L19) (AND (INT K) (= M (TIMES 2 K)))
      (0 ("HYP" () () "grounded" () ()))
    )
    (L22 (EVEN-COMMON-DIVISOR L19) (= M (TIMES 2 K))
      (0 ("ANDE" () (L19) "unexpanded" ()
        ("L21" "NONEXISTENT" "EXISTENT")))
    )
    (L21 (EVEN-COMMON-DIVISOR L19) (INT K)
      (0 ("ANDE" () (L19) "unexpanded" ()
        ("NONEXISTENT" "L22" "EXISTENT")))
    )
    (L8 (L8) (AND (INT M) (AND (= (TIMES (SQRT 2) N) M) (NOT (EXISTS-SORT (lam (VAR76 NUM) (COMMON-DIVISOR N M VAR76)) INT))))
      (0 ("HYP" () () "grounded" () ()))
    )
    (L12 (EVEN-COMMON-DIVISOR SQUARE-EVEN L8) (NOT (EXISTS-SORT (lam (VAR76 NUM) (COMMON-DIVISOR N M VAR76)) INT))
      (0 ("ANDE*" () (L8) "unexpanded" ()
        ("L10" "L11" "NONEXISTENT" "EXISTENT")))
    )
    (L11 (EVEN-COMMON-DIVISOR SQUARE-EVEN L8) (= (TIMES (SQRT 2) N) M)
      (0 ("ANDE*" () (L8) "unexpanded" ()
        ("L10" "NONEXISTENT" "L12" "EXISTENT")))
    )
    (L10 (EVEN-COMMON-DIVISOR SQUARE-EVEN L8) (INT M)
      (0 ("ANDE*" () (L8) "unexpanded" ()
        ("NONEXISTENT" "L11" "L12" "EXISTENT")))
    )
```

```
(L4 (L4) (AND (INT N) (EXISTS-SORT (lam (VAR79 NUM) (AND (= (TIMES (SQRT 2) N) VAR79)
(NOT (EXISTS-SORT (lam (VAR80 NUM) (COMMON-DIVISOR N VAR79 VAR80)) INT)))) INT))
 (0 ("HYP" () () "grounded" () ()))
 )
(L7 (EVEN-COMMON-DIVISOR SQUARE-EVEN L4) (EXISTS-SORT (lam (VAR79 NUM) (AND (= (TIMES
 (SQRT 2) N) VAR79) (NOT (EXISTS-SORT (lam (VAR80 NUM) (COMMON-DIVISOR N VAR79 VAR80)) INT)))) INT)
 (0 ("ANDE" () (L4) "unexpanded" ()
    ("L6" "NONEXISTENT" "EXISTENT")))
 )
(L6 (EVEN-COMMON-DIVISOR SQUARE-EVEN L4) (INT N)
 (0 ("ANDE" () (L4) "unexpanded" ()
    ("NONEXISTENT" "L7" "EXISTENT")))
 )
(L1 (L1) (RAT (SQRT 2))
 (0 ("HYP" () () "grounded" () ()))
 )
(L2 (EVEN-COMMON-DIVISOR SQUARE-EVEN RAT-CRITERION L1) FALSE
 (0 ("EXISTSE-SORT" ((:pds-term N)) (L3 L5) "unexpanded" ()
    ("EXISTENT" "EXISTENT" "NONEXISTENT")))
 )
(RAT-CRITERION (RAT-CRITERION) (FORALL-SORT (lam (VAR81 NUM) (EXISTS-SORT (lam (VAR82 NUM)
 (EXISTS-SORT (lam (VAR83 NUM) (AND (= (TIMES VAR81 VAR82) VAR83) (NOT (EXISTS-SORT
 (lam (VAR84 NUM) (COMMON-DIVISOR VAR82 VAR83 VAR84)) INT)))) INT)) INT)) RAT)
 (0 ("THM" () () "grounded" () ()))
 )
(L9 (EVEN-COMMON-DIVISOR SQUARE-EVEN L8 L4 RAT-CRITERION L1) FALSE
 (0 ("EXISTSE-SORT" ((:pds-term K)) (L18 L20) "unexpanded" ()
    ("EXISTENT" "EXISTENT" "NONEXISTENT")))
 )
(L5 (EVEN-COMMON-DIVISOR SQUARE-EVEN L4 RAT-CRITERION L1) FALSE
 (0 ("EXISTSE-SORT" ((:pds-term M)) (L7 L9) "unexpanded" ()
    ("EXISTENT" "EXISTENT" "NONEXISTENT")))
 )
(L3 (EVEN-COMMON-DIVISOR SQUARE-EVEN RAT-CRITERION L1) (EXISTS-SORT (lam (VAR85 NUM)
 (EXISTS-SORT (lam (VAR86 NUM) (AND (= (TIMES (SQRT 2) VAR85) VAR86) (NOT (EXISTS-SORT
 (lam (VAR87 NUM) (COMMON-DIVISOR VAR85 VAR86 VAR87)) INT)))) INT)) INT)
 (0 ("FORALLE-SORT" ((:pds-term (SQRT 2))) (RAT-CRITERION L1) "unexpanded"
    () ("NONEXISTENT" "EXISTENT" "EXISTENT")))
 )
(L13 (EVEN-COMMON-DIVISOR SQUARE-EVEN L8 L4 RAT-CRITERION L1) (= (POWER M 2)
 (TIMES 2 (POWER N 2)))
 (0 ("BY-COMPUTATION" () (L11) "unexpanded" ()
    ("EXISTENT" "EXISTENT")))
 )
(L15 (EVEN-COMMON-DIVISOR SQUARE-EVEN L8 L4 RAT-CRITERION L1) (EXISTS-SORT (lam (VAR88 NUM)
 (= (POWER M 2) (TIMES 2 VAR88))) INT)
 (0 ("EXISTSI-SORT" ((:pds-term (POWER N 2))(:pds-post-obj (position 2 2))) (L13 L16)
 "unexpanded"
    () ("EXISTENT" "EXISTENT" "EXISTENT")))
 )
(L14 (EVEN-COMMON-DIVISOR SQUARE-EVEN L8 L4 RAT-CRITERION L1) (EVENP (POWER M 2))
 (0 ("DefnI" ((:pds-term EVENP)(:pds-term (lam (X NUM) (EXISTS-SORT (lam (Y NUM)
 (= X (TIMES 2 Y))) INT)))(:pds-post-obj (position 0))) (L15) "grounded"
    () ("EXISTENT" "NONEXISTENT")))
 )
(L16 (EVEN-COMMON-DIVISOR SQUARE-EVEN L8 L4 RAT-CRITERION L1) (INT (POWER N 2))
 (0 ("WELLSORTED" ((((:pds-term (POWER N (S (S ZERO))))(:pds-sort INT)(:pds-symbol
 POWER-INT-CLOSED))((:pds-term (S (S ZERO)))(:pds-sort INT)(:pds-symbol NAT-INT))
 ((:pds-term (S (S ZERO))(:pds-sort NAT)(:pds-symbol SUCC-NAT))((:pds-term (S ZERO))
 (:pds-sort NAT)(:pds-symbol SUCC-NAT))((:pds-term ZERO)(:pds-sort NAT)
 (:pds-symbol ZERO-NAT)))) (L6) "unexpanded"
    () ("EXISTENT" "EXISTENT")))
 )
(SQUARE-EVEN (SQUARE-EVEN) (FORALL-SORT (lam (VAR89 NUM) (EQUIV (EVENP (POWER VAR89 2))
 (EVENP VAR89))) INT)
 (0 ("THM" () () "grounded" () ()))
 )
(L20 (EVEN-COMMON-DIVISOR L19 SQUARE-EVEN L8 L4 RAT-CRITERION L1) FALSE
 (0 ("WEAKEN" () (L29) "grounded" () ("EXISTENT" "EXISTENT")))
 )
(L17 (EVEN-COMMON-DIVISOR SQUARE-EVEN L8 L4 RAT-CRITERION L1) (EVENP M)
 (0 ("ASSERT" ((:pds-term (EVENP M))(:pds-nil)) (SQUARE-EVEN L10 L14) "unexpanded"
    () ("NONEXISTENT" "EXISTENT" "EXISTENT" "EXISTENT")))
 )
(L18 (EVEN-COMMON-DIVISOR SQUARE-EVEN L8 L4 RAT-CRITERION L1) (EXISTS-SORT (lam (VAR90 NUM)
 (= M (TIMES 2 VAR90))) INT)
 (0 ("DefnE" ((:pds-term EVENP)(:pds-term (lam (X NUM) (EXISTS-SORT (lam (Y NUM)
 (= X (TIMES 2 Y))) INT))(:pds-post-obj (position 0))) (L17) "grounded"
    () ("NONEXISTENT" "EXISTENT")))
 )
(L23 (EVEN-COMMON-DIVISOR L19 SQUARE-EVEN L8 L4 RAT-CRITERION L1) (= (POWER N 2) (TIMES 2 (POWER K 2)))
 (0 ("BY-COMPUTATION" () (L13 L22) "unexpanded" ()
    ("EXISTENT" "EXISTENT" "EXISTENT")))
 )
(L25 (EVEN-COMMON-DIVISOR L19 SQUARE-EVEN L8 L4 RAT-CRITERION L1) (EXISTS-SORT (lam
 (VAR91 NUM) (= (POWER N 2) (TIMES 2 VAR91))) INT)
 (0 ("EXISTSI-SORT" ((:pds-term (POWER K 2))(:pds-post-obj (position 2 2)))) (L23 L26)
 "unexpanded"
    () ("EXISTENT" "EXISTENT" "EXISTENT")))
 )
```

```
(L24 (EVEN-COMMON-DIVISOR L19 SQUARE-EVEN L8 L4 RAT-CRITERION L1) (EVENP (POWER N 2))
 (0 ("DefnI" ((:pds-term EVENP)(:pds-term (lam (X NUM) (EXISTS-SORT (lam (Y NUM)
 (= X (TIMES 2 Y))) INT)))(:pds-post-obj (position 0))) (L25) "grounded"
   () ("EXISTENT" "NONEXISTENT")))
 )
(L27 (EVEN-COMMON-DIVISOR L19 SQUARE-EVEN L8 L4 RAT-CRITERION L1) (EVENP N)
 (0 ("ASSERT" ((:pds-term (EVENP N))(:pds-nil)) (SQUARE-EVEN L6 L24) "unexpanded"
   () ("NONEXISTENT" "EXISTENT" "EXISTENT" "EXISTENT")))
 )
(L26 (EVEN-COMMON-DIVISOR L19 SQUARE-EVEN L8 L4 RAT-CRITERION L1) (INT (POWER K 2))
 (0 ("WELLSORTED" (((((:pds-term (POWER K (S (S ZERO))))(:pds-sort INT)(:pds-symbol POWER-INT-CLOSED))
 ((:pds-term (S (S ZERO)))(:pds-sort INT)(:pds-symbol NAT-INT))((:pds-term (S (S ZERO)))
 (:pds-sort NAT)(:pds-symbol SUCC-NAT))((:pds-term (S ZERO))(:pds-sort NAT)(:pds-symbol SUCC-NAT))
 ((:pds-term ZERO)(:pds-sort NAT)(:pds-symbol ZERO-NAT)))) (L21) "unexpanded"
   () ("EXISTENT" "EXISTENT")))
 )
(EVEN-COMMON-DIVISOR (EVEN-COMMON-DIVISOR) (FORALL-SORT (lam (VAR92 NUM) (FORALL-SORT
 (lam (VAR93 NUM) (IMPLIES (AND (EVENP VAR92) (EVENP VAR93)) (COMMON-DIVISOR VAR92 VAR93 2)))
 INT)) INT)
 (0 ("THM" () () "grounded" () ()))
 )
(L28 (EVEN-COMMON-DIVISOR L19 SQUARE-EVEN L8 L4 RAT-CRITERION L1) (INT 2)
 (0 ("WELLSORTED" ((((:pds-term (S (S ZERO)))(:pds-sort INT)(:pds-symbol NAT-INT))
 ((:pds-term (S (S ZERO)))(:pds-sort NAT)(:pds-symbol SUCC-NAT))((:pds-term (S ZERO))
 (:pds-sort NAT)(:pds-symbol SUCC-NAT))((:pds-term ZERO)(:pds-sort NAT)(:pds-symbol ZERO-NAT))))
 () "unexpanded"
   () ("EXISTENT")))
 )
(L29 (EVEN-COMMON-DIVISOR L19 SQUARE-EVEN L8 L4 RAT-CRITERION L1) FALSE
 (0 ("ASSERT" ((:pds-term FALSE)(:pds-nil)) (EVEN-COMMON-DIVISOR L10 L6 L12 L17 L27 L28)
   "unexpanded"
     ()
     ("NONEXISTENT" "EXISTENT" "EXISTENT" "EXISTENT" "EXISTENT" "EXISTENT" "EXISTENT"
      "EXISTENT")))
 )
(SQRT2-NOT-RAT (EVEN-COMMON-DIVISOR SQUARE-EVEN RAT-CRITERION) (NOT (RAT (SQRT 2)))
 (0 ("NOTI" () (L2) "grounded" () ("EXISTENT" "NONEXISTENT")))
 ))
(lemmata)
(agenda)
(controls
 (L19 (() () () ()))
 (L22 (() () () ()))
 (L21 (() () () ()))
 (L8 (() () () ()))
 (L12 (() () () ()))
 (L11 (() () () ()))
 (L10 (() () () ()))
 (L4 (() () () ()))
 (L7 (() () () ()))
 (L6 (() () () ()))
 (L1 (() () () ()))
 (L2 ((L3 L1) () () ()))
 (RAT-CRITERION (() () () ()))
 (L9 ((L16 L6 L7 L4 L1 L3 L8 L12 L11 L10 L13 L14 L17 L18) (L5 L2 L17) () ()))
 (L5 ((L6 L7 L4 L1 L3) (L2) () ()))
 (L3 (() () () ()))
 (L13 ((L10 L11 L12 L8 L3 L1 L4 L7 L6) () () ()))
 (L15 ((L13 L10 L11 L12 L8 L3 L1 L4 L7 L6) () () ()))
 (L14 ((L13 L10 L11 L12 L8 L3 L1 L4 L7 L6) () () ()))
 (L16 ((L6 L7 L4 L1 L3 L8 L12 L11 L10 L13 L14) () () ()))
 (SQUARE-EVEN (() () () ()))
 (L20 ((L29 L28 L27 L24 L23 L21 L22 L19 L18 L14 L13 L10 L11 L12 L8 L3 L1 L4 L7 L6 L16 L26 L17)
 (L9 L5 L2) () ()))
 (L17 ((L26 L16 L6 L7 L4 L1 L3 L8 L12 L11 L10 L13 L14 L17 L18 L19 L22 L21 L23 L24 L27 L28)
 (L17 L2 L5 L9) () ()))
 (L18 (() () () ()))
 (L23 ((L21 L22 L19 L18 L14 L13 L10 L11 L12 L8 L3 L1 L4 L7 L6 L16) () () ()))
 (L25 ((L23 L21 L22 L19 L18 L14 L13 L10 L11 L12 L8 L3 L1 L4 L7 L6 L16) () () ()))
 (L24 ((L23 L21 L22 L19 L18 L14 L13 L10 L11 L12 L8 L3 L1 L4 L7 L6 L16) () () ()))
 (L27 (() () () ()))
 (L26 ((L16 L6 L7 L4 L1 L3 L8 L12 L11 L10 L13 L14 L18 L19 L22 L21 L23 L24) () () ()))
 (EVEN-COMMON-DIVISOR (() () () ()))
 (L28 ((L27 L24 L23 L21 L22 L19 L18 L14 L13 L10 L11 L12 L8 L3 L1 L4 L7 L6 L16 L26) () () ()))
 (L29 (() () () ()))
 (SQRT2-NOT-RAT (() () () ())))
(plan-steps (SQRT2-NOT-RAT 0 L1 0 L2 0) (L3 0 RAT-CRITERION 0 L1 0)
 (L2 0 L4 0 L3 0 L5 0) (L6 0 L4 0) (L7 0 L4 0)
 (L5 0 L8 0 L7 0 L9 0) (L10 0 L8 0) (L11 0 L12 0) (L12 0 L8 0)
 (L13 0 L11 0) (L14 0 L15 0) (L16 0 L6 0) (L15 0 L13 0 L16 0)
 (L17 0 SQUARE-EVEN 0 L10 0 L14 0) (L18 0 L17 0)
 (L9 0 L19 0 L18 0 L20 0) (L21 0 L19 0) (L22 0 L19 0)
 (L23 0 L13 0 L22 0) (L24 0 L25 0) (L26 0 L21 0)
 (L25 0 L23 0 L26 0) (L27 0 SQUARE-EVEN 0 L6 0 L24 0) (L28 0)
 (L29 0 EVEN-COMMON-DIVISOR 0 L10 0 L6 0 L12 0 L17 0 L27 0 L28 0)
 (L20 0 L29 0) ))
```

15.4   System

What is the home page of the system?

<http://www.ags.uni-sb.de/~omega/>

What are the books about the system?
There is a book forthcoming and there are several journal and conference publications. An overview of recent publications gives the homepage. The most recent overview paper on the Ωmega project is:

[1] J. Siekmann and C. Benzmüller, OMEGA: Computer Supported Mathematics. In S. Biundo, T. Frühwirth, and G. Palm (eds.), KI 2004: Advances in Artificial Intelligence: 27th Annual German Conference on AI, LNAI vol. 3228, pp. 3-28, Ulm, Germany, 2004. Springer.

The article presented here represents work done in 2002. Related and more recent publications on the $\sqrt{2}$-case study in Ωmega (in particular [3] summarizes our complete work on the $\sqrt{2}$-case study):

[2] Solving the $\sqrt{2}$-problem with interactive island theorem proving:
J. Siekmann, C. Benzmüller, A. Fiedler, A. Meier, and M. Pollet. Proof Development with Ωmega: $\sqrt{2}$ Is Irrational. In M. Baaz and A. Voronkov (eds.), *Logic for Programming, Artificial Intelligence, and Reasoning — 9th International Conference, LPAR 2002*, number 2514 in LNAI, pp. 367-387, Tbilisi, Georgia, Springer Verlag, 2002.

[3] Solving the $\sqrt{2}$-problem (and its generalization) fully automatically with proof planning:
J. Siekmann, C. Benzmüller, A. Fiedler, A. Meier, I. Normann, and M. Pollet. Proof Development with Ωmega: The Irrationality of $\sqrt{2}$. In F. Kamareddine (ed.), *Thirty Five Years of Automating Mathematics*, pp. 271-314, Kluwer Academic Publishers, 2003.

What is the logic of the system?
Ωmega employs a higher-order logic based on Church's simply typed λ-calculus (with prefix-polymorphism). Furthermore, there is a simple sort mechanism in Ωmega.

What is the implementation architecture of the system?
Ωmega consists of several distributed modules that are connected via the MathWeb mathematical software bus. Different modules are written in different programming languages (e.g. the Ωmega kernel and the proof planner are written in Lisp, the graphical user interface is written in Oz).

What does working with the system look like?
There are different modes for the proof search:

1. Interactive Proof Construction with Tactics, Methods, and Calculus Rules.
   This is the level of proof construction displayed in this paper. Essentially it is like any other interactive, tactic-based theorem prover and definitely *not* the level we expect real mathematics to be represented. In fact, the whole purpose of the Ωmega project is to show that there is a substantially better way to prove theorems, namely at the proof planning level.
2. Interactive Island Proof Planning.
   In this mode, the user presents "islands", that is, intermediate statements in the potential proof sequence. The system then closes the gaps by proof planning. See [2] for a report about an island proof of the $\sqrt{2}$ problem.
3. Automated Proof Planning.
   In the best of all worlds the system finds a proof fully automatically by a hierarchical expansion of a high-level proof plan into a low-level logic proof. See [3] for a fully automated solution to the $\sqrt{2}$ problem, where we also introduce and automatically prove its generalization: the irrationality of $\sqrt[i]{k}$ for any $i, k \in \mathbb{N}$.
4. Calling External Reasoners via MathWeb.
   This is important for the $\sqrt{2}$ problem as well. Some gaps (subproblems) are closed by a computer algebra system, simple gaps in an island proof are closed by (fast and simple) first- and higher-order theorem provers and the proof planner also uses a constraint solver as an external subsystem.
5. Combinations of the above.

What is special about the system compared to other systems? The Ωmega system is a representative system in the new paradigm of *proof planning* and combines interactive and automated proof construction in *mathematical domains.*

The main purpose of the Ωmega project is to show that computer-supported mathematics and proving can be done at a more advanced and human-oriented level of abstraction as typically found in a mathematical paper or textbook. However, it can be used also just like any other interactive tactic-based system, as this article shows.

Ωmega's inference mechanism so far has been based on a higher-order natural deduction (ND) variant of a sorted version of Church's simply typed λ-calculus. The user can interactively construct proofs directly at the calculus level or at the more abstract level of *tactics* (as shown in this article) or proof planning with *methods.* Proof construction can be supported by already proven assertions and lemmata and also by calls to external systems to simplify or solve subproblems. A recent issue in the project is to replace Ωmega's ND calculus by a more human-oriented, sound and complete base framework that better and more directly supports reasoning at the logic and assertion level.

At the core of Ωmega is the *proof plan data structure* PDS in which proofs and *proof plans* are represented at various levels of granularity and abstraction. The proof plans are classified with respect to a taxonomy of mathematical theories, which are currently being replaced by the mathematical data base MBase. The user of Ωmega, or the proof planner Multi, or the suggestion mechanism Ω-Ants modify the PDS during proof development. They can invoke external reasoning systems whose results are included in the PDS after appropriate transformation. After expansion of these high level proofs to the underlying ND calculus, the PDS can be checked by Ωmega's proof checker. User interaction is supported by the graphical user interface LΩUI and the translation into natural language by the proof explainer *P.rex*.

Several first-order ATPs are connected to Ωmega via Tramp, which is a proof transformation system that transforms resolution-style proofs into assertion level ND proofs.

What are other versions of the system?
The most recent version is Ωmega 3.6.

Who are the people behind the system?
The list of Ωmega group members and affiliated researchers includes (many RAs work in Ωmega related research projects and only a few directly on the kernel of the system):

Serge Autexier, Christoph Benzmüller, Chad Brown, Mark Buckley, Lassaad Cheikhrouhou, Dominik Dietrich, Armin Fiedler, Andreas Franke, Helmut Horacek, Mateja Jamnik (now at Cambridge University, Cambridge, UK), Manfred Kerber (now at University of Birmingham, Birmingham, UK), Michael Kohlhase (now at International University Bremen, Bremen, Germany), Henri Lesourd, Andreas Meier, Erica Melis, Martin Pollet, Marvin Schiller, Jörg Siekmann, Volker Sorge (now at University of Birmingham, Birmingham, UK), Carsten Ullrich, Quoc Bao Vo (now at RMIT University, Melbourne, Australia), Marc Wagner, Claus-Peter Wirth, Jürgen Zimmer.

What are the main user communities of the system?
The Ωmega system is employed at: Saarland University and the DFKI (AG Siekmann), the University of Birmingham (Manfred Kerber and Volker Sorge), International University Bremen (Michael Kohlhase), Cambridge University (Mateja Jamnik), University of Edinburgh (Jürgen Zimmer).

What large mathematical formalizations have been done in the system?
The Ωmega system has been used in several other case studies, which illustrate in particular the interplay of the various components, such as proof planning supported by heterogeneous external reasoning systems. Publication references to these case studies are available in [1] (see above).

A typical example for a class of problems that cannot be solved by traditional automated theorem provers is the class of ϵ–δ–proofs. This class was originally proposed as a challenge by Woody Bledsoe and it comprises theorems such as LIM+ and LIM*, where LIM+ states that the limit of the sum of two functions equals the sum of their limits and LIM* makes the corresponding statement for multiplication. The difficulty of this domain arises from the need for arithmetic computation in order to find a suitable instantiation of free (existential) variables (such as a δ depending on an ϵ). Crucial for the success of Ωmega's proof planning is the integration of suitable experts for these tasks: the arithmetic computation is done by the computer algebra system Maple, and an appropriate instantiation for δ is computed by the constraint solver Cosie. We have been able to solve all challenge problems suggested by Bledsoe and many more theorems in this class taken from a standard textbook on real analysis.

Another class of problems we tackled with proof planning is concerned with residue classes. In this domain we show theorems such as: "the residue class structure $(Int_5, \bar{+})$ is associative", "it has a unit element", and similar properties, where Int_5 is the set of all congruence classes modulo 5 (i.e. $\{\bar{0}_5, \bar{1}_5, \bar{2}_5, \bar{3}_5, \bar{4}_5\}$) and $\bar{+}$ is the addition on residue classes. We have also investigated whether two given structures are isomorphic or not and altogether we have proven more than 10,000 theorems of this kind. Although the problems in the residue class domain are still within the range of difficulty a traditional automated theorem prover could handle, it was nevertheless an interesting case study for proof planning, since multi-strategy proof planning generated substantially different proofs based on entirely different proof ideas.

Another important proof technique is Cantor's diagonalization technique and we also developed methods and strategies for this class. Important theorems we have been able to prove are the undecidability of the halting problem and Cantor's theorem (cardinality of the set of subsets), the non-countability of the reals in the interval $[0, 1]$ and of the set of total functions, and similar theorems.

Finally, a good candidate for a standard proof technique are completeness proofs for refinements of resolution, where the theorem is usually first shown at the ground level using the excess-literal-number technique and then ground completeness is lifted to the predicate calculus. We have done this for many refinements of resolution with Ωmega.

What representation of the formalization has been put in this paper?
The problem has been formalized in POST syntax. The formalization employed knowledge provided in Ωmega's hierarchically structured knowledge base. However, because of the prerequisites posted for this volume, only the tactic-level proof is shown. This (logic) level of representation is important not least of all for the final proof checker. However, cognitively and practically far more important is the proof plan level of abstraction for a human-oriented mode of representation (see [2] and [3] above).

What needs to be explained about this specific proof?
Our aim was to follow our own (logic-level) proof sketch on a blackboard as closely as possible with the system. We replayed this proof idea in the system by partly employing interactive theorem proving in an island style, i.e., we anticipated some islands (some intermediate proof goals) and closed the gaps with the help of tactics and external reasoning systems. The results of the external system applications, such as the Otter proofs, have been translated and integrated into the central Ωmega proof object. This proof object can be verified

by an independent proof checker after expansion to base calculus level (natural deduction). The only tactic that can not be fully expanded and checked yet is by-computation, i.e. the computations contributed by the computer algebra system Maple. The translation of computer algebra proofs into natural deduction is an interesting problem on its own and we have work in progress.

16 B Method

Dominique Cansell

Formalization and answers by Dominique Cansell <cansell@loria.fr>.

16.1 Statement

```
!(n,m).(n:NATURAL&
      m:NATURAL
    =>
      (n*n=2*(m*m)<=>(n=0&m=0)))
```

16.2 Definitions

Definition of divide

```
divide(n,m)==(#k.(k:NATURAL & n=m*k));
```

Definition of coprime

```
coprime(n,m)==(!x.(x:NATURAL & divide(n,x) & divide(m,x) => x=1))
```

16.3 Proof

The B model

```
MACHINE
   m0
PROPERTIES
/* The well founded induction theorem it's an axiom */
   !P.(P<:NATURAL &
       !x.(x:NATURAL&!y.(y:NATURAL&y<x=>y:P)=>x:P)
     =>
       NATURAL<:P)

ASSERTIONS
/* it's a technical lemma used in the next one */
   !n.(n:NATURAL&
       #x.(x:NATURAL&n*n=2*x)
     =>
       #x.(x:NATURAL&n=2*x));

/* it's the difficult part of the theorem */
   !(n,m).(n:NATURAL&
         m:NATURAL
       =>
         (n*n=2*(m*m) => n=0));

/* the theorem, it's our statement */
   !(n,m).(n:NATURAL&
         m:NATURAL
       =>
         (n*n=2*(m*m)<=>(n=0&m=0)))
END
```

F. Wiedijk (Ed.): The Seventeen Provers of the World, LNAI 3600, pp. 142–150, 2006.
© Springer-Verlag Berlin Heidelberg 2006

Proof tree of the first proof obligation that is not proved automatically

```
cl
/*#x.(x: INTEGER & 0<=x & n = 2*x)*/
   xp
   ah(#x.(x: NATURAL & (n = 2*x or n = 2*x+1)))
   /*#x.(x: NATURAL & (n = 2*x or n = 2*x+1))*/
      se(n/2)
      /*n/2: NATURAL*/
         pp(rp.0)
      /*n = 2*(n/2) or n = 2*(n/2)+1*/
         pp(rp.0)
   rx(#x.(x: NATURAL & (n = 2*x or n = 2*x+1)))
   dcs(n = 2*x$0 or n = 2*x$0+1)
   /*#x.(x: INTEGER & 0<=x & 2*x$0 = 2*x)*/
      ds(n = 2*x$0)
      pp(rp.0)
   /*#x.(x: INTEGER & 0<=x & 2*x$0+1 = 2*x)*/
      ah(#k.(k: NATURAL & (2*x$0+1)*(2*x$0+1) = 2*k+1))
      /*#k.(k: NATURAL & (2*x$0+1)*(2*x$0+1) = 2*k+1)*/
         se(2*x$0*x$0+2*x$0)
      /*k+1<=x*
         /*2*x$0*x$0+2*x$0: NATURAL*/
            pp(rp.0)
         /*(2*x$0+1)*(2*x$0+1) = 2*(2*x$0*x$0+2*x$0)+1*/
            pp(rp.0)
      rx(#k.(k: NATURAL & (2*x$0+1)*(2*x$0+1) = 2*k+1))
      ah(k<x)
      /*k+1<=x*/
         pp(rp.0)
      pp(rp.0)
/*SUCCESS*/
```

Proof tree of the second proof obligation that is not proved automatically

```
cl
/*n = 0*/
   xp
   ph({n | n: NATURAL & !m.(m: NATURAL & n*n = 2*(m*m) => n = 0)},
      !P.(P <: NATURAL & !x.(x: NATURAL & !y.(y: NATURAL & y<x => y: P) =>
         x: P) => NATURAL <: P))
   /*{n | n: NATURAL & !m.(m: NATURAL & n*n = 2*(m*m) => n = 0)} <: NATURAL*/
      pp(rp.0)
   /*x: INTEGER & 0<=x & !y.(y: INTEGER & 0<=y & 1+y<=x =>
      y: {n | n: NATURAL & !m.(m: NATURAL & n*n = 2*(m*m) => n = 0)})
   => x: {n | n: NATURAL & !m.(m: NATURAL & n*n = 2*(m*m) => n = 0)}*/
      /*x: NATURAL*/
         pp(rp.0)
      /*m$0: NATURAL & x*x = 2*(m$0*m$0) => x = 0*/
         /*x = 0*/
            ct
            /*bfalse*/
               ph(x,!n.(n: INTEGER & 0<=n &
                       #x.(x: INTEGER & 0<=x & n*n = 2*x)
                     => #x.(x: INTEGER & 0<=x & n = 2*x)))
               /*#(x$0).(x$0: INTEGER & 0<=x$0 & x*x = 2*x$0)*/
                  se(m$0*m$0)
                  /*m$0*m$0: INTEGER*/
```

```
                    pp(rp.0)
                 /*0<=m$0*m$0*/
                    pp(rp.0)
        rx(#(x$0).(x$0: INTEGER & 0<=x$0 & x = 2*x$0))
        ph(m$0,!n.(n: INTEGER & 0<=n &
                #x.(x: INTEGER & 0<=x & n*n = 2*x)
                => #x.(x: INTEGER & 0<=x & n = 2*x)))
        /*m$0: INTEGER*/
           pp(rp.0)
        /*0<=m$0*/
           pp(rp.0)
        /*#x.(x: INTEGER & 0<=x & m$0*m$0 = 2*x)*/
           se(x$0*x$0)
           /*x$0*x$0: INTEGER*/
              pp(rp.0)
           /*0<=x$0*x$0*/
              pp(rp.0)
           /*m$0*m$0 = 2*(x$0*x$0)*/
              pp(rp.0)
        rx(#x.(x: INTEGER & 0<=x & m$0 = 2*x))
        ph(x$0,!y.(y: INTEGER & 0<=y & 1+y<=2*x$0 =>
   y: {n | n: NATURAL & !m.(m: NATURAL & n*n = 2*(m*m) => n = 0)}))
        /*1+x$0<=2*x$0*/
           pp(rp.0)
        ph(x$1,!m.(m: NATURAL & x$0*x$0 = 2*(m*m) => x$0 = 0))
        /*x$1: NATURAL*/
           pp(rp.0)
        /*x$0*x$0 = 2*(x$1*x$1)*/
           pp(rp.0)
        pp(rp.0)
   pp(rp.0)
/*SUCCESS*/
```

Another B model which is the basis of a different proof

```
MACHINE
   m1
DEFINITIONS
   divide(n,m) ==(#k.(k:NATURAL & n=m*k));
   coprime(n,m)==(!x.(x:NATURAL & divide(n,x) & divide(m,x) => x=1))
ASSERTIONS
/* it's a technical lemma used in the next one
   it's the same as the previous one using divide */
  !n.(n:NATURAL&
     divide(n*n,2)
     =>
     divide(n,2));

  /* The statement */
   not(#(n,m).(n:NATURAL & m:NATURAL1 & n*n=2*(m*m) & coprime(n,m)))
END
```

16.4   System

What is the home page of the system?

<http://www-lsr.imag.fr/B/>
<http://www.b4free.com/>
<http://www.loria.fr/~cansell/cnp.html>

What are the books about the system?

J.-R. Abrial. *The B Book - Assigning Programs to Meanings*, Cambridge University Press, 1996, ISBN 0-521-49619-5.

What is the logic of the system? First order logic and set theory. So we can have higher order logic because we can quantify on all subset of a given set like for the well founded induction theorem. Integers and Naturals are predefined.

What is the implementation architecture of the system? All tools of B4free are written in Logic-Solver. It is a language which looks like Prolog (inference rules and rewrite rules with tactics). Click'n'Prove is written in xemacs. The xemacs part drives only B4free. Proofs are managed by B4free.

What does working with the system look like? The proof obligation generator generates small proof obligations. Disjunction in hypotheses and conjunction in goals are splitted.

A first automatic prover can be used to discharged proof obligation. This first prover is rules based. To validate this prover a predicate prover was developed. This last prover is very powerful in set theory. It was added to the tool Atelier B and can be used for interactive proofs.

What is special about the system compared to other systems? With B we can prove theorems but we can also develop, using refinement, many models of a system. The proof accompany all the development. The proofs are invariant proofs and refinement proofs. We can add variables, invariants and events (which modify variables). Assertions are proved with properties (on constants) and invariants.

What are other versions of the system? The proof presented here was created using the tools:

- B4free
- Click'n'Prove

There are two other tools for the B method:

- Atelier B (ClearSy) <http://www.atelierb.societe.com/>
  B4free is an restricted version of Atelier B.
- B tool kit <http://www.b-core.com/btoolkit.html>

Who are the people behind the system? Jean-Raymond Abrial, Christophe Metayer, Laurent Voisin and Dominique Cansell.

What are the main user communities of the system? Many industrials use (or have used) the B method and associated tools like Atelier B: Gec-Alstom, Matra-Transport (now Siemens), RATP, Gemplus, Peugeot, ...

B4free is now used by many researchers in formal method and refinement and used to teach the B method.

What large mathematical formalizations have been done in the system? Set theory until Zermelo theorem (every set can be well ordered with the choice axiom).

The most important is the development of systems like:

- embedded system of METEOR which is the success story
- sequential and recursive progams
- producer and consumer protocol: PCI
- byte code verifier of the Java card
- distributed algorithms: IEEE 1394 leader election protocol and spanning tree detection
- pointer programs: Schorr & Waite: a garbage collector, Michael & Scott: the non blocking concurrent queue algorithm
- large system: access control, a press
- ...

What needs to be explained about this specific proof?

The model. The B method is a modeling language developed by Jean-Raymond Abrial. One can model a (close) system starting from an abstract model and adding new details using refinement. Variables and events which transform variables are defined in a model. Proofs (invariant and refinement) accompany all the development. B4free is a free and limited (not provers) version of Atelier B. Atelier B is a commercial set of tools for the B method (typechecker, proof obligation generator, automatic and interactive provers). Atelier B was developed and used to model the embedded system of METEOR (line 14 of Paris's subway).

Click'n'Prove is a proactive interface for B4free especially for the interactive prover.

For the "square root of two is not rational" challenge we have defined a model without variables and events. We have only modeled, in set theory, the well founded induction theorem in the PROPERTIES clause and a list of assertions. Assertions can be proved only using properties (of constants) and the invariant (empty in our case). Properties correspond to axioms and assertions look like theorems or lemmas (we can use the previous assertions to prove the next one).

In set theory we can define easily the well founded induction theorem with this following property:

$$\forall P \cdot \left(\begin{array}{l} P \subseteq \mathbb{N} \wedge \\ \forall x \cdot (x \in \mathbb{N} \ \wedge \forall y \cdot (y \in \mathbb{N} \wedge y < x \ \Rightarrow \ y \in P) \ \Rightarrow \ x \in P) \\ \Rightarrow \\ \mathbb{N} \subseteq P \end{array} \right)$$

It's our single axiom (we have already proved it in another development).

Then we have define a first lemma which is used two times to prove the difficult part of the theorem. This lemma express that if the square of a natural number (here n) is even then the given natural number (n) is even too.

$$\forall n \cdot \left(\begin{array}{l} n \in \mathbb{N} \wedge \\ \exists x \cdot (x \in \mathbb{N} \ \wedge n \times n = 2 \times x) \\ \Rightarrow \\ \exists x \cdot (x \in \mathbb{N} \ \wedge n = 2 \times x) \end{array} \right)$$

Then we can define the difficult part of the theorem which is the following

$$\forall (n, m) \cdot (n \in \mathbb{N} \wedge m \in \mathbb{N} \ \Rightarrow \ (n \times n = 2 \times m \times m \ \Rightarrow \ n = 0))$$

We have proved this lemma using the well founded induction theorem. We have instantiated P with this following set:

$$\{n \mid n \in \mathbb{N} \wedge \forall m \cdot (m \in \mathbb{N} \wedge n \times n = 2 \times (m \times m) \ \Rightarrow \ n = 0)\}$$

Then after proving this lemma it's very easy to prove the given theorem.

$$\forall (n, m) \cdot (n \in \mathbb{N} \wedge m \in \mathbb{N}) \ \Rightarrow \ (n \times n = 2 \times m \times m \ \Leftrightarrow \ n = 0 \wedge m = 0)$$

In the system one then writes this B model in an ASCII form (! for $\forall$, # for $\exists$, <: for $\subseteq$, ...). This is the "B machine" which is shown at the start of Section 16.3 on page 142.

Proof obligations. This machine provides five proof obligations (PO) because the last assertion is splitted in three PO $(n*n = 2*(m*m) \ \Rightarrow \ n = 0)$ which is the second assertion, $(n*n = 2*(m*m) \ \Rightarrow \ m = 0)$ and $(n = 0 \wedge m = 0 \ \Rightarrow \ n*n = 2*(m*m))$. Two of these tree PO (the first and the last one) are automatically proved by the B prover (force 0) and the second one is automatically proved by the B prover (force 1). The other PO need some interactions.

Proof. We explain the proofs with the three proof trees of the interactive proofs. These proof trees are provided automatically by the tool. [mk] and [zm] are buttons which are very helpful to replay a script (all command between two [mk]) or to hide a part of the proof tree (button [zm] for zoom). After each [zm] the current goal is displayed in a comment and after each [mk] an interactive command is displayed. Using Atelier B a user might type all the command but now with the Click'n'Prove interface this command is displayed after one click (most often), a mouse selection (for a witness or a parameter) followed by a click and sometimes type a parameter (using select & paste and/or using the keyboard followed by a click. For a better explanation, please, see the demo on this following web page <http://www.loria.fr/~cansell/demo.html>.

Next is the first proof tree. It finishes with SUCCESS. We have added some comments to explain all interactions which are not provided by a single click. When pp(rp.0) (or pp(rp.1), pr) is displayed then the current goal is proved by an automatic prover. The two first commands cl (it's a technical command which can be removed) and xp (for expert mode, a beginner mode exists) are provided automatically by the tool. dcs(a or b) launches a proof by case (case a then b)

```
[mk] cl
[zm] /*#x.(x: INTEGER & 0<=x & n = 2*x)*/
[mk]    xp
[mk]    ah(#x.(x: NATURAL & (n = 2*x or n = 2*x+1)))
```

It's the first interaction; we have type the text inside ah(.) only. We have added this new hypothesis which expresses that n is odd or even.

We need to prove it.

```
[zm]    /*#x.(x: NATURAL & (n = 2*x or n = 2*x+1))*/
[mk]      se(n/2)
```

For our second interaction we have suggested $n/2$ as a witness for the existential.

```
[zm]      /*n/2: NATURAL*/
[mk]        pp(rp.0)
[zm]      /*n = 2*(n/2) or n = 2*(n/2)+1*/
[mk]        pp(rp.0)
[mk]    rx(#x.(x: NATURAL & (n = 2*x or n = 2*x+1)))
[mk]    dcs(n = 2*x$0 or n = 2*x$0+1)
[zm]    /*#x.(x: INTEGER & 0<=x & 2*x$0 = 2*x)*/
[mk]      pp(rp.0)   /* if it's not ok try ds(n = 2*x$0) before */
[zm]    /*#x.(x: INTEGER & 0<=x & 2*x$0+1 = 2*x)*/
[mk]      ah(#k.(k: NATURAL & (2*x$0+1)*(2*x$0+1) = 2*k+1))
```

It is our third interaction; we have added a new hypothesis. The square of (2*x$0+1) is odd. x$0 is a fresh variable which is provided by rx(#x.(x: NATURAL & (n = 2*x or n = 2*x+1))) (remove existential).

```
[zm]    /*#k.(k: NATURAL & (2*x$0+1)*(2*x$0+1) = 2*k+1)*/
[mk]      se(2*x$0*x$0+2*x$0)
```

For the fourth interaction we have suggested 2*x$0*x$0+2*x$0 as a witness for the previous existential.

```
[zm]    /*k+1<=x*

[zm]      /*2*x$0*x$0+2*x$0: NATURAL*/
[mk]        pp(rp.0)
[zm]      /*(2*x$0+1)*(2*x$0+1) = 2*(2*x$0*x$0+2*x$0)+1*/
[mk]        pp(rp.0)
[mk]    rx(#k.(k: NATURAL & (2*x$0+1)*(2*x$0+1) = 2*k+1))
[mk]    ah(k<x)
```

It's our fifth interaction; we have added a new hypothesis $(k < x)$ where k is a fresh variable which is provided by rx(#k.(k: NATURAL & (2*x0+1)*(2*x0+1) = 2*k+1)) (remove existential).

```
[zm]      /*k+1<=x*/
[mk]          pp(rp.0)
[mk]        pp(rp.0)
 /*SUCCESS*/
```

At end we have 15 clicks (5 with text introduction). Next come the difficult lemmas. The command ph(E,!x.(P(x)=>Q(x))) intantiate the variable x of the universal predicate with the term E. First prove P(E) then prove the current goal under the extra hypothesis Q(E). The previous lemme is too long so we have write ... the first lemma .... The command ct launches a proof by contradiction.

```
[mk] cl
[zm] /*n = 0*/
[mk]    xp
[mk]    ph({n | n: NATURAL & !m.(m: NATURAL & n*n = 2*(m*m) => n = 0)},
          !P.(P <: NATURAL &....  y: P) => x: P) => NATURAL <: P))
[zm]    /*{n | n: NATURAL & !m.(m: NATURAL & n*n = 2*(m*m) => n = 0)} <: NATURAL*/
[mk]       pp(rp.0)
[zm]    /*x: INTEGER & 0<=x & !y.(y: INTEGER & 0<=y & 1+y<=x =>
          y: {n | n: NATURAL & !m.(m: NATURAL & n*n = 2*(m*m) => n = 0)})
        => x: {n | n: NATURAL & !m.(m: NATURAL & n*n = 2*(m*m) => n = 0)}*/
[zm]       /*x: NATURAL*/
[mk]         pp(rp.0)
[zm]       /*m$0: NATURAL & x*x = 2*(m$0*m$0) => x = 0*/
[zm]         /*x = 0*/
[mk]           ct
[zm]          /*bfalse*/
[mk]              ph(x,...  the first lemma ...)
[zm]              /*#(x$0).(x$0: INTEGER & 0<=x$0 & x*x = 2*x$0)*/
[mk]                se(m$0*m$0)
[zm]                /*m$0*m$0: INTEGER*/
[mk]                  pp(rp.0)
[zm]                /*0<=m$0*m$0*/
[mk]                  pp(rp.0)
[mk]              rx(#(x$0).(x$0: INTEGER & 0<=x$0 & x = 2*x$0))
[mk]              ph(m$0,...  the first lemma ...)
[zm]              /*m$0: INTEGER*/
[mk]                pp(rp.0)
[zm]              /*0<=m$0*/
[mk]                pp(rp.0)
[zm]              /*#x.(x: INTEGER & 0<=x & m$0*m$0 = 2*x)*/
[mk]                se(x$0*x$0)
[zm]                /*x$0*x$0: INTEGER*/
[mk]                  pp(rp.0)
[zm]                /*0<=x$0*x$0*/
[mk]                  pp(rp.0)
[zm]                /*m$0*m$0 = 2*(x$0*x$0)*/
[mk]                  pp(rp.0)
[mk]              rx(#x.(x: INTEGER & 0<=x & m$0 = 2*x))
[mk]              ph(x$0,!y.(y: INTEGER & 0<=y & 1+y<=2*x$0 =>
          y: {n | n: NATURAL & !m.(m: NATURAL & n*n = 2*(m*m) => n = 0)}))
```

```
[zm]                    /*1+x$0<=2*x$0*/
[mk]                        pp(rp.0)
[mk]                    ph(x$1,!m.(m: NATURAL & x$0*x$0 = 2*(m*m) => x$0 = 0))
[zm]                    /*x$1: NATURAL*/
[mk]                        pp(rp.0)
[zm]                    /*x$0*x$0 = 2*(x$1*x$1)*/
[mk]                        pp(rp.0)
[mk]                    pp(rp.0)
[mk]        pp(rp.0)
/*SUCCESS*/
```

At end we have 24 clicks (5 with a selected text and 2 with text introduction). To prove all assertions we have click on buttons 39 times and typed using keyboard seven text. Next are all texts (7) which are typed during the proof.

1. #x.(x: NATURAL & (n = 2*x or n = 2*x+1))
2. n/2
3. #k.(k: NATURAL & (2*x$0+1)*(2*x$0+1) = 2*k+1)
4. 2*x$0*x$0+2*x$0
5. k<n
6. {n | n: NATURAL & !m.(m: NATURAL & n*n = 2*(m*m) => n = 0)}
7. x$0*x$0

where 2*x$0+1, 2*x$0 and n*n = 2*(m*m) => n = 0 are obtained by select and paste.

17 Minlog

Helmut Schwichtenberg

Formalization by Helmut Schwichtenberg <schwicht@mathematik.uni-muenchen.de>. Answers by Helmut Schwichtenberg and Ulrich Berger <U.Berger@swansea.ac.uk>.

17.1 Statement

```
all x,p,q.2===x*x -> x===p#q -> F
```

17.2 Definitions

Definition of `RealEq` *and* `===`

```
(add-ids
 (list (list "RealEq" (make-arity (py "real") (py "real"))))
 '("all x,y.all k abs(x seq(x mod(k+1))-y seq(y mod(k+1)))<=(1#exp 2 k) ->
        RealEq x y"))

(add-token
 "==="
 'pred-infix
 (lambda (x y)
   (make-predicate-formula (make-idpredconst "RealEq" '() '()) x y)))

(add-idpredconst-display "RealEq" 'pred-infix "===")
```

17.3 Proof

```
(load "~/minlog/init.scm")
(mload "../lib/numbers.scm")

(set-goal (pf "all p,q.SZero(q*q)=p*p -> F"))
(ind)
(auto)
(assume "p" "IHp")
(cases)
(auto)
(save "LemmaOne")

(set-goal (pf "all p,q.2==(p#q)*(p#q) -> F"))
(use "LemmaOne")
(save "LemmaOneRat")

(aga ;for add-global-assumption
  "RealRatTimesComp"
  (pf "all x1,x2,a1,a2.x1===a1 -> x2===a2 -> x1*x2===a1*a2"))
(aga "RatRealEq" (pf "all a,b.a===b -> a==b"))
(aga "RealEqTrans" (pf "all x,y,z.x===y -> y===z -> x===z"))
```

F. Wiedijk (Ed.): The Seventeen Provers of the World, LNAI 3600, pp. 151–157, 2006.
© Springer-Verlag Berlin Heidelberg 2006

```
(set-goal (pf "all x,p,q.2===x*x -> x===p#q -> F"))
(strip)
(use "LemmaOneRat" (pt "p") (pt "q"))
(use "RatRealEq")
(use "RealEqTrans" (pt "x*x"))
(prop)
(use "RealRatTimesComp")
(auto)
(save "Corollary")
```

Proof term of LemmaOne

```
((((|Ind| (lambda (q) (lambda (u55) u55)))
   (lambda (p)
     (lambda (|IHp58|)
       (((((|Cases| p) (lambda (u62) u62))
         (lambda (n290) (lambda (u63) ((|IHp58| n290) u63))))
        (lambda (n291) (lambda (u64) u64))))))
  (lambda (n286)
    (lambda (u65) (lambda (q) (lambda (u66) u66)))))
```

Proof term of Corollary

```
(lambda (x)
  (lambda (p)
    (lambda (q)
      (lambda (u69)
        (lambda (u70)
          ((((|LemmaOneRat| p) q)
           ((((|RatRealEq| 2)
             (* ((|RatConstr| p) q) ((|RatConstr| p) q)))
            ((((((|RealEqTrans|
                  ((|RealConstr| (lambda (n300) 2))
                   (lambda (n300) 1)))
                 ((|RealTimes| x) x))
                ((|RealConstr|
                  (lambda (n299)
                    (* ((|RatConstr| p) q)
                       ((|RatConstr| p) q))))
                 (lambda (n299) 1)))
               u69)
              ((((((|RealRatTimesComp| x) x)
                 ((|RatConstr| p) q))
                ((|RatConstr| p) q))
               u70)
              u70)))))))))))
```

17.4   Proof of Lemma 1, Using Unary Numbers

```
(load "~/minlog/init.scm")
(mload "../lib/nat.scm")

; "Even" and "Odd"
(add-program-constant "Even" (py "nat=>boole") 1)
(add-program-constant "Odd" (py "nat=>boole") 1)
```

```
(add-computation-rule (pt "Even 0") (pt "True"))
(add-computation-rule (pt "Odd 0") (pt "False"))
(add-computation-rule (pt "Even(Succ n)") (pt "Odd n"))
(add-computation-rule (pt "Odd(Succ n)") (pt "Even n"))

; "Double"
(add-program-constant "D" (py "nat=>nat") 1)

(add-computation-rule (pt "D 0") (pt "0"))
(add-computation-rule
  (pt "D(Succ n)") (pt "Succ(Succ(D n))"))

; "Half"
(add-program-constant "H" (py "nat=>nat") 1)

(add-computation-rule (pt "H 0") (pt "0"))
(add-computation-rule (pt "H 1") (pt "0"))
(add-computation-rule
  (pt "H(Succ(Succ n))") (pt "Succ(H n)"))

; "CvInd"
(set-goal
  (pf "(all n.(all m.m<n -> Q m) -> Q n) -> all n Q n"))
(assume "Prog")
(cut (pf "all n,m.m<n -> Q m"))
(assume "QHyp")
(assume "n")
(use "QHyp" (pt "Succ n"))
(use "Truth-Axiom")
(ind)
(assume "m" "Absurd")
(use "Efq")
(use "Absurd")

(assume "n" "IHn")
(assume "m" "m<Succ n")
(use "LtSuccCases" (pt "n") (pt "m"))
(use "m<Succ n")
(use "IHn")
(assume "m=n")
(simp "m=n")
(use "Prog")
(use "IHn")
(save "CVInd")

; "LemmaOneAux"
(set-goal (pf "all n,m.n*n=D(m*m) -> m*m=D(H n*H n)"))
(assume "n" "m" "n*n=D(m*m)")
(simp "TimesDouble1")
(use "DoubleInj")
(simp "<-" "n*n=D(m*m)")
(simp "TimesDouble2")
(simp (pf "D(H n)=n"))
(use "Truth-Axiom")
(use "EvenOddDoubleHalf")
(use "EvenOddSquareRev")
(simp "n*n=D(m*m)")
(use "EvenDouble")
(save "LemmaOneAux")
```

```
; "LemmaOne"
(set-goal (pf "all n,m.n*n=D(m*m) -> n=0"))
(use-with
  "CVInd"
  (make-cterm (pv "m") (pf "all n.m*m=D(n*n) -> m=0")) "?")
(assume "n" "IHn" "m"  "n*n=D(m*m)")
(cases (pt "0<n"))
(assume "0<n")
(use "ZeroSquare")
(simp "n*n=D(m*m)")
(cut (pf "m=0"))
(assume "m=0")
(simp "m=0")
(use "Truth-Axiom")
(use "IHn" (pt "H n"))
(use "LtSquareRev")
(simp "n*n=D(m*m)")
(use "LtDouble")
(use "DoublePos")
(simp "<-" "n*n=D(m*m)")
(use "SquarePos")
(use "0<n")
(use "LemmaOneAux")
(use "n*n=D(m*m)")
(use "NotPosImpZero")
(save "LemmaOne")
```

17.5   System

What is the home page of the system?

<http://www.minlog-system.de/>

What are the books about the system? There is no book on Minlog at present. However, the paper "Minimal Logic for Computable Functions"

<http://www.mathematik.uni-muenchen.de/~minlog/minlog/mlcf.ps>

describes the logical basis of the system. There is a reference manual

<http://www.mathematik.uni-muenchen.de/~minlog/minlog/ref.ps>

and a tutorial (by Laura Crosilla)

<http://www.mathematik.uni-muenchen.de/~minlog/minlog/tutor.ps>

What is the logic of the system? Minimal logic, hence (via ex-falso-quodlibet and stability axioms) also intuitionistic and classical logic are included. Quantification over higher order functionals (of any finite type) is possible. There are also (parametric) type variables and predicate variables, but they are seen as place-holders for concrete types and comprehension terms, i.e., they are (implicitly) universally quantified (this is sometimes called ML-polymorphism). To keep the system predicative and moreover proof-theoretically weak (i.e., conservative over Heyting arithmetic), quantification over type and predicate variables is not allowed. Inductive data types and inductive definitions with their usual introduction and elimination rules are present. Of course, the latter in general increases the proof-theoretic strength.

What is the implementation architecture of the system? The system is written in Scheme (a Lisp dialect). Types, terms, formulas and proofs are separate entities. Terms and (following the Curry-Howard correspondence) also proofs are seen as λ-terms. There is a simple proof checking algorithm, which guarantees the correctness of a generated proof object.

What does working with the system look like? The standard LCF tactic style is used. David Aspinall's "Proof General" interface has also been adapted (by Stefan Schimanski).

What is special about the system compared to other systems? The intended model consists of the partial continuous functionals (in the Scott-Ersov sense), so partiality is built in from the outset. Program extraction can be done from constructive as well as from classical proofs; the latter uses a refined form of Harvey Friedman's *A*-translation. A proof that an extracted program realizes its specification can be machine generated.

Function (or better: program) constants (again of any finite type) have user-defined computation and rewrite rules associated with them. Using Scheme's evaluation, terms are normalized ("normalization by evaluation") w.r.t. all standard conversion rules (β, η, recursion, user-defined computation and rewrite rules), and terms with the same normal form are identified. This feature can shorten proofs drastically, as seen in the example above. Rewrite rules are to be viewed as part of the proof object, but, in the current version of Minlog, are not kept as part of the proof term. The system supports working in proof-theoretically weak theories, in order to have control over the complexity of extracted programs (this is work in progress).

What are other versions of the system? There is only one supported version. The current one is 4.0.

Who are the people behind the system? The Munich (LMU) logic group, and the Swansea logic group.

What are the main user communities of the system? The main user communities are in Munich and in Swansea.

What large mathematical formalizations have been done in the system? The intermediate value theorem in constructive analysis; the usage of concrete representations of the reals (as above) allowed extraction of a usable program to compute $\sqrt{2}$ (20 binary digits in 10 ms). Higman's lemma (Monika Seisenberger). Correctness of Dijkstra's and Warshall's algorithms. Program extraction from a classical proof of Dickson's lemma (Ulrich Berger).

What representation of the formalization has been put in this paper? In the proof of Lemma 1 and the statement about $\mathbb{R}$ using binary numbers, what is presented is the complete tactic file producing the proofs terms shown. In the proof of Lemma 1 using unary numbers, for brevity the (easy) proofs of the auxiliary lemmas have been left out. They should be part of the standard library, and can be found in the file examples/arith/sqrttwo.scm of the minlog directory.

What needs to be explained about this specific proof? The short proof of Lemma 1 (only five commands) is due to the fact that arguing with even and odd numbers in the context of a binary numbers is particularly simple (see below for more details). On the other hand, binary numbers are a must (for efficiency reasons) when working with rationals.

To provide a clearer picture of how working with the system is like in less fortunate circumstances, a proof of Lemma 1 for unary numbers is included as well.

The file numbers.scm contains definitions of the (binary) positive numbers n, m, p, q ... with constructors One, SZero and SOne, the integers i, j ... with constructors IntPos, IntZero and IntNeg, the rationals a, b ... seen as pairs i#n of an integer i and a positive natural number n, and the reals x, y ... seen as pairs of a Cauchy sequence of rationals and a modulus. Equality deserves special attention:

- – = is the structurally defined equality for positives and integers,
- – == is the decidable (equivalence) relation on the rationals, and
- – === is the (undecidable) equivalence relation on (the chosen representation of) the reals.

Here are some more details on the proofs.

Lemma 1 (binary): $\forall p, q. S_0(q * q) = p * p \to F$. Since the proof is by induction on binary numbers the following sub-goals are created (writing $1, S_0, S_1$ for One, SZero, SOne respectively):

?2 $\forall q. S_0(q * q) = 1 * 1 \to F$
?3 $\forall p. IH(p) \to \forall q. S_0(q * q) = S_0(p) * S_0(p) \to F$
?4 $\forall p. IH(p) \to \forall q. S_0(q * q) = S_1(p) * S_1(p) \to F$

where $IH(p) \equiv \forall q. S_0(q * q) = p * p \to F$.

Goal ?2 is solved by normalizing $1 * 1$ to 1 and hence $S_0(q * q) = 1 * 1$ to F. Similarly, in goal ?4 the premise $S_0(q * q) = S_1(p) * S_1(p)$ normalizes to F since $S_1(p) * S_1(p)$ normalizes to a term of the form $S_1(\_)$. The premise $S_0(q * q) = S_0(p) * S_0(p)$ of goal ?3 normalizes to $q * q = S_0(p * p)$. Consider the possible forms of q: $1, S_0(r)$, or $S_1(r)$. In the first and last case $q * q$ normalizes to a term of the form $S_1(\_)$ hence the equation normalizes to F. In the second case the equation normalizes to $S_0(q * q) = p * p$ which implies F by the induction hypothesis. The system does all this fully automatically, except for the case analysis on q.

Lemma 1 Rat: $\forall p, q. 2 == \frac{p}{q} * \frac{p}{q} \to F$. Up to normalization this is identical to Lemma 1, since $2 == \frac{p}{q} * \frac{p}{q}$ normalizes to $S_0(q * q) = p * p$.

Global assumption on equalities on the rationals and the reals. Here the fact is used that the rationals are coerced into the reals.

Lemma 1 (unary). The 12th command, (use "IHn" (pt "H n")), reduces the goal $m = 0$ with the help of the induction hypothesis $\forall m.m < n \rightarrow \forall k.m * m = D(k * k) \rightarrow m = 0$. The argument (pt "H n") is *not* –as one might think– used to instantiate the first universal quantifier, $\forall m$, but the second one, $\forall k$, which is the only quantifier left uninstantiated after matching the goal with the head of the induction hypothesis.

Author Index

Lecture Notes in Artificial Intelligence (LNAI)